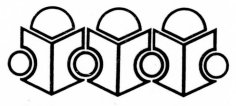

Sound, Self, and Song:

Essays on the Teaching of Singing

by
EARL WILLIAM JONES

THE SCARECROW PRESS, INC.
METUCHEN, N.J., & LONDON
1989

British Library Cataloguing-in-Publication data available

Library of Congress Cataloging-in-Publication Data

Jones, Earl William, 1921-
    Sound, self, and song.

    Bibliography: p.
    Includes index.
    1. Singing--Instruction and study. I. Title.
MT820.J66   1989   782'.007   89-6419
ISBN 0-8108-2221-0

Adam's Song

I am Adam, dust and clay,
I tend the very sod
From which I rose, Creation's Day,
In wonder after God.

I sing because I might bequeath
Some sureness, wondered clean,
Of sun above, or soil beneath,
Or Singing Man between.

Shaping praises out of sound
In songs of birth and death,
I sing because I have not found
A better use for breath.

— Jones

To my son, Gwilym, and my daughter, Bronwen,

and, with gratitude, to my brother, Lyman,

the real writer in the family

I have learned much from my teachers,
more from my colleagues than from my teachers,
and more from my students than from all of them.

The Talmud

CONTENTS

1. In the Beginning Was the Larynx   1

2. Singing's Original Sin   5

3. Bel Canto and the Species-Specific Sound   12

4. First Meeting   24

5. Class Lessons and Group Therapy   72

6. Class Lessons: Coda   103

7. Two Teachers   108

8. Singing in Our Schools   118

9. Perfect Singing   141

10. The Spontaneous Cure   152

11. The Bel in Bel Canto   195

Related Reading   214

Index   219

Chapter One

In the Beginning Was the Larynx

I am that final thing,
A man learning to sing.

— Roethke

In the beginning was the Larynx; the Word came much later!
So reads the first line of the singer's litany, properly invoking the
Muse and stating the essence of our understanding of the nature
and uses of our vocal equipment. But our personal perceptions
and the nature of language are such that the simpler an idea, the
more sentences it takes to explain it. What follows are a lot of
sentences intended to support the axiomatic value of that title-
sentence, and to expand on its applications to the study and the
teaching of singing.

Much has been written on the precise physiological
functionings of each component of the vocal apparatus, and of the
resultant acoustical phenomena. There are many books offering
methods for teaching, time-tested, on how to sing, some so well
written that they offer as much as any writing can to help the
singer. It would be more than redundant, even foolish, to
duplicate these or to try to improve on them. The best one can do
with the best of these is to quote them whenever they apply to our
studio practices and our students' problems.

But much more can always be said about the probable causes
and possible cures for bad singing, and much about verifying or
invalidating teaching methods. Much remains to be written about
those motives other than artistic, of transference attitudes, those
pulls in the air from psychological currents flowing through the
studio and classroom, and about "what's behind what's behind
what's behind" what is going on in the studio, practice room, and
recital hall.

Much more is to be said about the parallel between
psychotherapy and voice teaching, and the application of group
analytical techniques in class voice lessons, about what both
teacher and student might know about each other even before the
first meeting – the a priori imperatives.

1

And there is much to be said about the semantic slippage in studio terminology, in definitions of talent, affectivity, trainability, and in the application of the revelations of vocal science to the actual teaching of singing.

And crucial in its effects on our art is our culture's schizoid split between cognitive and affective modes of experience, that division between thought and feeling, intellect and emotion, which has led educators to exalt "discipline" and "cognitive gain," while downgrading the values of imagination, reducing our art to an extra-curricular "activity." A singer must protest.

And little in the literature, written by voice teachers, has been risked about what actually constitutes vocal beauty. Of course we recognize it when we hear it, but a teacher of singing ought to attempt a more thoughtful explanation, more worthy of the art than the usual superficial tautologies, such as "sheer loveliness," or "that which pleases the ear." For we pursue that beauty everyday and assume it as the goal and confirmation of our teaching. And in that pursuit and assumption is a profounder implication: our sense of beauty as a survival mechanism identifying our species.

And all these matters should be set forth and argued by those of us "inside" the art. For singers have, for the most part, left such evaluations and justifications to "outside" experts, the journalistic critics, the musicologists, historians, aestheticians, and philosophers, who, more often than not, apply intellectual abstractions to the art we experience with an undivided body, brain, and spirit.

Contributing to the discussion among colleagues is always valuable; subsequent efforts at clarification keep the debate lively and add to the collective wisdom. It can keep us from falling into semantic certainties, and from the side-effects of overdosing on jargon. It can keep us from a reflexive defense of method, often indulged in by voice teachers as if one's method involved one's personal morality. A continuing effort to explain ourselves helps to melt frozen concepts into fresh and flowing perceptions, in those we are trying to convince as well as in ourselves. And, of course, all this relieves some of the self-consciousness in offering "another book" about singing.

But this is meant to be a "different book" about singing, neither method nor manual. These are, rather, essays out of experience, intended to illuminate any approach to the art, by whatever method. And the title sentence, "In the beginning was the Larynx; the Word came much later," is meant to serve as a premise for diagnosis and therapy, as a hypothesis for generating research, as a foundation for those values by which we judge vocal beauty and artistic performance, as a reference to that transcendent experience as members of an appreciative audience, and most certainly as a validation of the singers' joy in their own performance.

There will be cautions and comforts for beginning singers whose present delight in singing brings them to seek greater expressiveness, whom we should always think of as "young artists," as, indeed, they should always consider themselves. Precious time can be saved at the outset if only the "right" teacher can be found. These essays are intended to help identify a "right" teacher, and, at the same time, intended to help the student cultivate the irrational-rational working faith in the teacher, so necessary for surviving the difficult process of redefining the self-as-singer, without sacrificing the joy.

For experienced singers who may have slipped or styled themselves away from the paths of vocal righteousness, there will be reassurances. Most of these know, or need to know, and all need reminding, that any vocal difficulty is an indication for a return to the earliest lessons.

It is assumed that the teacher who reads these essays possesses the requisites for teaching: the musical, technical, and artistic training, a facility in languages, an up-to-cruising grasp of the problems and promises of vocal science, a wide acquaintance with song literature, performance experience, minimal proficiency at the piano, and, above all, an authentic "calling" for the teaching.

But there are meant to be special implications for the young teacher, and the artist-turned-teacher, who may yet have to learn that a method which helped them may not have broad application in their teaching, and that a terminology refined for their own uses may even have a negative value for most of their students.

Teachers of singing need an evolving vocabulary of adjectives, an unusual appreciation for analogy, metaphor, imagery, a life-long love affair with the language. Converting intended meanings into useful understandings requires numberless ways for saying the same things. These essays offer some.

All of us teachers of singing deal with the same physical and aesthetic problems. We generally aspire to similar standards. We agree on which are the best voices, the best students, the best performers. Unanimity departs, however, when we try to identify the best teachers. It departs altogether on how they go about teaching. Many paths have been trodden in quest of the Grail of Bel Canto. These essays retrace one such personal quest – a pilgrimage.

I mean this to be a book I would like to have read when I was a young student. It surely is a kind of book I wish I could have read as a young teacher, back at a time when I only imagined myself qualified to teach. I mean it to celebrate the memory of all those students who have helped me learn to teach, and at whose expense I am still learning to be "that final thing."

Chapter Two

Singing's Original Sin

*She called her husband
in a kind of song.*

– Shapiro

From Genesis it seems we are to understand that language was conferred on man as a gift, along with creation's other blessings. It is an assumption common to creation myths and still powerful as a popular conception. Ordinarily we think and act with a kind of folk-faith – philosophers call it "naive realism" – that things are pretty much what they seem to be. Our use of speech certainly seems "natural" enough. We talk constantly to others and to ourselves. Nothing seems unusual or dramatic about that. So it is easy to understand that the makers of legends would not likely think it necessary, or worthwhile, to bother explaining something so familiar. They surely would know that they could not write, or recite, the great stories without language, and that no one could read, or listen, without it. Considering the enormity of other events in a "creation," language might easily seem too common a thing for special notice.

But for teachers of singing, and all lovers of language, the magnificent Genesis story is deeply profound when interpreted to mean that our First Father did not become "Man" until he acquired language, which truly set him apart from the other creatures. With language, only Adam was able to reflect on notions of yesterday, tomorrow, good, evil. And from an inordinate pride in that superiority came the abuses that brought about his Fall. That interpretation has inexhaustible inference.

All of us find it fascinating, at times, to speculate about what the first actual word might have been. But all such efforts are futile; the origins of speech disappear into the ancient mystery we have come to call "prehistory," and further back to the time before the "Word" expelled us from innocence into our irreversible self-awareness.

5

From what we know of egocentricity we might easily imagine the first word to have been "I." Enter Adam, wandering through his lovely park, musing,

> I am Adam, Eden's Prince,
> Held in God's high opinion
> Above the lower-lived,
> Sole fitted for dominion.

using the present indicative in a naively exalted context, with a necessarily personal reference.

But in "The Recognition of Eve," poet Karl Shapiro tells us that the first word was "thou," and it is Eve who speaks. This is a deeper insight; the generous expression of the human capacity for altruism. And it is more accurate. One thing we do know for certain about language is that it is a communal achievement. Alone, one would not invent it. Adam's musings would have had some non-verbal form, while still single of his kind.

Milton did not think so. In "Paradise Lost" Adam says,

> To speak I tried, and forthwith spake.
> My tongue obeyed, and readily could name
> Whate'er I saw...

And later, when God brings the animals to him for naming,

> I named them as they passed, and understood
> Their nature; with such knowledge God endued
> My sudden apprehension...

It is easy to identify with Adam's "forthwith," sensing the spontaneity of everyday speech. The "sudden apprehension" may well have been the only means by which Milton could ever explain to himself his own amazing flow of words.

There are a few references to language in Genesis. Adam listens and understands when God speaks. Then a direct reference: Adam names the animals, which confirms the author's understanding of the importance of an ability to use verbal labels.

Later comes the Tower of Babel story, which illustrates a crucial function and limitation of language: a shared language unites and identifies an ethnic group, different languages divide us. So, we are to understand that language may be universal but it is cultural, not biological.

Suppose Genesis read, "...Let us make Man in our own image, *giving him the Arts of Language*..." with that emphasis making it clear that speech is an art, not instinctive; acquired, not given. Then we might not forget that language use may be learned well or badly, that it can be unlearned and relearned, that the only "given" is a potential for learning.

Or maybe Prometheus should have stolen a few verb forms from the gods, a theft worthy of a Titan. That would have justified the jealousy of the gods, and the punishment would have fit the crime. Stealing fire was a petty theft; a mere human hero would sooner or later have discovered fire, like Charles Lamb's roaster of pigs. But our human hero would have needed language to tell his companions about the discovery; verbal communication, so much more subtle and efficient than mime and gesture, would have eliminated the necessity for each generation to rediscover.

Why did Prometheus steal fire and not the "Word"? Because dependence upon language is so absolute that it is still common to assume it as inseparable from its uses. The very medium used to tell the story – right under our noses – can be literally overlooked. And this is where most vocal problems begin.

But we should not be too hard on Prometheus. Appearing in ancient Egypt as the god Toth, he is said to have invented writing, and his very name means "foresight," which depends upon an ability to abstract, presumably using language symbols. There are other profound implications in the myth: the folly of inordinate pride, the dangers of ambition, the destructive potential of technology when information exceeds understanding. And the uses of fire still separate man and animal. The assurance of that separation remains as much a part of the comfort felt, sitting in front of a wood-burning fireplace, as the consolation of the radiant warmth. To understand that man, only, could turn, face, and learn to exploit a terrible fear he had shared with all animals is an idea dramatic enough for any great legend.

Surely the discovery of fire was an act of early genius, but not of the order that invented language. As Suzanne Langer reminded us in her *Philosophy in a New Key* "Discovery is not creation... naming things is Man's first creative act... to give a concept, an object, or an experience a name, however irrational, unscientific, poetic, illusory, is to bring a vision into repeatable focus... the notion of giving something a name was the vastest generative idea ever conceived."

With this naming power, man had a limitless number of devices for grasping and interpreting daily experience, to shape and reshape it, remember it, predict it, to compare and even invent it. With this power he rose from innocence to awareness, from the rigid patterns of instinct to flexibility and freedom of choice. Surely this is one of the glorious meanings in the Genesis legend for any singer:

> Adam found his Godly voice
> Left to us is Adam's choice.

But Adam abused the little knowledge he had. And we have inherited that weakness. We do so in assuming our verbal functioning as "given," as is. We choose manners of speech which interfere with efficiency of physical function, and we distort the loftier purposes of language by mistaking naming for knowing. So, in our version of the myth it might be said that we not only abuse the design, offending the designer, but we seem often to believe that our "Word" expresses a final truth, an unforgivable offense to an ineffable Creator. We think the little knowledge we have is All. That is the original sin, and thus:

> In Adam's Fall
> We sinned All.

In all Adamic innocence we begin taking voice lessons and that first disapproval, or that first hearing of a recording of one's own voice, is an agonizing expulsion from a personal Eden.

This is why Genesis might have read "... teaching him the Arts of Language..." and why Prometheus ought to have stolen "I Am," "He Is," "They Are," along with the fire. For that audacity,

in the voice teacher's version, the punishment would have been
isolation to an unaesthetic practice room, condemned to vocalize
an eternity of nine-note scales on the vowel "AH."

Voice teachers ought to deplore the fact that "myth" has come to
mean that which is untrue, and that psychologists have labeled
compulsive lying as "mythomania." Myths hold truths which
cannot be revealed in other forms. They remind us that there was a
human history, spiritual and emotional, prior to the Word. We
ought to remember that poetic myth always precedes science,
having great power to predict, and at the foundations of the purest
of sciences is the poetic expression of intuitive hypotheses. So,
we may know that art directs science – not the other way around.
As artists we ought to insist that science is myth, maturing.

For myth has its uses in the studio. By inquiring about
students' hopes, why they like to sing, why they want to study,
who are their favorite singers, what they read, what other interests
they have, in an effort to learn who they really are (or think they
are): teachers come to some sympathetic understanding of the
students' myths, without which their teaching will be ineffective,
for they will otherwise merely rely on their "Word," their
methods, their myths. And the trouble with this, as Bronowski
reminded us, is that the nature of myth is such that the holders of a
myth do not believe it to be a myth, which describes those teachers
of singing who protest a perfect faith in their one-and-only
method, while departing from it daily in their teaching.

The best voice teaching is a yeasty mix of science and myth.
We use "science" to help students revise their myths, and our
own. But we must always be ready and able to resort to creative
myth-making to describe the process in ways that have meaning to
others.

In any case, our opening axiom is not myth, but observable
fact. The larynx was functional before we were vocal. We are
vocal before we are verbal. The Word came much later. And since
its coming it has given direction to our cultural evolution. No
wonder we mark the beginning of "history" with its coming. No
wonder we need reminding that our cultural history is much older
and must have included dance, drama, ritual, and, surely, kinds of
song.

When it came the Word brought with it all manner of physical malfunctionings and misconceptions, cultural and individual. In our uses of the Word each of us is able to distinguish ourselves by adopting personal vocal and verbal styles. We represent ourselves as whom-we-wish-to-be to whomever we wish to impress. We cultivate vocal and verbal eccentricities to represent ourselves as whom-we-think-we-ought-to be. And in this cultivation of personal styles, more often than not, we compromise efficiency of function and fail to notice. And this forgetting, or ignoring, is the first cause of bad singing, of limited technique, poor habits of speech, of unproductive practice, of non-idiomatic song composition, and of the temporary enthusiasms for a great many unbeautiful, even destructive, singing styles.

And although this surely might seem enough to attribute even to a first cause, there is more: the failures of communication due to semantic slippage, the mistaking of descriptions for directives, confusing verbal representations with reality, and believing our best definitions are more than metaphors. So, every day, we go about imposing our vocabulary and syntax on our students, on our art, our culture, on the cosmos.

Our opening axiom lumps all these abuses under the error of the "Given Word," which encloses and perpetuates prejudices, prevents perception, distorts experience, and, as chief defender of the students' egos, offers heroic resistance to our instruction.

Teachers of singing talk constantly about "freeing the voice." This means enabling the singer to sing with the natural ease the vocal apparatus displays in its more primitive functionings, in which, through long evolutionary practice, there is a parsimonious efficiency appropriate to the design and properly adjusted to the needs. It means "freeing" the voice of physical and psychological inhibitions which upset the easy and natural coordination. It means discovering and identifying with a fundamental tone production, a basic sound for each voice which allows for a full use of the instrument "free" of those technical inadequacies which confine the untrained singer to a limited personal "style." It means becoming capable and worthy of our great inheritance of song.

Originally, "original sin" meant losing one's way through ignorance or lack of skill, and this still applies to all vocal faults resulting from the errors of the "Given Word." Vocal grace and redemption comes from daily meditation on the axiom:

In the beginning was the Larynx; the Word came much later!

Ignoring this is singing's original sin.

CHAPTER THREE

Bel Canto and the Species-Specific Sound

*Song is the forgotten
language of the soul.*

– Jung

When the Word came it was overlaid, so to speak, on mechanisms and functions already ancient. This means that a healthy and effective method for the teaching of singing must be consistent in its references to the Larynx-Word order. It means that vocal beauty and technique are dependent upon simulations and exploitings of prevocal and preverbal functions. It means that the lessons and practice involve recapitulations of an evolutionary process. It means that we do not begin the study of singing with the Word.

"In the beginning was the Larynx; the Word came much later" is a premise for developing and applying any teaching method, as well as for guiding the student's practice. It implies a sequence of functional "stages" in the progression from Larynx to Word, stages that the teacher and student will isolate and focus upon with particular attention from time to time as required by specific vocal problems. And these stages may be identified by an alliterative teaching device, the "Five S's": Silence, Sound, Signal, Symbol, and their final fusion into Song.

"Silence" refers to the most basic of prevocal activities, producing no perceptible, certainly no intentional sound. A prototype one-way valve, the larynx kept water out of the lungs of amphibious ancestors, sphinctering in the processes of swallowing and breathing. And, as anyone knows who has endured a laryngeal spasm after having inhaled an odd bit of particulate matter, the valve can still, whenever necessary, assert the primacy of its earliest survival functions over any of its later social uses. Deep beneath our consciousness it remains faithful to its original charge; if not, there would be very little dinner conversation.

"Sound" refers to the acoustical phenomena associated with other life-preserving uses. We can "hear" the valve slip while

12

lifting, throwing, climbing, in the huffs and puffs of strenuous exertion. And there are audible accompaniments of other biological happenings: the coughings, snortings, belchings, chewings, smacks, and gurgles. There are hiccoughs, sneezes, gasps, hisses, yawns, gulps, and other such sounds having no communicative intent and requiring no significant response. And these involved the larynx, soft palate, jaws, tongue, teeth, lips, sublingual and abdominal musculature, lungs, and diaphragm in various concerts of functions later applied to phonation, and later still to articulation.

"Signal" refers to sounds which, somehow, came to have survival significance, and that "somehow" remains a difficult and debated problem for linguistic theorists. The "Signal," unintentional at first, perhaps only identified one member of a species to another. But "somehow" it came to be intentional, influencing the behavior of others. Among the earliest of these are what Bronowski called "one-word sentences": Hunger! Danger! Enemy! Mate! All indications of immediate states or conditions, and all responded to with the stereotyped behavior that identifies a species – the species-specific sounds.

One example serves: The gregarious prairie dog of the western plains of the United States has two such "one-word sentences" for Danger! One apparently meaning "enemy from above!" signifies a predatory hawk or eagle, and every one within hearing immediately dives down the most convenient burrow. Another apparently means "enemy on the ground!" for everyone, alerted, stretches erect to locate the intruding snake, fox, or coyote. What marks these sounds as signals is that no member of the species is free to go about its business, musing perhaps about Old Nuisance over there, always complaining about something.

Likewise, human signals have not been meant for discussion or debate, but for action. We were "selected for" prompt and correct reaction; survival depended on immediate empathy, on perception inseparable from response. Indifference would have meant great evolutionary risk. We are still "moved" by those signals, moved to the kinds of responses that identify us as members of the human species.

Well of course, what could or should be more affecting than the sound of another human voice? When Eve "called her husband in a kind of song," Adam knew he was no longer single of his kind, and we inherit that understanding. Our signals are direct presentations of imperatives which transcend cultural differences, voicing the emotional material deep in our racial memory, and deeper still in our bio-genetic strata, signifying life and death. And preserved as the "pathos" in the singing voice they are heard directly by the heart and resonate in the bone.

It was the color and quality of these sounds which, for Aristotle, expressed the passions of the soul, and had, for Pliny, an irresistible power to win hearts. For Jung, these sounds contained the archaic properties originating in the "cradle of Mankind." So, we are alerted, arrested, alarmed, aroused by the sounds of other human voices calling up milleniums of responses to grief, joy, anger, danger, love, and loss. And so affected, we think with our emotions, identified by the fears and fascinations that give significance to all human living: the ineffable mysteries, tragedies, sorrows, and delights which are the essence of all song. No wonder we "weep to hear."

That "signal" is the source of song can be inferred from the anthropological evidence of the association of song with magic, with mystic ritual, with social celebration, and with formal worship. It is signal that accounts for the similarities found in the folk music of separated cultures, and which explains why so much folk music is associated with action and dance. It is signal that makes music more important to a greater number of people than literature or any other art. It is signal that makes it acceptable for us to sing words that would seem utterly ridiculous when simply said. And it is the absence of signal that makes abstract statements awkward in song – we set poetry to music, being closer to signal. And it is signal that all instrumentalists strive to imitate in performance, which is why the singing teacher holds it to be a perversion of the art when singers are required to imitate instruments. Every element of music is a signal expression.

And it is just because signal preceded syntax that we find it so difficult to define "vocal beauty." We say that the beautiful sound was dark, bright, silvery, golden, shining, shimmering. We say it was tender, sweet, flowing, warm, rich. We find it exciting, moving, stirring, charming, commanding, borrowing terms from our sensual experiences and their associated motor responses. And this necessity for borrowing does more than illustrate the limitations of the "Word"; it is precisely what makes singing the necessary and powerful expression of feelings otherwise unexpressible. If "It" could be said, who would sing? Children are especially alert to signal, responding more to vocal color than to verbal content. This is presumptive proof of a keen survival skill that gets blunted, later, against the "Word," because of the growing requirements for paying more and more attention to information. But teachers of singing must retain that innocence of ear, or relearn it through experience, for any incongruities of signal and substance are causes of and clues to vocal interferences. More, these are specific indications of psychological states which affect and define relationships between teacher and student. It is the "pathos" in the students' speech that expresses what they are "really" saying, revealing who they are in their own estimation, important indications of talent and trainability.

Singers need a profound intuitive and intellectual understanding that we still live and move in the Signal era. They practice the everyday proofs, exploiting the differences between wails and whines, cries and croons, moans of delight and those of pain, interjections of joy and those of calamity. Their practice is a disciplining of these signals into a spontaneous expressiveness. Their interpretive powers cannot range beyond their appreciation for the emotionally accurate signal, and their capacity for being affected by it. Words may become the singer's medium, but the signal remains the message.

Finally, came the "symbol," the word of our opening axiom, the achieving of an ability to flap the air in certain ways with the tongue and to arrange agreed upon sounds in the variety of constructions that make up a language. The Word, the power of naming, the "vastest generative idea ever conceived," the tool for holding in mind all manner of abstractions substituting for objects and events out of the present reach of the senses. Without the Word we would have remained another part of the landscape; with it we have been enabled to discover a past, envision a future, to control and even create our own environment, and, for better or worse, choose the direction of our cultural evolution.

Generally, the interest of singing teachers in speculating about language acquisition has been narrowed to the applications of the term "natural" to the vocal functionings of their students. We have tolerated a loose application of that term because we "know what we mean by it." A student having a minimum of difficulty with vocal technique is a "natural" talent. Some students sing "naturally" into the upper ranges; some have pleasing speaking voices we think "natural." But this careless use of the term has contributed to a general impression that real singing is reserved to the fortunate few "naturals." And so close an identification of "natural" with "talent" stops us short of a closer examination of how the mechanisms are affected, and what interferences are learned, in the process of acquiring speech.

Anyone with a professional interest in the uses of the voice ought to become associated with the increasing interest among linguists in the nature and "deep structure" of language, an interest particularly excited by the early writings of Noam Chomsky and his followers and detractors. At the center of theoretical debate is the problem of reconciling theories of language acquisition with generally accepted evolutionary theory. Did human speech evolve from animal cry, or was there an evolutionary leap into language? Our answer to that question directly affects our use of the vocal mechanism.

Those who maintain a conservative view of the theory of evolution argue that new functions are not anticipated, but are mutations grafted onto older uses and retained when successful, and refined by use. Such a process does not prepare for future uses; it can only "reward" present adaptations. Something not present can't be "selected." Therefore, the immense distance between involuntary cry and intentional call can only be explained by an enormous stretch of evolutionary time. Language must have been acquired in a gradual, uninterrupted process. Any break, gap, or leap in the process, however small, would discredit the evolutionary theory altogether. Evolution implies continuity; there had to have been continuity from cry to call, from signal to symbol.

But others believe that the Word could have appeared as a quite "sudden" event, by an extraordinary evolutionary leap that only humans could have made, made possible by an evolving complexity in our brain. In the evolutionary process there must have been a sudden arrival – a relatively rapid occurrence on a paleontological scale – at some critical level of complexity resulting in a quantitative change in our nervous systems which created a potential for language, a predisposition, an evolutionary readiness. For whereas the signal required immediate and "thoughtless" response, this greater complexity of neural networks in the brain allowed for "delay loops" for a processing of sounds, a separation of perception from action, pauses for reflection. And in this sense, since a ripeness for speech was "pre-wired" in the brain, it may be argued that there has been no gap in the evolutionary process, and that such leaps are possible as functions of complexity. Biological structures may thus appear before a full realization of potential use; evolution may provide a kind of surplus potential for strategies of survival.

Still, how did speech actually begin? Some argue that those natural signals would have been repeated over and over, being called up again and again in the repeatings of common activities of hunting, working, celebrating, mourning. Could not these sounds have become crystalized around such events, evolving into symbols? The simplicity of this assumption is tempting, but cannot explain the mechanism of speech acquisition nor the fact that signals have remained presentational while symbols became representational.

Or, did man "make" speech along with his making of other tools? Making any tool surely involves anticipation, some sense of "I can use this later," which would have been true even of bending down to pick up a stone to throw at some threatening animal. And it may have been this ability to conceive a "later" that conferred such a great selective advantage on man. It seems to explain the otherwise incredible growth of the neo-cortex, an explosive growth out of proportion to that of brain structures representing other body parts and functions in, anthropologically speaking, so short a time.

An abstraction, like the Word, would be the very tool needed for holding the "later use" in mind. Were vocalisms transformed into verbalisms for such a purpose? We do know that the speech centers in our brains expanded and developed concurrently with those centers for manual dexterity and forethought. It seems impossible, then, not to recognize a relationship between the Tool and the Word; both are abstractions. And we know that early man had other means of symbolizing; he made markings on bones, paintings on cave walls, and, as we know from inherited myth, he practiced ceremonial ritual, mime, dance, and surely a "kind of song."

But from the naive to the poetic, effects of the "Given Word" are easily recognizable in early, and persistent, theories of the origins of speech:

Speech is the invention of man! This is unarguably true, but affords no explanation of the nature of the accomplishment. Nevertheless, it is a theory that has had powerful apologists. Plato, for instance, maintained that speech was man's invention, the obvious result of superior intelligence. And, carrying that conviction further, trusting in the superiority of his own intelligence, he insisted that Greek was the most perfect language; others were barbaric.

Speech was the gift of God! Wherever there has been a theological imperative to regard the book of Genesis as a literal and authorative account of Creation, there has been no room for debate; only this unarguable statement of faith. But even an allegorical interpretation of the account presents language as given. And even the most liberal theologies have insisted on a clear separation between man and other life-forms, and language has always seemed a clear proof of that though this proof has been eroding as we learn more about the communication systems of whales and dolphins. Secularized into a kind of folk-faith the "Given Word" operates pervasively as an uncritical and unconscious assumption, influencing our attitudes toward speech and our understanding of the mechanism making up what we now call "vocal equipment."

We may find ancient markings on ancient bones and evidence of the earliest uses of fire, but never, of course, any verbal artifacts to help us understand anything about the beginnings of language. Even among living "primitives" language is anything but primitive. So, it is easy to understand why Dante thought there could not have been such a thing as a primitive language; he believed that Adam spoke Hebrew, too perfect a language to have been a human product.

Speech was lucky accident! A fortuitous, ontological happening, growing out of an obvious social need to be understood. And this tells us what we already know about its usefulness, but nothing to clear up the mystery of its invention and acquisition.

Speech began with oral gesture! And became audible as the lips, jaws, tongue unconsciously followed the movements of the hands, arms, and body? This seems to be related to theories that speech may have developed out of the infant's "struggle behavior," out of the sounds involuntarily made in the process of mastering its muscle coordination. Some have thought that language may have originated from later sounds that accompanied deliberate communicative gesturings and, later, as speech became more and more refined, gestures were dropped – reduced perhaps, but never dropped. Here, at least, is a reminder for singers of the importance of authentic body language and gesture for song interpretation.

Max Muller introduced lectures on linguistic science with a delightful, tongue-in-cheek, summing up of previous theories of the origins of language:

- The Ding-Dong Theory. Speech began with the inherent, natural connections between words and the things stood for.
- The Bow-Wow Theory. Speech developed from onomatopoetic origins.
- The Pooh-Pooh Theory. Speech grew out of the involuntary, emotional interjections of early man.
- The Yo-Heave-ho Theory. Speech began with the noises associated with communal labor. (Some have thought this the source of song.)

But, seriously, Muller suggested that the origins and acquisition of language must have been the result of the powers of abstraction that only man had. But this raised a question: If abstracting depended upon the manipulation of symbols, and if symbols depended on an abstracting ability, then which came first? And our feeling that this is a "real" problem is another illustration of our profound dependence upon language as a depiction of reality; we feel we must choose either-or. But we need to understand that it is only the nature and limitation of language that make the chicken or egg choice out of a purely linguistic paradox. If there must be an answer, it is, of course, "Both!"

The either-or feeling should remind us that speculation about the nature and acquisition of language is complicated by the fact that language is a primary instrument of our thought processes. (Some have insisted it is the exclusive instrument.) We have to use the Word to theorize about and to study the Word. How can we be sure the analysis is not limited, distorted, or somehow qualified? There are semantic "somehows" by which we seem to become whatever we "say" we are. And for teachers of singing this can take forms of believing that singing and its teaching are just what our particular pedagogical terminologies say they are. And, of course, any analysis of language may be further skewed by the fact that its use has affected, and been affected by, our cultural evolution in ways that have caused cultural evolutions to move in different directions and at different rates from "natural" evolution. And on the periphery of this debate are those who believe that our use of speech has already affected and will continue to affect our physical evolution, causing the mouth, larynx, and lungs to show structural adaptations for speech. And opposed to these are those who insist that speech can never be other than that which is permitted by the natural structure.

One thing is obvious; we speak long before we are able to think about language, and this makes its acquisition seem like breathing or walking. But it is not at all like those activities, and not at all like learning to play the piano or to ride a bicycle. About all we know for sure is that language is not "given," appears to be latent, and can be acquired only by living in an environment of language use.

Those who argue for a "pre-wired" readiness remind us that children seem to generate as much language as they imitate, which means that speech acquisition cannot be explained as a process of simple imitation. Children, everywhere, make up all manner of novel statements, the novelty of any one of which is enough to discredit all behavioristic explanations, all notions of simple conditioning. Such novel usage often strikes us as poetic. But then, as Robert Frost reminded us, "All language is fossilized poetry."

Children seem to understand complicated rules of grammar without any instruction – those from whose examples they learn may know little or nothing about grammar – and make spontaneous generalizations which seem only to have been made possible by some innate grasp of language structure, as if they knew such things in advance. In every language they say things like, "She hitted the cat." Or, "I goed downtown." And these seemingly simple generalizations are accomplishments separating the human child from the infant animal by an immense evolutionary distance, or an incredible leap.

We know that infant vocalisms are identical at birth, whatever the race or culture, and only in later months does a child begin to favor localisms. And if singers are ever to sing beautifully they must come to understand what all parents learn from efforts to understand their infant's needs; first words are not ever for naming, but for expressing. And when they are able to sing beautifully there are powerful reasons why they love to sing songs like Brahms' *O Wüsst Ich Doch Den Weg Zurüch*, expressive as it is of the desire to return to innocence. Audiences respond for the same reasons; the loss of innocence is the price paid for the "Word," for with it comes the expulsion from Eden, with it man became the uncomfortable, amphibious "more than beast, less than angel."

With the "Word" came the dualisms which have made all human history a bruising in the gauntlet of intuition and intellect, the hyphenating of thought-feeling. And with this has come a hubris, in the form of an inordinate reverence for "rationality," for "pure" knowledge, resulting in the technical feasibility of our species self-extinction while, and perhaps because, our appreciation for affect remains where it was in classical Greece. The "Word" makes us forget that our "enemies" are only those whose songs we have not learned. In that hyphenated space between thought and feeling is a wasteland of alienation and spiritual disease, educational imbalance, and crucial for us, derogation of the arts.

But what an achievement! Fire was fine, but the Word was divine! And the "somehow" of its acquisition seems all the more amazing when we consider that it was accomplished by exploiting the earlier functions of what we have come to call a "vocal apparatus." Somehow, nearly the entire inventory of our physical parts proved adaptable for the purpose, using air to activate, the "cords" to vibrate, the larynx and supraglottic airspaces to resonate, the basic mechanisms once having only biological functions came to have cultural ones. Acquired, somehow, little more than half a million years ago, the Word came later. Indeed, it is the very latest use to which we have put the larynx.

Of course there is not insistence on the use of the specific terms: silence, sound, signal, and symbol. It is just that our pedagogical contexts always need broadening, using terms from other disciplines, from other fields associated with students' experiences and interests, especially when we find ourselves repeating our standard teaching jargon with increasing frequency and lessening effect. "God speaks Analogy and Metaphor / We speak in Images or not at all."

We might reduce the "stages" to three; silence and sound logically making one, and think of them as mechanical, emotional, and intellectual. Or, as physical, psychological, and personal. We can relate these three to the nature and development of our three-part brain: the oldest, the "reptilian" brain which we have kept in common with all animals, the nerve center for monitoring and controlling silent and sound functions with such a smooth mechanical efficiency. Later, the limbic brain, the center for "fight or flight" responses, and for generating, receiving and responding to the signal's affect. And at last, the neocortex, the highest, latest accretion, with centers for analyzing, symbolizing, for speech.

Or, we can describe these stages as involuntary, intermediate, and intentional, and their functions as survival, social, and stylistic. Or, reduced to two, as autonomous and artistic. But however described, an understanding of these "stages" is important for singers, particularly young singers, so anxious to be expressive, so enraptured by song, so isolated in the personal aesthetics of music-making that the desire to sing inhibits and overpowers the free functioning of the vocal equipment.

From time to time the study will focus on one or another of these stages. We can approach the students' technical problems with explanations and illustrations that the silent and sound functions are "below" emotion, providing, in the students' own internal experiences, the best models for the coordinated muscular activity they are to emulate in their singing. And when the problems of interpretation arise we may remind them that the signal, saturated with emotion, remains the best model for authentic expressiveness. And the symbol, "above" emotion, is to be consulted for objective analysis, reality testing, for an intelligent understanding and communicating of the music's form and text.

All such terms are useful; the ability to enrich the teaching language with fresh associations and imagery is a critical gauge of the teacher's art. But we must never forget that all such separations into "stages" are no more than teaching conveniences, conceptual aids. Every singer knows, or must learn before he sings well, that there must be a seamless fusing of mechanical efficiency and authentic pathos with an intentional expressiveness. The earlier stages are assimilated and then transcended in song.

This is what is meant by Bel Canto.

Chapter Four

First Meeting

Myself when young did eagerly frequent
Doctor and Saint and heard great argument
About it and about...

— Omar Khayyam

Any voice teacher may be fortunate enough, occasionally, to have a student with exceptional gifts for singing; some have traded heavily on that good fortune. But a proper judgment of a teacher's effectiveness can be made only after hearing a large and representative number of his students in performance.

The new student cannot make such a well-founded judgment, having been impressed, perhaps, by the performance of a single student, or having learned something of the teacher's reputation by seeking out the opinions of a few other students. The trouble with this is that singers' opinions of their teachers are rarely objective and may not be at all reliable. Most singers – not just the beginners – have tender egos which seem to be toughened by the belief that they are studying with the "right" teacher, by which they often mean the "only" teacher. In any case, whatever new students infer of the character and competence of prospective teachers, it is almost certain that they will have "heard" those aspects of attitude and approach which relate as much to their emotional as to their vocal and artistic needs.

So, the choice of a teacher is usually irrational, and may be altogether unfounded; there might not be another teacher within a convenient distance, or a particular teacher just happens to have an opening in her schedule. Young students often cannot afford the fees of teachers they might prefer. Or, they may be arbitrarily assigned to a teacher about whom they know nothing at all, as is often the case in institutional teaching.

Finding the "right" teacher, especially the first teacher, is a critically important event in the young singers' career, and is almost always a matter of luck. But the odds for both student and teacher might be improved by a consideration of what may be going on in the minds of both at a typical first encounter.

24

First, it must be understood that cosmic events are less important to the young singer – and should be for the teacher – than the beginnings of this artistic association. They are about to become bound up in each other's personal and professional lives, and both are to be transformed in the process. Students come in ambivalent mixes of eagerness and anxiety. Having had some joyful experience with singing, they come wanting, hoping, perhaps expecting to hear that they have beautiful voices, great talent, and fine futures as singers. But they come also to reveal their weaknesses, real and imagined, vulnerable to the judgment of one with the impressive aura of "teacher," whose opinion of them at this moment is by far the most important on earth.

Teachers have their own apprehensions. They will not be able to say how long the study may take, though they will be asked that question in one form or another. They will not be able to promise success, though that question will certainly pervade the studio atmosphere, even unasked. And now, once more, they must consider accepting a responsibility combining that of teacher with rabbi, parent, confessor, confidant, critic, analyst, fellow-artist, and a further list of required roles limited only by their empathy and imagination. And all these will be lived-out, played out, in a wonderful variety of mixes, at levels of intensity depending on the needs of a student and the dynamics of the moment. To fail in any of these roles is to inhibit the student's growth toward artistic maturity. To evade any of the roles is just that, evasion.

If a new student proves to be unusually talented, a teacher's apprehension will be increased, probably in direct proportion to the delight. For now there is the responsibility for the outcome of a most precious possibility. And if the student seems not to be so talented, at this first hearing, the apprehension is little less, for now there is a responsibility for any error of judgment, any failure to liberate such talent as there may be.

An experienced teacher can rely on a working definition: Talent is a high degree of interest. And a student whose abilities may not be immediately apparent shows a significant interest by coming for instruction, the quite considerable interest needed to endure the anxieties of this first meeting. Beginners are to be given the benefit

of all early doubts; the experienced teacher will remember the
many students whose inhibitions seemed too great, at first, ever to
be overcome. Yet, later, this only confirmed an extraordinary
sensitivity. Their interest had been powered by a need for
expressiveness strong enough to survive more than the ordinary
risks in the study. And, once given a taste of vocal freedom,
brought out of the agonies of repression into the exhibitionistic
joys of performance, their characteristic sensitivity helped make
them persuasive interpreters of vocal literature. Ah, the powerful
need for self-expression can make an artist out of the most
inhibited.

A high degree of interest remains the most positive force in
overcoming whatever the present limitations. The teacher will be
alert to any of its early indications. Such students will show a
more than usual insight into their own vocal problems. They are
likely to know who all the pre-eminent singers are, surely those of
their own vocal classification, whom they can identify by their
distinctive sounds. They will be eager for performance
opportunities and inquire about them. They will ask specific
questions about the music, or the technique, and be keenly
attentive, with a glint in the eye, to the answers. They will have
shown initiative in choosing repertoire, and likely will have
prepared more than one audition piece. They may be more
conversant than the average student with the literature for piano,
violin, and orchestra. They will have been collecting a library of
music, spending all they can afford on recordings. They will
volunteer to usher at local concerts and opera productions in order
to be in the presence of the great singers.

And while all these are indications of talent, there are cautions
which longer acquaintance will have to dispel; the highly interested
students are also likely to aspire to the most difficult repertoire,
which will be indicated by the choices prepared for this first
hearing. They are most likely to have been trying too hard, and
will continue to do so, to force their immature voices to be worthy
of their precocious taste and criticism. Still, a teacher can hardly
hope for anything better than a studio full of such students.

But will this new student be one of those obviously talented
ones of another common sort? One of those "best singers" from
whatever school he attended? One who has done too much

performing too soon. Encouraged by parents for their substitute fulfillment? Exploited by a high school music teacher – a non-singer – for being the best talent available? Another of those who has sung all the leading roles in school productions, coaxed and coached to sound as much as possible like the "star" – another non-singer – who made the original recording? Among such "talents" will be some who may have won scholarships for having performed "so well for their ages." And often these recipients of extravagant praise for their early successes have little reason to be dissatisfied with their present abilities. But such "successes" may have arrested both their technique and artistry, and may very well impede their progress. Many such young singers have not had the important experience of having had to earn either their sound or their expressiveness, and may lack a discipline commensurate with their gifts. They may have learned their music by listening to recordings, being "quick studies," and perhaps the learning of music has come so easily that they have not felt a need to look at a score with their whole minds. They may be careless in their musicianship as standards are raised. They may have difficulty memorizing as the song literature becomes more demanding. It may take all the teacher's skill and patience to bring such students to face the superficiality of their involvement in the art. The plodders who must earn every inch of their progress may overtake them. Will this new student be Hare or Tortoise?

Or, will this be one of the mildly neurotic, typically attracted to the arts as substitute expressions for imagined personal or social inadequacies? Some of these will be able to shed a repressed personality by assuming the role of performer, and the singing can be a safe, healthy, constructive compensation. But it may be one of the more severely neurotic, attracted to the art for similar reasons, but afloat in fantasy, out of touch with objective assessments of technical faults, relying on eccentricities of tone production and style in a defense of the neurosis, offering the greatest resistance to instruction and change.

Will this new student's innate expressiveness have survived the deprivations of the typical early educational experience? So few arrive with their artistic intuitions intact. The repressive atmosphere of most early educational institutions stifles creativity, offering little exposure and experience in expressiveness, neither recognizing nor prizing creativity. Alas, talent for singing is not nearly so rare as generally thought. Indeed, it is widespread, but only a small portion of it survives that early awful averaging.

Will this new student show some of the attributes, other than intense interest, in the teacher's broader definition of talent: open-mindedness, curiosity, readiness for self-analysis, more than an intellectual grasp of what she does, emotionally accurate responses to the music, more than a superficial understanding of poetic texts? The teacher may hope that this student will be a genuine sensitive-exhibitionist with a healthy ego and normal vocal equipment.

So musing, the teacher waits for the new student to arrive; waiting, because of a primary pedagogical principle: Never arrive at the studio after a student! Teachers who are late for appointments give the clearest possible indication of a lack of interest in the student's problems and progress. A student can only think that the teacher would rather be somewhere else.

And a profound *a priori* assumption ought to be in the waiting teacher's mind: Students rarely come to this first meeting or to their early instruction with the psychic maturity and personality integration which enables them to think of the teacher simply as "teacher." In fact, most mature singers return to their teachers for more than remedial help with vocal technique or for artistic coaching: for them the teacher is also shaman and guide. But the young *always* come with a need for establishing a satisfactory emotional relationship with the teacher.

Psychologists identify this emotional necessity as "transference," and all writings of the nature and function of transferences ought to be required reading for voice teachers, and referenced for every class in vocal pedagogy. For transferences bloom in the one-to-one setting, doctor's office or singing teacher's studio, because of the prestige differentials and the intimacy of the associations.

This means that immature students will have acquired certain techniques which worked, or seemed to have worked, in getting along with significant persons in their pasts. And the successes, even the relative successes of these techniques may have resulted in a kind of psychological inertia which prevents them from perceiving differences in new relationships, just as the premature praise for the "talented" young singers can arrest their progress. Old behavior patterns will be re-enacted, "transferred" to the studio. Students will cast the teacher in a variety of roles, familiar to them, using behavioral patterns that "worked," up until now.

The teacher must understand that the young student will have a very limited capacity for adjusting to this new relationship; the teacher must make the adjustment. And the intensity of the transference need will be more than an index of the student's psychic health and maturity; at this beginning the student's faith in the teacher will be emotionally determined, almost totally dependent upon the teacher's sensitivity to the proper transference role. Where there is no such faith there will be no efficacy, no "magic" in the teaching.

No matter how rational the teacher's method, the approach must be determined by the student's present reality. The two can meet only at the student's emotional and artistic locus. All teaching begins there. And "there" the teacher becomes exemplar and persuader, Merlin to Arthur, Dedalus to Icarus, Fairy Godmother to Cinderella, the ubiquitous and mysterious "helper" of the folk tale who appears at just the right time to lead the young hero safely through trials to triumphs.

So, throughout the early instruction the student's analytic and objective capacities may be approached only by an emotionally valid teaching role. But, even later, when teachers may think their work properly consists of criticism of old concepts and the provisional presentation of new ones, they should be reminded of Jung's admonition that around every concept there will always be a "halo" of unconscious associations.

Observing the intensity of transference relationships brought Jung to the belief that love was essential to the process of learning. And surely every teacher of singing, worthy of the title, understands this, having often had occasion to celebrate the joys of surrogate parenthood without having to endure the distresses of the actual role. But even the most purely professional regard for the students must take some form of accepting their present realities, allowing them to remain in their "pasts," for the present, gaining their confidence, allowing time for the transferences to develop, after which the teacher may begin to bring them into a more authentic present. This acceptance allows for self-esteem, crucial in the nurturing of young artists. No purely "objective" method can achieve this; teachers apply themselves with their methods.

How will a teacher apply himself? Through intuition, which he may hope has been enriched and confirmed by experience, he will insert himself into the students' emotional and artistic contexts, perceiving with them. None of the students' misconceptions will be much modified by any lofty separation, or with repetitions of trusted jargon, or with admonishments to "Work harder!" Or, "You must come to terms with your problems!" Or, "Will you never grow up?" Experience teaches us to waste no reliance on the students' present will power. And, besides, there are certain risks in such expressions of our own extremities; a slightly more mature student, told to "Work harder!" is entitled to respond, "Yes sir (or Ma'am) but at what, and how, exactly?"

Where there is an equal command of other requirements for the teaching, it is the sensitivity to the transference which explains why one teacher may be so much more successful with a particular student than another may have been. Insensitivity to the transference drives many students from studio to studio, searching for a teacher who more nearly suits the present emotional need. Voice teachers often attribute this "drifting" to the students' lack of talent or discipline; the students are left to rationalize it as best they can, not often to their own psychological or artistic advantage. Any improper response to students' immature distortions of perception ought to be a disqualification for teaching. Teaching will be ineffective where the transference is simply denied.

Recognizing the transference need is much more than a psychological necessity; there are pragmatic values. Because the relationship may fill a real gap in the young student's development, the teacher is in a position to exploit the student's idealized trust. This brings an earlier and easier acceptance of the teacher's analyses and descriptions. The experienced teacher knows that the efficacy of any vocalises that might be assigned will not be in any objective detailing of their values, not in any analysis of their desired effects, and not merely in their practice, however religious. If they are to be effective there must be an "emotional accuracy" in their presentation. This is to say that the teacher must prepare the student to trust the recommended practice techniques and materials. It means that the teaching must always have more than an intellectual significance. Otherwise, students will simply continue trying to make their "old" voices do the "new" things, further ingraining the unnecessary expectations of a tedious process of "vocal development."

Of course the teacher will not put all the egos in one basket; there must be an alertness for clues to the particular nature of a transference need: What persona is being presented? How does the student relate to authority? With poise? Inordinate respect? Brash familiarity? How does he use the teacher's title? Mr.? Ma'am? Doctor? Professor? Maestro? How often and with what inflection? Is the teacher to be the unapproachable authority? First name buddy-buddy? Is the student anxious to identify with the teacher's strength? With an excruciating desire to please? Nodding with every comment? Quick to adopt the teacher's jargon? Does a student apologize for her vocal limitations? With references to accomplishments in other fields? Is the teacher to respect her as a person even though she lacks talent for singing? Is the teacher to be the confirmer of the student's poor opinion of herself? Does the student interrupt, anticipating criticism?

Does she stand close? Touch? Stand off? Are there gestures, body language appeals for approval, affection, for love? Is the teacher the parent-who-punishes? The strict parent who withholds love? The teacher's response to the stern-parent transference is to be particularly delicate, since part of the student's psychic weakness requires authority while another part wants to be free. There will be alternating failures of confidence and forms of rebellion.

Are there fantasies of professional success? Is the teacher to be the indulgent parent? Is the student here to please a parent who holds impossibly high standards? Are there guilty expectations of failure? Is the teacher the parent-to-be-punished for imposing unrealistic demands? Does the student protect herself by rejecting instruction? Is the teacher ally or adversary?

Ah, but the teacher ought never to be in too great a hurry to accept a transference role. A slight reluctance, a temporary ambiguity about the relationship, will cause the students to reveal themselves more clearly. The teacher, after all, is going to ask the students to suspend or change their notions of vocal beauty and control, to give up their present technique and criteria for performance, and, in fact, to alter their very personalities in the process. Delaying the acceptance of the indicated transference role can imply that a satisfactory relationship depends upon the student doing all these things, willingly.

In discussing and acknowledging the desirability of "rapport," voice teachers often are making oblique and unconscious references to transferences. But generally the term "rapport" has only the vague connotation of some form of sympathetic understanding, something that happens, or not, when teachers and students "hit it off," or not. And an implication is that students have an equal responsibility for establishing the rapport, or that they must have the kinds of personalities which make for such lucky and harmonious relationships. But devising strategies for handling transferences is the teachers' responsibility, and this requires more than ordinary rapport. What is needed is an enlightened empathy, near as possible to Henri Bergson's "inserting oneself into the duration of and coinciding with" a student. This is the kind of empathy which ought to affect the timing, the manner, and the language in which the teaching material is to be presented.

But nothing in our pedagogical training or performance experience prepares us for a conscious recognition of, response to, and proper resolution of transferences. And this has serious effects on the accuracy of our assessments of intrinsic motivation, and on our abilities to engage and exploit it. When a transference goes unrecognized, "rapport" is difficult to establish, and then the teaching temptation is to question the student's character or commitment. We can easily mistake an apparent absence of motivation for an actual absence of talent. Doing so, our definition of talent becomes: presumptive evidence of the fewest teaching problems.

That definition of talent does a great disservice to the art, justifying a high drop-out rate and an almost exclusive dedicating of teaching energies to the presumably most talented. Yet, it is a definition arrived at quite naturally; almost all voice teachers come to the teaching by way of their own proficiency in the art.

That proficiency is important but it is an insufficient promise of success, either for the teaching or the learning. It prepares us easily to recognize it in others, but not necessarily for transmitting it.

Perhaps all teachers of singing ought to be administered an Orphean Oath, promising to lose no one to the art, pledging that students at any level of talent and interest are to be taught to capacity, "Quarts with quarts, pints with pints," so to say. All will do the art some service.

A few "case histories," actual except for invented names, can illustrate some transference effects and typify kinds of students who might easily be neglected as inadequate talents. Similar examples are to be found, and heard, in private studios everywhere, everyday.

Daddy's Little Girl

Marion, at her first lesson, sang with one of those clear young voices that can spin out a long, lovely pianissimo with an angelic beauty. There appeared to be no major problems beyond the fact that her voice was immature, which time would remedy. Her musical talent appeared worthy of high expectations and fairly firm motivational shoves.

She was particularly devoted to the portamento as the most important element of her personal expressive style. At one of her early lessons I began an effort to convince her that it was one of those singer's "effects without causes," to be used sparingly, judiciously, even where indicated by a composer. To dramatize the point I pressed her to repeat and repeat a particular phrase, directing her attention each time to the slurring anticipation which over-sentimentalized a musical line that cried out for a clean advance from note to note.

She stood behind me reading the music over my shoulder as I played the accompaniment. (An obvious lesson for teachers who accompany: Students must stand where they, and the music, can be seen.) I played the short interlude leading up to the phrase, twice, three times, but she did not sing. I turned to see her utterly forlorn, in tears.

As a young teacher this was the first time that one of my students had wept during a lesson. I jumped up from the piano bench, embarrassed, chagrined to have so upset such an innocent young lady. I tried to comfort her with awkward and apologetic repeatings of "That's alright, my dear," and ended the lesson early to allow her to recover. I spent the rest of the afternoon and much of the evening accusing myself of insensitivity, thoughtlessness, of ungentlemanly and probably unprofessional behavior.

But then came one of those too brief and rare strokes of sanity, a recollection of having recently read something, somewhere, about transference, as it occurred in the one-to-one analytical setting – for teachers of singing perhaps the most important of Freud's insights – and began to berate myself not for meanness but for having fallen so easily and unconsciously into the role of Forgiving Father who always makes things "alright" for his dear daughter.

Marion was petite, very pretty, looking younger than her 18 years. She spoke on a slightly too-high pitch, with trace inflections of the petulant child. Very likely she had always gotten what she needed, or wanted, from her father – affection, approval, and all manner of material expressions of his regard – by remaining an appealing child. And who could resist? Not an inexperienced singing teacher whom she had so sweetly forgiven with a smile meant to melt the heart of a statue. I had been turned into another such "father" with an exquisite expertise, well-practiced, and perhaps not altogether unconscious.

The remembered reference was to a primary principle of psychoanalytic practice: the analyst serves, when appropriate, as an absolute barrier against which the infantile and inappropriate behavior patterns of the patient eventually prove ineffective, after which the patient might become ready to seek other more open and productive means of expression. And the application to the teaching of singing was clear: at times it must be the function of the singing teacher to serve as the rock-solid critic against which the immature assumptions, conceptions, and techniques of his students will shatter.

An opportunity to test the insight came soon after. My "darling daughter" came to a lesson not having prepared a song she was supposed to have memorized, a song well within her musical and vocal capabilities. We started the song several times, and each time she stopped at the same place, unsure of her next entrance.

I offered a fairly formal lecture on expectations for diligent practice, and soon, as before, came the tears. But this time I was prepared with an innocence of my own, saying, "I am impressed and very pleased to see that you can take your work so seriously that you can weep about it. Now, take a moment to collect yourself and we will study this song together."

It would be nice to be able to write that she immediately became a superior student and eventually a famous singer. She did not. But soon she became a much better student, gaining in confidence by accepting greater responsibility. And eventually she sang very well, becoming a dependable performer with one of those lovely, lyric voices, so effective in the Haydn oratorios. Presently, she is doing excellent work as a professional soloist in a first-rate church choir.

The Young Bass

Edward was slender, smaller than average, with a history of precarious health as a child, growing up with feelings of physical and social inferiority to other boys his age. Highly intelligent, he had found a valuable compensation in academic achievement of such precocity that his parents had been encouraged to permit him to skip a grade in elementary school. He remembered being proud of that recognition but it had been ill advised, insuring that he would remain, throughout his schooling, the youngest, smallest, and, as he believed, the weakest boy in his class.

Though he excelled in his studies, his greatest pride was in his singing. He had earned a reputation as a small celebrity for his solo performances as a soprano in a local boy's choir. Upon arriving at high school his greatest ambition was to be a member, perhaps even a soloist, with the "Mens' Glee Club," but he was not yet 14, still singing with his unchanged voice.

Still, he simply had to sing, and for the first two years of his high school career he was the only boy in what seemed a sea of girls, singing soprano in the school's large general chorus, enduring the social embarrassment and his classmates' teasings.

But he continued his academic compensation, establishing and maintaining his position at the head of his class, winning respect and finally friendships in his junior and senior years, co-authoring a senior musical play, and finally becoming assistant director of the Mens' Glee Club, a signal honor for outstanding seniors.

It had not been until late in the summer preceding his junior year that his change of voice occurred, that maturation having been slower than average, perhaps due to his earlier ill health and perhaps somewhat further delayed by the success and familiar feel of his soprano singing. He remembered spending the rest of that summer testing his voice daily to see just how low he could sing, and was overjoyed to hear himself "sing" a low F. As soon as school opened he auditioned for the Glee Club and, on that happiest day of his life up until then, he was not only accepted but was assigned to the bass section by a non-singing choral director who was undoubtedly happy to have a new, intelligent, musical, motivated "bass."

At last it was not so painful to be the youngest and smallest. He now had a strong, six-foot-two bass voice. Lowering his larynx and growling out a dark, pharyngeal sound, he reveled in the "richness" of his "adult" voice. The labored production made it nearly impossible for him to vocalize above a middle C, but that, to him, was confirming proof that he was indeed a real "bass."

So, he began his formal voice study having sung for two years as a bass in that glee club, and having switched to the bass section in the youth choir of his church, where he often performed as a soloist, receiving the kinds of praise he welcomed most, the essence of which was, "What a big voice for so young (small) a man!"

But sensitivity of a high order was immediately apparent. And musicianship! There had been piano lessons, much playing by ear, an independent study of music theory, and, from an omnivorous reading habit, an impressive amount of general information about music history, composers, operatic plots, and lives of famous singers.

Asked what singer he most admired, he immediately named Alexander Kipnis, and waited to see what effect this name had on the teacher – since it was a name unknown to most of his own contemporaries. Kipnis, the long-retired Russian bass whose low

D rattled the springs in the fourth balcony seats, and whose old 78 rpm recordings Edward had searched out, collected, re-recorded, and, alas, imitated.

His intelligence and desire made him a teacher's delight; he always came well prepared for his lessons, having perfectly memorized any assigned songs, having informed himself about the composers' times, places, and significant contributions to the song form. And he often brought along songs he had discovered for himself. He loved sight-reading through volumes of song literature, and two years of high school German had helped prepare him to be enraptured by Schubert and Schumann lieder. A delightful student indeed, but how to disengage his ear and ego from that artificially dark caricature of a bass sound?

At the first meeting he stood ramrod-straight with a military rigidity, and, larynx nearly disappearing below his collar; he spoke well below an optimal frequency with the formality of one not yet 19 wishing to be 40. It was clear that he was anxious to be considered, or considered himself, or expected to be treated as an adult. He preferred, it seemed, the company of adults, still socially insecure with his peers. It appeared that he wanted to put an unhappy childhood as far behind himself as possible. And this was confirmed by his obvious pleasure in being addressed as "Mr." "Edward" was acceptable; the diminutive "Eddie" not at all.

A productive relationship was established by exploiting his longing for maturity, for "equality," by assuming a wisdom and experience beyond his years. Then, gradually, often casually, arranging for him to discover that his "equal," the teacher, was an authentic adult whose academic grasp obviously exceeded his own, who sang easily higher, and more importantly, lower than he. His "equal" obviously admired the high, soft, lyric singing of the best of the low voices – even that of Kipnis, relative to the immensity of that voice.

Throughout the process there were constant appeals to his innate artistry, with an introduction to the beauties of the standard vocal literature – the "standard" literature so full of requirements for ranging higher and softer than Edward imagined he was able to sing, or would not be able to sing until he was older and stronger. The songs he had prepared for his audition had been transposed a third lower than their original keys; he had scored them for

himself. Now, an adult was sharing with him an assumption, not
at all necessary to dwell on, that adult singers perform those songs
in the proper keys, and that of course composers understood the
capabilities of properly produced voices.

In this atmosphere of "equality" Edward slowly, and then more
rapidly, responded to the absence of praise for the dark sound,
and to the encouragement for efforts to settle on an optimal
speaking frequency. Gradually he began to hear with "equal" ears,
acquiring a new sense of vocal reality in an association of
increasing informality which eventually became a first-name
relationship.

As it happened, his health began to improve soon after the
beginnings of his voice study. He began a program of exercise
and developed a sturdy singing physique, becoming an excellent
swimmer and a better than average tennis player. In these activities
he learned what it truly meant to experience an efficient,
coordinated, complete use of his body, and his long-repressed
competitiveness found a satisfying outlet. His earlier rigidity, from
efforts to appear strong and vigorous, had prevented the relaxed
intake of breath needed for singing; he had simply tensed
everything he had, striving for a black belt in Bel Canto.

Identifying with his teacher, he began to trust and later to enjoy
the lighter feel, the greater ease, and the expressive beauty of his
higher, lyric voice. It would never be a voice of operatic caliber,
but he became an excellent recitalist, especially effective in the
performance of lieder. And, perhaps because of the insights
gained through the struggle to overcome his own problems, he
became a valuable high school choral director, and a more than
"equal" singing teacher.

The Hypochondriac

Bradley was a young tenor with a small, strained sound that
was incongruous with his tall, lean physique. On short
acquaintance one could always tell when he felt some conscious
concern for, or some unconscious association with his next
performance; he would clear his throat – a primary "no-no" for
any professional user of voice – with an Uhmm, Uhmm, Uhmm,

always three times, testing to be sure that his voice was "still there." This he did with increasing frequency as the performance date drew near, and by the time the day arrived he would have cleared his throat into an irritating laryngitis. "Ah," he would complain, "Why is it, always, just as I get an opportunity to sing, I get a sore throat?" He attributed it to a combination of unstable health and general bad luck, having become unaware of the unconscious tic.

Longer acquaintance confirmed an accident-prone personality, often involved in minor mis-steps, bruised from walking into furniture, bumped against car doors, trippings on rugs, turned ankles on uneven sidewalks, and two minor auto accidents. It seemed that he was often out of "present time," either rethinking past problems or worrying about future ones, failing to attend to immediate activities, senses dulled to objects and events in the actual present.

Difficulties with vocal technique were complicated by a perfectionism with which he approached any activity – a crippling attitude for any singer, and this was reinforced by a hypochondriasis, or perhaps was its cause, as if his body punished him for his unforgiving demands with more colds, flus, and allergies than usual. Significantly, his father had been a fine amateur tenor, and Bradley had repressed a considerable resentment, thinking he might never be able to sing so easily, and this further contributed to his conviction, perhaps its primary cause, that nothing he might do would ever be quite good enough. Performance proved too disappointing. He turned to a successful career in educational administration where his penchant for ordered and detailed perfection was an asset. As principal of a large inner-city high school he insisted on hiring a vocal specialist for his music program, and not once during his administrative tenure did his school's choral groups, which he sometimes enjoyed conducting, fail to win superior ratings at festivals.

Don't Call Me "Miss"

Laura was a large girl, somewhat overweight, lacking a singer's energy. Unhappy about her height, she slumped in the crook of the piano with an appearance of chronic fatigue. She did not like the formal "Miss," wanting to be called "Lolly," and better still, "Lolly-Polly."

She spoke with a high, breathy voice, attaching diminutive suffixes wherever possible. She affected a slight lisp and often reverted to a kind of infantile auto-echolalia; things were "nice-nice," or "bad-bad." Her pet dog, Tiger, was "Ger-ger." She invented diminutive versions of her friends' names.

She was an only and very dependent child, and at 20 still lived at home. Her parents, "Mummy and Poppy," were much older than those of her peers; Laura had been born late in a marriage long after hopes for having children had been abandoned. Her parents had been apparently as indulgent as grandparents.

There was a genuine interest in singing; her room had always been furnished with state-of-the-art sound systems and she had a large collection of vocal recordings. And there was intelligence; her academic record had been above average. But she sang, or "crooned," a breathy soprano, breaking even short phrases to catch a breath. An endomorphic, unathletic type, she seemed never to have experienced the feel of resistance to collapse accompanying a complete closure of the vocal folds.

She was ordinarily a passive student, but occasionally when pressed to make a more vigorous sound she would respond, tantrum-like, by shouting at the pitch and pouting, "Is that what you want me to do?" But the increased effort she felt she was making was not equaled by a significant increase in volume, there being no solid fundamental, the "highs" not being reinforced by clear formants because of the breathy production. Sounds produced by a near closure, or by an accidental break into the authentic lower register, were "not pretty."

To rule out organic causes or results of the breathy, incomplete closure, she was sent to a laryngologist who reported that the vocal folds appeared normal and recommended a general physical examination. A hypothyroid condition was discovered and treated and her vitality dramatically improved. But her psycho-vocal problems persisted, resisting the efforts of several teachers who, understandably, found the transference role – Indulgent Parent who indefinitely prolongs the dependency – beyond their patience, understanding, or competence.

But later, after psychological counselling, Laura found a satisfying relationship with a "motherly" teacher who was able to guide her toward singing a maturing and acceptable mezzo-soprano. And later still, as a young matron, Laura formed a music committee in a women's club, organized a variety of fund-raising activities, and presided over an annual awarding of scholarships for young singers in her community.

The Rare Talent

Arthur was over six feet tall, elegantly handsome, with the body and grace of an Olympic athlete, and a wide-ranging baritone of rich, rare, ringing masculine beauty. He had sung from an early age without any awareness of problems with technique. If ever there was such a thing, his was a "natural" voice which obviously was going to be able to encompass any of the baritone literature, lyric, heroic, opera, or oratorio. It was a talent of such magnitude that nothing, it surely seemed, stood in the way of a great performing career, of international recognition and acclaim. It was impossible to believe that he could ever sing for anyone who would not be profoundly stirred by the magnificence of the voice.

But his was a limit case. Alas for singing teachers who can only hope to find themselves associated with such a student once in a teaching career. He appeared incapable of accepting praise. Positive comments – there could hardly be negatives – were received with suspicion, frowns, dark doubts that would not be dispelled, bordering on depression and resentment.

He drifted from teacher to teacher, never staying with one more than a few months, never finding what he seemed, perversely, to want, a teacher who accepted his curious self-abnegation. Enthralled by the glorious sound, each new teacher immediately made enthusiastic predictions and plans for great performing success; only a saintly teacher would have been untempted to consider how wonderfully a teaching reputation might be enhanced by such a student.

Arthur sometimes fantasized about a performing career, but never seemed able to commit himself to the whole-hearted effort required. When he did bring himself to attempt an important audition, he appeared unprepared, not having mastered and memorized his music, physically apologetic. "Fine voice... but...!" Something in him seemed to prefer failure. He sought career opportunities unrelated to music, singing only occasionally for his local church or in local amateur productions. Until, at age 45, he began a belated, still lukewarm effort toward professional performance, with moderate success. He left behind many a disappointed singing teacher who sighed over the ironies of talent without ambition, ambition without talent, dreaming of the day when just the right mix arrived at the studio door in one package.

Perhaps it was the sheer beauty of Arthur's voice that made it so difficult for any of his teachers properly to understand his emotional need, or to consider for a moment his self-denial in order to help him outgrow it. How in the world could anyone with such a voice have any problems?

Hearing that voice it would have taken a great technical effort not to be impressed, awed. But some teacher should have spent less time on admiration and, instead, insisted on a stern discipline of study in those areas where he might have agreed with Arthur that there were serious lacks, one who might have said, "Ah, well, you have a healthy and beautiful voice. Good. Be thankful for that. But that is only the beginning and far from enough. You must understand that you need to know just how and why you produce such sounds in order to keep them. And you have an immense amount of work to do on languages, repertoire, acting, body movement, style. There will be years of coaching, preparing roles for successful auditioning."

Arthur might have responded, having been "located" much nearer to where he, himself, believed he was, with much to be done to be worthy of his natural gift. He might have welcomed the time it was going to take; time to earn a level of self-confidence nearer to that which others seemed to have in him.

This form of transference role acceptance might have resulted in a more enduring relationship with a teacher, and in the kind of emotional trust Arthur needed to gain and confide some insights into the sources of his doubts and denials. His problem might have been so simple as to be overlooked: From the time he first opened his mouth to sing for anyone he had been unbearably burdened and bewildered by the expectations of everyone. All he ever got was praise.

The Late Bloomer

Tom stood stiffly, singing with enormous tension, forehead wrinkled, face flushed, larynx high, shoulders hunched up, chest caving in, and belly muscles so cramped that a railroad spike could hardly have been driven into him with a ten-pound sledge, and a restricted flow of air that flattened the pitches more and more toward the end of each phrase.

He could be approached only by the gentlest of suggestions, and these had to be offered as if in reference to singers in general, not directly to him. Direct comments were taken, it appeared, as harsh criticisms of his character and drove him into flurries of defensive explanations for what he had done. Even gentle suggestions were anticipated, or deflected, with ready rationalizations for not having performed perfectly. It was not that he "didn't know how," or "didn't understand," but everything he did had to appear intentional and reasonable. "Well, I didn't want it to be nasal, so I tried to give it more room." Or, "I lowered the back of my tongue to see if that would help." Or, "I just tightened my 'support' a little more that time." Or, "Well, I was trying to put the sound a bit higher up in my head." Or, "I was concentrating on widening my ribs a little more to get a better breath." Or, "I just meant to get a better pronunciation of the vowel." And any such comment might have been made when all he had been asked to do was to sing a legato arpeggio without moving his lower jaw.

He seemed incapable of a spontaneous, uncritical effort, or of following simple directives. He was always adjusting, fixing, interjecting, defending, expecting difficulty and proving it. This fragmented attention to irrelevant detail prevented a coordinated act of phonation and the kind of calm, alert readiness for recognizing any sound that might be promising and new. This made it difficult to judge his innate musicality and expressiveness, although it was apparent from his conversation that he had an unusual appreciation for poetry, for painting, and for the expressive singing of others.

When told that a particular sound was better than before, he would respond with something to the effect that, "It didn't feel at all the way you described." Or, "But that was so far back in my throat." Or, "Wasn't that what you called 'nasal' before?" As if implying that it had been the teacher's inadequate descriptions and criticisms, all along, that had kept him from finding the right sounds.

Indeed, there seemed to be sufficient reason to consider Tom unteachable, but the resistance and rationalizings came to have another interpretation upon learning that no one else in his large family, for generations, had had any interest at all in music. His father, dominating and, Tom thought, "impossible to please," was particularly skeptical and scornful of Tom's interest. He had agreed to pay for a "practical" education, but certainly not for voice lessons. "Why can't you take up something useful?" It was so overwhelmingly important for Tom to succeed that he struggled to sing by stringing a series of defensive devices together with a "Can't you see I am trying, Papa?" Or, for the teacher, "Can't you see what a good student I am?"

But his vocal problems were not merely psychological; a high school teacher had mis-classified him as a tenor, and had even contacted Tom's father in an effort to persuade him to allow Tom to take private lessons, implying considerable potential and future success as a tenor. Tom could produce some deceptively pleasing sounds on the higher pitches, but the collection of inhibiting devices needed to "get there" made him unable to sustain them.

He made some progress toward an improved tone production in the studio, but when he performed, his audiences were filled with disapproving fathers, mothers, brothers, sisters, cousins and aunts. All his constrictions asserted and his sagging intonation made performance an ordeal, for him and his audience. After two years of study, discouraged, he gave up the effort, apparently accepting his father's advice about "practicality." He left school, joined his family-owned business, discouraged, but never quite reconciled to the defeat.

Fifteen years later, now presiding over the family business, financially secure, his father retired, Tom returned to the study of singing, now as an avocation. Calmer and mature, and having listened to much singing in the interim, he accepted the proper classification as a baritone. And within two more years he performed an impressive *Elijah*. Now he sings as a regular member of an opera company chorus, as a church choir soloist, and auditions for every local and regional semi-professional musical production. In fact, he sings anywhere, anytime, for anyone who will listen, and with the obvious and deserved satisfaction that comes from having finally slain the old dragons of defeat and discontent.

*   *   *

As the student progresses toward a technical and artistic maturity, toward an equality with the teacher, the problem becomes one of ending the transference. Ah, when to kick the fledgling out of the nest? When to destroy the student's dependence on the teacher? Perhaps none of us is ever skilled enough for this, and there are no objective methods for determining the proper time. We can only take comfort in the thought that intuition, after all, is much older than analysis, and managed our survival long before logic-come-lately. The principle is simple enough: The transference is to be ended when it no longer contributes to the learning. And then the teacher should be, intend to be, as careful not to extend the dependency beyond its positive value as he, or she, was, earlier, not to refuse the role when it was needed.

It may never be necessary or appropriate to explain to a student what the transference has been, although an effective teacher has, in a sense, been "explaining" it all along by preparing the student for new perceptions. The transference will be brought to the students' awareness by showing them how and why they relied on distortions of their vocal experience, why the problems persisted, what might be done about them, and without them. But a "psychological" explanation may never be attempted, or needed. Students come to understand, without being told directly, that their interferences have been "disguises" for the expressiveness they felt insecure in revealing.

There is another *a priori* certainty: The students' problems will be further complicated by counter-transferences. Alas, voice teachers have emotional needs of their own which may be masked or displayed as personal styles. And many of these are not likely to have positive values for the teaching: Why do they like one

student so much more than another? Why are they so patient with
one and so short with another? Regardless of talent? Why do they
so enjoy some lessons and dread others? Why are they so anxious
about accepting a particular transference role?
  Do they ever have difficulty remembering their schedules?
Their students' names? Are they vaguely uncomfortable with
some? Do they suffer anxieties related to competence? Are they
upset when asked a question they cannot answer? Do they feel it
necessary to impress their students? Their colleagues? Are they
ever tempted to "show off" during some lessons? Do they dislike
teaching beginners? Advanced students? Have they ever been
envious of a student's superior talents?
  Do they dislike admitting mistakes? Are they reticent about
discussing fees? Unduly flattered when a student says something
like, "I can't seem to find the right sound in the practice room, but
I always find it here with you"? Do they find themselves repeating
stock phrases learned, perhaps, from some dominating teacher in
their pasts? What is it about a particular student that makes a
teacher feel angry, gratified, frustrated, jealous?
  Does a teacher ever assign song literature too difficult for a
student? What is it that makes one fairly modest and another
blatant about their professional careers? Are there ever implied
apologies for not having had a performing career? Has one ever
found himself tempted to force student voices into his own vocal
category? Does one sing too often during the lesson? Too seldom?
Are they ever jealous of other teachers? Of other teachers'
students? Why is one so reluctant to release her students to another
teacher? Does she ever seek out social relationships with her
students? And what about erotic overtones? Have we never sensed
our craft ebbing?
  There are strong teachers who have "fathered" generations of
students, and many of these students, years later, still find
themselves repeating the fatherly dictums often without the
fatherly insights. And there are "motherly" teachers who revel in
the role, encouraging their students to remain dependent,
anxiously overseeing their diet, dress, even their social lives, in a
kind of live-in studio atmosphere. Authority figures require
dependents and can continue the dependency, albeit

unconsciously, perpetuating the vocal problems. Ah, is the student means or end?

The Positive Papa

No one remembered how, when, or by whom the title had been conferred, but he was "Dad" to everyone on campus; never "Professor," or "Doctor," just "Dad." And it never seemed to occur to any of his students, until perhaps many years later, that he needed and prided himself in the role, and that if he had not originated it himself he did nothing to discourage it and much to reinforce and sustain it.

Myths of his powerful persona attracted and affected students even before their first meeting with him. They approached with the awe and respect due a latter-day Victorian Papa, and, on longer acquaintance, came to do so with genuine affection and the authentic respect his teaching deserved.

He used the paternal authority to inspire and liberate the talents of generations of anxious-to-be-accepted young students. Later, they would discover that nothing he ever said about the art ever turned out to be misleading or untrue.

He taught by pointed aphorism, always immediately applicable and always proving to have more profound implications as his students matured in the art: Musicianship can be judged by the treatment of the anacrusis. The first appeal is to the eye. There will always be a crescendo of emotional intensity as you sing into a harmonic suspension. Sing always toward the most important word in the phrase. Color the adjectives. The strongest effect of a rubato will be in the return to tempo. The musical line is always, always, moving toward or away from a climax. Placement? All vowels should sound as if produced by the same instrument; minimize the physical and acoustical differences. Interpretation? What situation might you find yourself in that would result in the spontaneous expression of the text? Conducting? Take Wagner's advice: Find the melody in every bar.

Those who began their study with him had lifelong occasion to be grateful that the transference was used to discipline and to teach. A more dependent student might receive more attention but

only when the dependency was warranted also by talent and
earned by commitment. All had to work diligently to prove worthy
of his paternal and artistic regard. At times his passion for making
music with his most talented students led him to spend more time
on repertoire than on technique, but he was a superior coach and a
peerless accompanist: "What key do you want this in?"

The Negative Papa

Another powerful personality, an Irish mystic, tall, handsome,
imposing, a noted choral conductor and voice teacher who, one
season, might stand before his choir, arms raised, eyes closed in
intense meditation, still as a statue until everyone's attention was
riveted, breathless, and then, out of the dramatic silence, would
roar, "What tempo am I thinking?" And this with the utmost
conviction, his own and that of his awed singers, that he was
releasing vital inner forces which communicated his thoughts to
the deserving. "Rapport, Rapport," he would demand, and those
who had guessed wrong felt disgraced, their lack of sensitivity
making them unworthy of so great a spirit.

But, season to season, practicality might alternate with the
mystical. The entire secret of singing was in some singularity of
technique: "Everyone down on the floor! On your backs! Hands
on your belly, and Shout! Shout! Shout!" Or, "Everyone around
the piano and on every high note Lift! Lift! Lift the piano off the
floor!"

One year it might be: "Remember the Holy Book! In the
beginning was the Word! Now concentrate, heart, mind, and soul
on the meaning of every word and the technique will follow!" But
the next year it might be "Vowels! Vowels! We sing not words,
but Vowels!" One season it was "No trace of Vibrato! We seek a
perfect purity, a cosmic uniformity, an immense and oceanic
oneness!" And the next it was "Everyone in this choir must think
himself a world famous soloist!" Sometimes all music was to be
memorized, sometimes "Why should not singers, like other
musicians, read from the score?"

He was indeed an exciting choral conductor; one season with
great gesturings and ballets of body movement, and another it was

to be the smallest of hand movements, "Dignity, after all!" with movements invisible to the audience and requiring the spellbound attention of the singers to see and follow. But who he was and what he was doing in front of the choir was, in all seasons, surely much more important than the music.

Every eccentricity of emphasis was presented with the solemnity and nearly the effect of divine revelation, each the perfected and final insight of the master. Students were either too awed to detect inconsistency or they blamed themselves for failing to grasp the whole.

He raised crops of faithful imitators, which happens when the teacher is, or seems to be, more important than the teaching. And the teaching becomes harder and harder to adapt to later experience. The dogmatic presentation and the unquestioning acceptance has, rather, the effect of forcing later experience to adapt to it. His many disciples, fired with apostolic zeal, went out into the world evangelizing, usually without the master's seasonal flexibility.

*　*　*

So it is, along with the joyful fulfillments of music making and the attentiveness to vocal and artistic interests, these transferences and counter-transferences may be powerfully operant, dominating the studio atmosphere. Indeed, sometimes much of what passes for studying or teaching is actually the acting out of transferences. And in these relationships are all the archetypal rumblings: fear, love, rejection, betrayal.

New students should understand that the quality of this encounter is as important as the teacher's knowledge, training, or method. They ought to be prepared at least to recognize two contrasting forms of counter-transference: the technically friendly, insecure teacher, and the antiseptically professional authoritarian.

Insecure teachers will have eccentric versions of this meeting, seeking the students' approval, overplaying the role of friend, or indulgent parent, and underplaying the role of teacher. Anxious to establish a personal version of the relationship to come, these teachers may be the early winners of the popularity contests, but later prove to be runners-up. Intelligent students ought to sense the overtones of artificial friendship; healthy students will have come seeking an authority, not an equal. Sensitive students should sense the talking-down, the patronizing use of student jargon, the abuses of reassurance; they ought to expect a low standard of achievement.

Insecure teachers' comments will be safe, tentative, even after hearing the student sing, because they will be waiting for the student to exhibit qualities and attitudes to which they can comfortably relate. They will not carry the initiative far enough for the immature student, and may well be unconsciously fearful of the confident or talented ones. They are likely to begin "teaching" too soon, with disconnected comments rather than with coherent patterns. They may not recognize, or be reluctant to accept a transference need. Students may sense difficulties in making either personal or professional connections with the vagueness; they may respond to the friendliness and suspect that their difficulties in understanding the teaching must be due to their own dullness.

Conversely, this may be the time when the authoritarian feels he must exaggerate his formality – though often this is the time for the most spontaneous approach. The authoritarians' contexts require the early establishing of a wider prestige gap between themselves and the students. They will not waste time exploiting a transference, nor encouraging a personal relationship. They will not begin their teaching at the student's locus, but from their own. Their descriptions sound like directives, their methods may be asserted as exclusive, and their principles are likely to be presented as implicit references to the great distance to be traveled to the artistic realms, and their students' musical and artistic naiveté will be exploited as reminders. Students may feel deprived of such artistic and personal dignity as they might have, and talented students, consciously or not, may rebel, disliking the teacher as a person without being in a position to admit it even to themselves. They may begin the study with guilts about their shortcomings and attitudes toward a prestigious teacher.

The authoritarian atmosphere may be reinforced in overt or subtle ways, easily rationalized by both teacher and student as indications of respect for high standards. The teacher may dwell a little too long, or too often, on the successes of former students, or on the reputations of his own former teachers as exclusive custodians of the great Bel Canto tradition, inherited from an impressive genealogy of earlier anointed masters. Studio walls may be festooned with autographed photos of greats and near-greats who stare in silent disapproval at the neophyte's impertinent approach to the castle of the Grail.

Authoritarian teachers are most likely to sing too soon, and too often thereafter, demonstrating artistry and command before students are afforded any insights into the possibilities for achieving such command themselves. And this may seem less of a demonstration of the teacher's joy in performing – which is always contagious and a great teaching device – than an implied "You see, this is how it is supposed to be done." The teaching vocabulary may be limited, restricted; the teaching may heavily depend upon imitation. Students are likely to show striking similarities of tone quality, mannerisms, and interpretations. These teachers may be reluctant to accept students who are judged to be without obvious talent, and will easily attribute failures of instruction to the students' limitations. They will delay dissolving dependencies; it is not in their interest to have students outgrow them.

It should be clear, here, that the term "counter-transference" refers to any inappropriate feelings, perceptions, or responses on the part of teachers, expressive of psychological rather than pedagogical needs. Obviously these can have deleterious effects on the learning. Effective teachers must be able to test their own realities, understand their own motives, and be conscious of the implications of their actions, attitudes, and approach. These are not expected to be saintly, but, being conscious, can be kept from clouding up the studio atmosphere. Otherwise, they will significantly help, or appear to help, only those students whose specific needs and psycho-orientations comfortably relate and respond to their own particular needs.

Effective teachers will be prepared to recognize and accept the proper transference role; infantile egos may respond only in an utterly non-threatening atmosphere, while those egos which have outgrown artistry may need a sterner disciplinarian. Only the truly rare and talented ones simply need a "teacher."

In adjusting to the proper transference role the teacher must avoid confronting students with something they may not be ready to accept or handle. The teacher must speak from an attitude, at a level, and with a language that students can understand from where they now "are." Jung suggested that we ought to love our students, and, in doing that, we must adjust our communicative styles and content, personal and professional, to whatever their capacities to accept.

The truth is that the best teachers do indeed come to love their students, and it is not an exaggeration to refer to this as the love of a spiritual parent, fulfilled by contributing to the student's growing power for the creative expression of a unique self. And it is no wonder that students often return the love; the teacher is liberating them, and can be, at best, the healthy, helpful, understanding, accepting "parent" the student may never have had.

Certainly there must be a prestige differential in the teacher's favor if there is to be progress, but prestige comes with the title, as a "given," and is usually already enough. There will be differentials of age, accomplishment, experience, and reputation. Students usually come to this audition anticipating a breadth of knowledge and power in the teacher – likely over-rating it. Transferences may position a teacher just short of divinity. They can afford to think of themselves as elders, senior partners, fellow-artists. They need not be concerned with the power of authority, having that natural authority inherent in the role of teacher. And the greater this natural authority the less is the need for its display. Nor need they, in advance of any indications of a student's need, display an anxiety to establish a friendship; they are simply friendly. They ought not set out to crush an already tender artistic ego, but should accept the students' present emotional and artistic status in order to help them grow beyond their present bounds.

In "auditioning" the teacher, students should be ready to suspect all unwarranted praise, and be just as ready to defend their own artistry. They should be skeptical of such assurances as, "Everything is just fine," with a vaguely implied something like, "Stick with me and I'll have you in the Met!" – maybe the towel concession in the men's room – and be just as distrustful of, "Ah, we must begin all over again," or, "Now you must forget everything you know about singing!" They should suspect any method presented as "exclusive," and especially so when it is presented with an emotionally satisfying, near mystical solemnity. They should distrust any language of approach and instruction which obscures the simplicity of either the theory or the act of singing.

But alas, students are easily impressed, because they want to be, need to be. And years after their first study, sadder and wiser, many students have come to realize that their technique, such as it may have been, had, at best, been no more than taken apart and put back together again. Indeed, they may have come "out by that same door" wherein they went – with perhaps an altered terminology.

Axiom for beginners: Seek out a teacher who is more anxious to adapt the method to the student than the student to the method. Students should trust themselves to know, after a very few sessions, whether or not a particular teacher will be able to help them. The trouble with this is that most young singers, and many older ones as well, find it very difficult to trust their own intuitions, to appreciate that internal melody of self.

Axiom for teachers: New students will be hearing their intentions. They will bring with them all their particular distortions of perception, all their "Given Word" errors, Milton's ignorance of the phylogenic facts of the vocal event, and Adam's ignorance of the ontogenic. They will likely have forgotten, if they ever knew, that they have "chosen" their present usages. And whatever interferences these have caused in their speech will probably be exaggerated in their singing. But they will have been "getting along" with their present use; people understand them, their voices "work," and the workings are familiar, trusted, precious, and probably have been praised. They will hear beauty and sense control in their singing because they intend both and believe they are doing only what seems to be required. Much of the teaching will be a comparing of intent with actual result.

Another teaching truism: Students do not come to have their voices changed in any way! What they really want is to be shown how to do all those wonderful things the great singers do, with their present voices. No matter what they say in self-criticism, or about the desirability for change, no matter how keen their intellectual grasp of their vocal problems, no matter how talented and cooperative, how discriminating in their judgment of the singing of others, they do not want to have their voices changed. The experienced teacher is prepared for inertia, resistance, rationalization, and rebellion.

The new student arrives. Personal judgments begin with a "sizing up" and a sparring for connections. With the amenities of introduction are all the first impressions of appearance, sex, dress, posture, body language, all of which reveal or mask the "who" is to be taught. And teachers should be interested in the students' responses to the studio itself; this is the place where they spend most of their time, the atmosphere and furnishings reflect their interests, taste, and character. Is it modern, traditional, conventional, contemporary in its decoration? Straight lines or curves? Rugs, drapes, in fabrics of what color and design? Orderly, cluttered, symmetrical, neat? Every detail offers a clue to the teacher's personality. And the student absorbs, by a kind of aesthetic osmosis, the close connection between the teacher's decor and psyche. A "field" is thus established in which the student has an immediate sense of "whom" he will be relating to, which makes the relating easier. Further, since teachers thus reveal much about themselves, the students will find it easier to do likewise.

In turn, students will already have revealed much about themselves in their reactions. What do they first notice? The Picasso print? The books? The abstract sculpture? The potted plants? The antique chair? Much can be inferred of their alertness, intelligence, interests, educational and cultural backgrounds, all important indications of "who" will be taught.

It should be obvious that the quality of this important first meeting is impaired, and the subsequent teaching suffers, when the teacher does not have a permanent studio of his own, or must share a studio with another teacher, as is often an economic necessity in institutional teaching. Worse, a singing teacher ought never to be required to teach singing in an ordinary classroom, generally an unaesthetic environment unsuited to the art, certainly unsuited to the close one-to-one relationship. The singing teacher's best work requires a personal place, not an expedient one, a "significant" place, a place in which the transferences can be established, an aesthetic atmosphere, and a familiar acoustical setting.

Diagnosis begins with the teacher's first impressions of the student's speaking voice and the earliest inferences drawn from the language behavior. This is a time when voice teachers have cause to regret the meagerness of their knowledge of the relationship between speech and personality, beyond the general understanding that any deviations from "normal" will be symptomatic of some disturbance that may affect the teaching, and which might be an indication of the proper transference role. They may regret that a thorough analysis of the student's vocal-verbal habits is beyond the competence of contemporary vocal science. But it may be somewhat comforting to know that it is also beyond the competence of contemporary psychology. And, because of this, once more the singing teacher must accept the challenge of dealing with some unquantifiables which will forever keep the teaching from becoming a "science," much as psychology itself has failed so to qualify, except in the terms of those reductionists who continue laboring to harvest a few figs from thistles in the arid academic deserts of behaviorism. In any case, whatever the singing teacher's command of vocal science, it will have less application to this first meeting than an experienced sensitivity of ear for affect, and an intuitive recognition of and response to the student's locus.

Conscious or not, teachers will infer a personality from the newcomer's vocal behavior; an intuitive inference which, we may hope, may be balanced, reinforced, and partially objectified by experience. But inexperienced teachers who wish to test the validity of their responses might well prepare themselves by reference to Paul Moses' *The Voice of Neurosis,* an excellent refreshment for the experienced as well. Undervalued at the time of its publication, this work has deserved increasing respect among voice teachers and therapists. It suggests approaches to psychotherapy through analyses of vocal-verbal behavior. But unfortunately, its development into a formal methodology awaits a much closer cooperative research effort by specialists in these fields, or the unlikely arrival of another Moses, of as many parts, prepared in psychology as well as laryngology, with a profound understanding of music and musicians, and a particular, indulgent love for singers. Moses has been one of the very few laryngologists able to "hear" what a visual examination might be expected to reveal; the only one to attempt relating functional and organic vocal symptoms to psychiatric syndromes.

The teacher listens for "audible scars" while the students are being careful putting into words that which will be too revealing and self-expressive. What self do they want to present? What needs are hidden behind the proprieties of studio conversation? What "unspeakable" feelings of defensiveness, of fear? What does the student consider situationally proper to say? And, since omissions are also related to personality needs, what are they careful not to say?

But objectively: What about articulation? What failures of fluency affect the function, perhaps even the structure of the mechanism? Is the articulation precise, complete? Marred by tension in the jaw? A lazy tongue? A disregard for consonants? A gliding, slurring, or drawling that stains the purity of phonemes? Is the rate of speech normal, appropriate to the substance and emotional content of the message and situation? Is the rate affected by shyness, submissiveness, conformity, or insecurity? None of these latter being promising indications of talent for singing. Or, is the rate too fast? Cluttered? From anxiety? Habit? Neural deficit?

Are there articulation faults related to environmental variables: family speech traits, educational, economic, ethnic backgrounds? Are there evidences of transitory vocal-verbal fads which identify the student as one among peers? Alas, the rarity of efficient articulation ought to be caution enough for those teachers fond of saying to their students, "Sing as you speak!" For indeed this is likely to be just what most students do, accounting for their special vocal problems. Some singing teachers offer a related, but more mystical pronouncement: "Sing as you live!" But, alas, most of us must do much better than that.

Faulty speech is frequently heard in a divergence of registers; there may be a weakening in the middle ranges and a forcing toward the top. This can be "seen" as well as heard in the struggle behavior of the muscles involved. Extreme examples are heard in the tone production of the typical "pop" singer who, lacking vocal technique, restricts the expression of powerful emotions to the narrow limits of conversational range, or resorts to the "falsetto" sound inappropriate for the message – if not the style. Speech habits are forced to damaging pitch and intensity levels. This forcing of conversational voice production is often heard among actors who, having insufficient vocal training, seem unable to find and use the sounds of authentic passion, those "head register" whines and wails, the proper signal-expressions of genuine conflict and crisis. These, too, push the conversational habit toward destructive levels.

So, "Sing as you speak" is a phrase to be reserved for the very fortunate few whose voices seem to be "naturally" free, which means that somehow they managed an earlier, easy and efficient tone production. These are the ones whose occasional appearance reinforces the general misconceptions about being "born with a voice." They are not typical, which ought never to surprise a teacher of singing. It is the other way around; singers acquire beautiful speaking voices as a by-product of their study of singing.

However, there can be an element of useful truth, after all, in that carelessly overused phrase, if the teacher goes on to illustrate that speech approaches singing as the emotional content increases and intensifies. A teacher can certainly say that students will notice that singing, when it is "right," feels very much like vehement speech, that their bodies, while singing properly, might recognize the feel of "emergency level speech." It might even be appropriate in the privacy of the studio – perhaps sotto voce at a voice teachers' convention, but probably never in print – that singing can feel like an "elegant" yelling. For years many fine voice teachers have found it wonderfully helpful to insist that there are no "high" notes, only "peaks" of human emotion.

But ordinarily, speech is a poor, undependable model for singing, being affected by intention, leveled out for the sake of abstracting, kept deliberately to a narrow range of expressiveness for the sake of transmitting mere information, and, having been acquired very late in our evolution, vulnerable to even slight emotional disturbances.

"Sing as you speak" was given great currency and conviction by some early music psychologists, notably Carl Seashore, who misled several generations of singers and voice teachers – and large numbers of parents who were persuaded of the validity of his tests for musical talent. He insisted that singing and speech were to be equated, that they were subject to identical laws, developed from similar training processes – mostly imitation. It appeared to him that the only significant difference had to do with pitch and duration. "Only" indeed. Singing was simply speech in musical phrases. There was no recognition that speech and singing were altogether different adaptations, of the fact that evolution has been a parsimonious process in that many of its designs have proved to be adaptable for multiple, complex, and even seemingly contradictory functions.

And what about the newcomer's vocal "quality"? One thing is certain; voice teachers have good reason to insist that vocal "quality" cannot adequately, even usefully, be described simply as a distribution of energies among certain frequencies in an acoustical spectrum. That is so, but the definition is without "teaching meaning" for most voice teachers, and utterly without meaning for beginning students. Quality may be described purely as the bias of a listener, but it is obviously related to our perception of personal warmth, coolness, alertness, dullness, all of which help identify a transference need.

Is the quality "normal"? Which is to say pleasing, appropriate to the student's age, sex, background and general appearance? Or are there audible scars of competitiveness, impatience, aggressiveness, hostility, cynicism, reserve? Is it nasal? Denasal? Does the smothered pharyngeal sound represent apology, timidity, withdrawal, or mere habit? The singing teacher will have to intuit a basic sound unaffected by any such accretions.

Is there breathiness? Why do the vocal folds fail to impede the flow of air? Pathology of the leading edges? Protrusions, nodules, polyps, any of those "bumps" on opposing surfaces which are usually the results of some form of chronic abuse?

Such conditions may not be very far advanced; the teacher must listen for even slight indications of incomplete closure. What might be the history of this symptom? Did it disappear with voice rest? And return with a resumption of misuse? How much of this study will amount to vocal rehabilitation?

Even among non-singers the voice is one of the commonest sites for emotional stress. The voice is, after all, a function of respiration, and stress modifies patterns of breathing. Is the breathiness, or roughness, due to emotional or situational stress? Is the teacher hearing the "real" voice now meaning the student's usual voice? Had the breathiness once been intentional and now become habit? Is it related to sexual identity? What causes the hypovalvular functioning in which the folds vibrate but do not produce a clear sound? And has this caused structural change?

Any suspicion of abnormality or pathology, as detected by the teacher's experienced ear, should be referred to a competent laryngologist, "competent" meaning one experienced in the treatment of singers. Any laryngologist will be familiar with the worst of these functional and organic problems, with the protrusions which prevent an easy mid-line closure of the folds, causing the speaker to compensate with increased force. Extreme examples are heard in the damaged voices of athletic coaches, sports fanatics, drill sergeants, tense junior high school teachers with discipline problems, teenage cheer leaders, children with aggressive playground habits, and "pop" singers, folk-singers, and "belters" whose living depends on vocal abuse.

In the worst cases the speaking voices may be almost destroyed, sounding as if the folds had been shredded and fringed. And, alas, all these abusers could do all these things without bleeding from the throat, with even a minimum of voice training. Some argue that they might lose their individual styles if they underwent training, and accept the painful trade-off. But for all these, "style" is a collection of technical inadequacies. Style, properly, is in the head, not the neck.

But the singing teachers usually deal with subtler versions of these problems. Their concerns are for guiding the student toward a "normal" usage, "normal," here, meaning a usage efficient according to structure and design, and in comparison with others of the same age and sex. And for this the teacher should always be ready to seek the advice of a laryngologist who has learned to listen as well as look, and one who pays very close attention to what a student says about his own voice. For, in fact, hoarseness, roughness, or breathiness in the sound may not be at all "visible" to the laryngologist. The larynx and folds may appear perfectly healthy. And, ironically, many magnificent sounding voices "show" various forms of structural abnormality. The guiding wisdom, then, is conservative treatment. Surgery on the vocal folds, once commonly practiced for nodes and "bumps," is often unsatisfactory and does nothing to alter the speech habits which caused them. And the least scarring of the muscle tissue may result in an asymmetrical oscillation in the wave-like motion of the folds.

Speech and vocal therapy, followed by re-training, are almost always the proper indication. Most of these conditions are not serious if the singer is young and healthy, and if the therapy and training are timely. The difficulty is that young singers often are more concerned with satisfactory self-expression than with vocal health; they often accept roughness and hoarseness after vigorous vocal use as normal, because their voices seem to recover quickly.

The teacher will elicit and interpret a complete history of vocal use, knowing from experience that a student's description is not likely to be precise; responses to the teacher's questions may reveal as much about psychological states as they do of physiological problems. But the teacher will want to know what demands the student has put upon his voice. What has been the frequency of episodes of hoarseness? Of colds and sore throats? Of allergies? What medications? Which worked? Was there dryness or dehydration from decongestants? Was voice rest helpful or ineffective? Did the student cope, when hoarse, with aphonic whispering, without a closure? Or with a "stage whisper" that may have aggravated the condition? And what does the student think about his own ability to alter present usage?

A student might say, "My voice tires easily," or "seems to be husky in the morning," – a common result of the previous day's misuse. And the teacher must note the important distinction between the symptoms of hoarseness and fatigue. The noisy, scratchy roughness of the hoarse voice is probably due to some pathology on the leading edge of the vocal folds and will be treatable with conservative use. But vocal "fatigue" is likely to be more serious, especially if there have been cycles of recovery and recurrence, for these may be indications of some more general, perhaps even hormonal pathology.

The student may say, "I get this 'tickle' or 'scratch' in my throat when I try to sing high, or loud," and again the problem is likely to be on the leading edge of the folds, perhaps from an uncoordinated resistance to breath collapse. But when she says, "My voice 'hurts' after I sing for a while," the reference is to muscle tension which may be due to something other than overuse, anything from general hypertension to a long list of less likely causes: bruxism, temperomandibular joint, premenstrual hormonal imbalance, chronic dehydration – few students ever drink enough fluids. There is a high price paid for having a human instrument.

Is there a harshness, a stridency in the sound? Hypervalvular functioning? Do the folds open and close too violently? Is there a great increase of subglottal breath pressure? A resistance to airflow? A characteristic "pinching" of the sound? This is a common cause of chronic inflammation and vocal cord "bumps." Yet these can be the sounds of choice for those students who hear only forcefulness and like what they hear because it "sounds like" the great voices they so admire. Such sounds are almost always accompanied by, or caused by shallow, high breathing. The upper chest heaves with the inhalation, greatly increasing the tension in the entire laryngeal area. These students have something to learn about "belly breathing," the timely relaxation of the abdominal muscles that permits a complete inhalation; they must come to understand the authentic source of the forcefulness they so desire.

Is the speaking voice too soft? The incomplete phonation of modesty? Or too loud? The loudness of pseudo-authority forced through thickened folds? Intensity varies with the speaker's mood and the subjective perceptions of the listener. But it also varies with the student's psychological perception of the "distance" to or from the teacher, personal or professional. Is the softness intentional? A desire for intimacy? Or for distance? Is the loudness that of aggression? Assertiveness? Defensiveness? The teacher will have to intuit a proper level, remembering, of course, that most singers speak with a greater intensity than most situations require. And there is more to this sound than meets the ear; the singer's artistic equilibrium depends upon sensing that rumble and ring, the primary assurance that all's right with a personal and artistic world. And, as every teacher ought to know, the vitality of the singer's speaking sounds is not only necessarily narcissistic, it is ever so much easier on the vocal folds.

With the student's first words the teacher will have noted the fundamental frequency of the speaking voice. This is a crucial element in all early diagnosis, for any failure to have learned, or "chosen," to speak on an optimal frequency is one of the primary causes of vocal trauma. Much will depend upon the strength of the student's identification, physical and psychological, with the present pitch level and the reflexes which have come to support it. Does the student use much or little of the potential range? Is the pitch too high? Too low? There are revealing relationships between pitch and personality beyond those obvious primitive references of elevated pitch with excitement and lowered pitch with anxiety. Is there a consistent inflective pattern, indicating confidence, poise, personality integration? Or are the inflections narrow or erratic? Within what range? Is there a lack of color or emphasis on adjectives and qualifying adverbs? Tentativeness? Insufficient interest? Non-excitory personality? An absence of affectivity?

Perhaps this new student is a young female who has chosen to be represented by a high, breathy speaking voice – a fairly frequent choice. And perhaps she has had much praise for her "sweet" singing. Or maybe she is one who has been misclassified as a soprano by a high school music teacher – likely not a vocal specialist – who felt it logical to assume that her true voice was defined by whatever pitches she seemed able to reach at the time of the testing. Ah, if she could reach the high notes at all she must be a soprano! If she has trouble halfway up the octave from middle C, she must be an alto! And it can be worse; if she can phonate a G or F below the middle C, ah, then she can sing along with the tenors. And since non-singing directors do not often consider it necessary to test the voices periodically, a young singer may come to the the first private study with years of experience singing with the "wrong" voice.

Is there an exclusive use of the upper "light mechanism," with a partial closure of the folds? And the typical elevation of the larynx? Vocalizing downward, such voices do seem to disappear around the middle C, the "head voice" being pulled down and pushed vainly for volume – another prime cause of vocal wear and tear. Such singers are not likely ever to come away from a choir rehearsal without a tighter, higher, breathier speech. An optimal speaking frequency ought to be approximately a quarter of the way up from the natural bottom of the phonating range, but this singer may presently be unable to vocalize down to the pitches where she should be speaking, let alone to the voice's lower physiological limits. An inexperienced teacher can easily be misled, hearing only what he "hears."

Has this young singer even heard the authentic sound of her "heavy mechanism," the so-called "chest voice"? Probably not. Can she find it with the teacher's help? Perhaps, with patience. If she does will she be more alarmed than pleased? Probably. Certainly, if clinging to the immature sound represents psychological resistance to maturing, which may have been reinforced by the experience of having sung most of the "high" solos in her high school concerts.

It is easy for a singing teacher to be charmed by the pretty sounds of such an eager young singer, even though those "sweet" sounds are produced with considerable tension. And it can be tempting to exploit that singular sweetness by avoiding the dramatic song literature and the lower tessitura. But the experienced teacher will appeal to the maturing musicianship and the desire for greater expressiveness by acquainting the student with the great range of song literature she will be able to perform with her "grown-up" voice. It is important to realize that in most cases the vocal production stiffens and narrows in compass if the singer continues to cling to the immature, pseudo-lyric sound. The angelic soprano who cannot be persuaded to produce a full-bodied A or G below middle C, and to phonate nearer to the physiological limits, down perhaps to an E or E^b, will have an increasingly uncomfortable singing career. What is indicated is concentrated experimental and discovery work in the studio, coaxing, coercing the voice down, down into the beginnings of that warmer, womanly, "mother-of-us-all," complete sound, so thrilling in song and so comfortable in speech. There may be disagreement among teachers about the most proper treatment of such young "lyric" voices, but here it is asserted that the desired sound is "there" to be found, as an enrichment for the upper voice and as the foundation for a perfected technique. The young singer may not yet have heard such a sound from herself; the experienced teacher hears it before it is "there."

Perhaps this new student is a young male who speaks above an optimal frequency as a result of self-misclassification, or as an indication of a reluctance to accept mature responsibility, or perhaps some ambivalence about a social role, or ambiguity about a sexual identity. Or, more likely in this present culture, this may be one of those young males who speaks on pitches much nearer the lowest of the potential range, with more than the usual crackling "fry" to which normal voices fall at the ends of sentences. There will likely be a reflexive lowering of the larynx at the instant of phonation. Here, "low" does not mean relaxed; there will be considerable sublingual tension as the larynx is pulled down, and there might well be a history of chronic vocal roughness, fatigue, morning inflexibility, and a need for long "warm-ups." Such a speech habit, carried over into singing, will often result in a shouting approach to the higher pitches. Many young male singers feel that there is no choice but to sing louder as the pitch rises. And these "heavy" sounds can feel internally satisfying, huge and rich to the singer and perhaps in a small studio, or even close-up on a stage. But there will be a mushiness that will not carry much past the third row of the recital hall, and the sound will be lost altogether in the thinnest orchestral texture. But the muscularity involved sorts well with a young male's sense of masculinity; it can represent assurance, command, and control. It can be very difficult for them to separate the feel from the acoustical result, and hard to convince them that one simply needs to become an efficient resonator, that force at the source of the sound is not the goal.

A preference for this "rich" sound is not only a problem for the young singer; many mature singers have been misled, having sung successfully on their youth and health, equating the internally perceived sound with dramatic expression, and have had promising careers cut short. How to convince the student to, as some old master teacher put it, "Sing on the interest, not on the principal." The experienced teacher becomes a specialist in the treatment of "Bassitis," and, of course, "Altoitis," for many young women with naturally low voices can be profoundly in love with that dark, hollow sound.

Experience confirms that most students, hearing their speaking voices recorded for the first time, are startled, surprised, sometimes truly dismayed, to hear that the pitch is "too high." And many non-singers report the same general impression. The implication seems to be that we tend to hear our recorded voices as "high" because of a long-term cultural preference for "low." From

many vocal histories the teacher will learn of conscious efforts –
and infer unconscious efforts – to "do something" about speaking
voices. Perhaps a parent, a friend, a high school drama or speech
teacher once advised the student to "lower" the speaking voice.
And, most likely, what those critics actually meant referred to the
quality of the sound rather than the pitch, to an enrichment of the
sound rather than a "lowering." A strong physical and
psychological identification with the culturally, or personally
preferred lower sound can make the "higher" sounds seem
strange, unnatural. How to get the ego attached to higher
fundamental frequencies?

Students who have never experienced "freedom" in the
production of their speech as a result of speaking on an optimal
frequency will surely have difficulty even conceiving of "freedom"
as a possibility in singing. And the improper speech habit can
persist, undoing all the careful studio work; such habits may have
originated from psychological problems which may have been
resolved long ago, no longer available to the student's memory –
but the habit persists.

Interest in optimal speaking frequencies is another reminder of
the voice teacher's need for cooperative research with psycho-
linguists. Some questions for considering: Why has authority been
so long associated with a low voice? Has it been since the Mother
Goddess was displaced by a Male God? Where matriarchal
societies gave way to male domination? Since Victorian times,
when Papa sat at the head of the family table, the unquestioned
authority on all matters? From the infant's earliest encounter with
authority figures associated with the lower, adult voices?

Why, at least until very recently, would any dramatic
representation of the voice of God have to be the lowest, richest,
rollingest, darkest voice available? Why is God a Bass? He has
not always been so considered; why and when did his voice
change? Why is it that, in so many primitive cultures, it has
seemed that the gods would not speak in the vulgar "chest voice"
of ordinary human conversation, and not even in an ordinary
language. The Shaman in his magic trance, and a worshiper in
mystic rapture speak in "tongues," in song.

In Handel's time gods and heros were thought to be properly,
and more dramatically, represented by unnatural and powerful

male sopranos, those unkindliest cut of all, the Castrati, who carried the art of florid singing to what must surely have seemed superhuman heights.

Yet, later, Stravinsky confirmed his genius by scoring the voice of God neither as a high nor as a low voice, but both at once, using two voices paralleling octaves apart, representing the voice of a more complete, complex God: "In Our image, Male and Female."

The first truly popular radio "pop" singer was a light, lyric soprano – why are there none such at present? Why have nearly all radio and television commercial announcers had low voices? And almost none of these females? What is meant by the more recent "pop" convention, the unisex sound that makes one ask, "Is it a male with a high voice, or a female with a low voice?" What might be the psychological, sociological, and even the political implications – to say nothing of the artistic – of the pervasive use of "falsetto" by adult male "pop" singing groups? Beyond the lack of a "legitimate" technique? Is it that the "Establishment" is a bass? Is this one way in which independence is declared? Responsibility evaded? Adolescence prolonged? And what may be the long-term effects of androgynous vocal styles on the vocal mechanisms?

But of course, listening to the new student, the teacher will not rely altogether on the ear. What is revealed by the body language? Are the gestures too large to be authentic? Are they repressed? Out of place? Is the smile at the wrong place in the sentence? Are there twitchings, tics, blushings, pallor, dryness of mouth, hyperventilation? Standing at ease? Stiffness or slackness of posture? Tense formality or flaccid passivity? All these reflect some level of effective intensity in the student's feelings, being "real" responses to the teacher and situation. How will these affect the singing and interfere with the requirements of style and characterization in performance?

Do the eyes widen in interest and wonder? Eyebrows narrow in distrust, defense, doubt, disbelief? Are there frowns, downcurlings of lips in resistance? Eyebrows raised in irritation? Or a controlled absence of expression? A fear of presenting the wrong face? These archetypal expressions have universal meanings, often more the essence of the message than the Word. The teacher should know that these and all such para-linguistic signs may be accurate indications of the student's responses to the teaching, and the teacher. But where any of these have become tics, habitually associated with producing the sound, an audience will surely misunderstand the artistic intent and be uncomfortable with the incongruities. What eccentricities are to be eliminated? Ah, there was the baritone who raised one eyebrow at the highest note in each phrase, and raised both when approaching the passagio into the upper register. There was the soprano who trilled with her eyebrows. And a tenor who always raised himself on tiptoe for notes above the staff.

But the verbal behavior has offered more than clues to the student's self-image and sensitivity; the subject matter of this first conversation has not been idle. There are transference indications in the answers to the teacher's questions: What are the students' other interests? And the teacher might hope that these would include literature, drama, dance, athletics, science, all indications of sensitivity, experience with a coordinated use of the body, and a disciplined intellect. What voices do they like? Who are their favorite singers? What do they consider to be their greatest vocal problems? What technical exercises have they been working on? What songs? Have they a favorite song? Do they play piano at all? Another instrument?

And finally, a crucial question: "Why do you want to sing?" And the teacher will think it a healthy response if, without reflection, the student shows an interest in a performing career. This implies at least a measure of ego-strength and may be an early indication of talent; the motivation is strong, intrinsic, and there is the promise of trainability. Teachers should welcome this response and decide later whether or not the desire is realistic.

There will be those who rationalize their answers, expressing doubts about their talents, who say they are not necessarily interested in singing careers, who expect to "teach rather than perform." These answers are revealing; students may be responding with what seems to them to be a proper humility, or they may be preparing themselves, and the teacher, for failures to practice.

There may not be the ego-strength to endure the rigors of the training. There may be too frail a faith, or expectations for the teacher to prop them up at every step of the way. They may think their humble gifts do not justify their secret desires for a career. They may be preparing an escape route for the time when a lack of progress confirms their present poor opinions of themselves. There will even be those who expect, even "demand" a confirmation of that opinion from the teacher.

So, singing teachers must remember that those patients who are to be helped by their psychiatrists must be "healthy" neurotics, those with egos strong enough to endure the deprivations of the analytic situation where, for long periods of time, there may be no gratification, satisfaction, approval, or apparent progress. And learning to sing perfectly parallels that analytical process; students must be "healthy" in just that same sense, strong enough to endure the stresses of the studio situation in which they may be deprived of approval for their familiar sounds, and may, for what seems like very long periods of time, be deprived of making music altogether. It would not be at all surprising to find a comparable record of success and failure in the two fields.

A healthy confidence will be confirmed by the study, and overconfidence can be modified if the student is intelligent and talented. But the tentative responses may indicate an inability to survive the criticism and challenge, implying a repression of belief in the self, a belief absolutely required for singing. How appropriate the estimate of self the teacher must intuit, and adjust the teaching accordingly.

So, the teacher learns of the new student's judgment, taste, concepts of singing, self-classification, and goals. Now, do the answers reveal a clear understanding of past teaching? Does the new student quote his former teacher? Has there been a strong transference relationship? What was its nature? Was it dissolved? Are there indications of resistance to new teaching approaches? Can a relevant application of past instruction be incorporated into the new? Without a violent change being apparent to the student?

All the foregoing may have taken only moments, but already the teacher has enough information to begin reconstructing his method for this new student – and for each new student his method must be either reconstrued or reinvented. The language of description and directive will have to be reconstituted to suit the present understandings of this individual. This is why the teacher has been so alert to the student's verbal behavior and general language interest and ability. Is that interest merely practical? Or is there a love for language? Is it used descriptively or with a stringing of cliches? Is there a use of metaphor? Does the student know a metaphor when used? Just what may be the level of semantic sophistication? Is there a paucity of associations? How will this affect interpretive ability?

Experienced teachers know they must speak as many "languages" as they have students. And they will be challenged to use, directly or analogously, practically everything they know and have ever felt. They must combine every resource of intuition and intellect, all their reading and experience, however indirect, however far afield from the problems of singing, and apply it all to the student's context. They must have much more in common with a student than singing, in order to teach singing. They must seek out shared meanings among fields of common interest and select a language of useful analogy.

Teaching success is directly related to analogical skill; students can be lifted out of their present limited contexts of understanding only through analogy. Connections must be made between the familiar and the foreign, and they will grasp something presently beyond their perceiving by associating it with something now known. This might be something so simple as relating the efficiency desired for singing to the efficiency of "form" in athletic performance. And the teaching power of such associative connections must never be undervalued out of any concern for "scientific" accuracy.

The desired rapport is more quickly established and more easily maintained if the teacher plays piano well enough to accompany for this first hearing, and this remains a significant teaching advantage through much of the early training. The timing, the mood, and the rhythm of the teaching is freer, more flexible, uninterrupted by the necessity for communicating with and through a third party. The students risk less in their self-revelations; the subtleties of the transferences are much better exploited one-to-one.

But where to begin? With singing! The teacher intends to have the student sing a song, or a few songs, before beginning any serious investigation of tone production problems, and surely before any indoctrination into a new terminology. After the singing whatever positive aspects have been noted may be commented upon. Perhaps there is " a good basic quality," or a "nice sense of phrasing," or a "sensitivity to the text," or "well prepared," if any of these can be truthfully said. This is not to give any false assurances; the immediate concern is to reduce the anxieties of this first hearing in order to hear the most revealing indications of the student's mechanical and conceptual problems. The teacher will want to assess the student's present artistry.

So, for the moment, the teacher's intent is to convince the student that this hearing is for him, the teacher. "I want to get familiar with your voice," or, "Sing another song for me," or, "Sing this again and let me listen," reminding the student that this is a hearing, implying that this is not a performance, that there is no need to impress the teacher. The teacher simply reflects a desire to hear more in order to be able to help. It is not necessary, at this point, to call attention to wrong notes, or mispronouncings; a prepared student will know if he makes mistakes; a less well prepared student will know his musicianship is limited. Specific comments and criticisms of details may only increase the anxiety of the audition. Where talent warrants, musical lapses and academic details can be addressed later.

The teacher will encourage the auditioning students to sing other songs, or to repeat the same song, assuring them that "this is for me," or, "I want to know you better," or, "this key seems comfortable for you." And with the other songs, or with the repetitions, a reduction of anxiety will allow a clearer indication of abilities. The non-critical attitude is crucial at this first hearing for an obvious reason: No matter how stressed, students are not going to sing a deliberately ugly sound, and the teacher wants and needs to hear the clearest versions of their present best.

With a second or third repeating of a song the teacher might choose to sing along with an anxious student, not to demonstrate how the song should be sung, but to show that he also loves to sing, remembers singing this song and joins in because he enjoys it. This can be wonderfully reassuring for young students, giving them a chance to "audition" the teacher. Often, nothing can be so relieving as this spontaneous proof that the teacher loves both the art and the teaching. But the "singing along" will not have the proper effect if employed merely as a technical teaching device; it must be an authentic expression. The student's antennae may also be out, sensing any artificiality in the teacher's behavior. Students must not sense that teachers are "showing off," demonstrating how badly they, themselves, have done by doing it so much better. Students must not ever be made to feel that they might never be able to equal that performance.

Assaults on the student's taste are not to be a part of this first hearing; it will be difficult to repair the emotional and artistic damage involved. To be carefully avoided are any such slips as, "That old song again?" Or, "Don't you have anything better to sing?" Or, "Ah, we must get right to work on a better repertoire!" Significant meanings in "Old," or "Anything better," or, "Work," may call up images of joyless drudgery ahead, when there should be anticipations of freedom and joy in the process. Authentic criticism comes, later and naturally, and much of it will come from the students themselves as their emerging taste and skills require "better" songs and greater artistry.

Such are the generalities upon which the teacher meditates while preparing to meet and teach a new student; generalities from experience and intuition, from practice and performance, which have become the principles from which the teaching flows appropriately and apparently spontaneously. These may no longer be "technical," but ought to remain available to the consciousness so that teaching strategies may be adapted to the student's emotional and artistic terrain.

Now, out of all these visible and invisible threads, the teacher begins to weave some order and begins the work. Personal relationship has begun, the professional and artistic begin. There are clear indications of what the future work with this student will be. So begins the process of transforming all the emotional and artistic risks into the excitement of exploration and discovery, into a growing love for the art, for greater powers of expression, with teacher and student as partners in the pursuit of the Canto Ergo Sum.

CHAPTER FIVE

CLASS LESSONS AND GROUP THERAPY

So I sung the same again
While he wept with joy to hear

— William Lake

Whether we know it or not, wish it or not, deny it or delight in it, teachers of singing are psychoanalysts and psychotherapists. Not to know this, or wish it, and perhaps even not to delight in it only means that we are less effective, not just in the analysis and therapy, but in the teaching of singing. The terminologies may differ but the practices parallel and overlap. Both are unlearning and relearning processes in which the student-patient is guided toward a healthier expressiveness.

Early in this century psychologists involved in linguistic research noted relationships between neuroses and language behavior, that speech disorders revealed personality disorders, and that any change in personality was reflected in speech. They found that diagnosis was facilitated and treatment could be monitored by observing and analyzing language behavior. These early findings had primary reference to the language behavior of neurotics and psychotics, but the conclusions still ring with relevance for teachers of singing whose work, directly or indirectly, always involves speech therapy and semantic refinement.

But, isolated in our artistic specialty, we have been slow to relate the work of psycho-linguists to the theory and practice of the teaching of singing. Slower, certainly, than we have been in attending to the results of recent research in the "harder" sciences of physiology and acoustics. Of course we know that verbal behavior has significance for our work; teachers and students talk to each other all the time. But it is less obvious that we are constantly adjusting our teaching in response to the students' language behavior, theirs not being ours. And, for most of us, this has been an intuitive adjustment with only a superficial understanding of the psychological clues offered.

We know, for instance, that a "healthy" student's speech is generally appropriate, whatever the occasion, and we notice gross incongruities of content and context in the neurotic's speech, inappropriate to the occasion, or to the student's appearance, age, sex, or background. But within the verbal behavior are more significant clues to the student's psychological "set." We might learn from the psycholinguists why and when language behavior indicates resistance or readiness for instruction, and how to recognize attitudes which might inhibit practice or performance. Our inferences of affectivity might be more accurate, our expectations for progress more realistic. We might become more sensitively aware of "who" we are teaching.

We ought to confer with psycholinguists on the deeper meanings of vocabulary skills, distortions of grammar and syntax, redundancies, "filler phrases," and other verbal tics, about any language behavior out of tune with the occasion. For these reveal much more than a level of literacy or clarity of thought; these are direct presentations of states of psychic strength and health, important indexes of talent for singing.

We need a "third ear" for hearing through the ego-protective verbal disguises of our students. And, in turn, we might offer the psycho-linguists the most sensitive ears on earth, surely, for sensing subtle variations in vocal quality, helping them to hear through the ego-protective disguises of their patients. For they have been slow to appreciate that having some of the voice teacher's training might enable them to "hear" into some of the shadowy recesses of their patients' psyches, learning to do some of their research "by ear."

Careers spent discriminating among the slightest shadings of pitch, intensity, and timbre ought to be the best, if not the only possible training for hearing the "audible scars" of neuroses, those tell-tale incongruities between meaning and melisma. Teachers of singing are as hypersensitive to "signal" as experienced psychiatrists are to "symbol," and they have had to be as intuitive in their response to vocal behavior as we have been to the verbal.

Isolated in its specialty, traditional psychiatry depended almost entirely on the content of a patient's speech for its diagnoses. Treatment was a "talking out" of the problems. Criteria for judging progress were changes in language behavior. Some analysts were so dependent upon the talking-out process that they refused patients who presented severe emotional or physiological difficulties in the verbal exchange.

The "talking-out" had other limitations: it was expensive, it might take years, and it was often ineffective. More recently those limitations have led to the development of "adjunctive therapy," a process which can be carried out in groups, in which both diagnosis and therapy involve the patient's efforts in painting, sculpting, dance, drama, and tentatively, music. Psychiatry has learned what singers have always known: The Word is never enough; singing begins at the limits of speech. And, we are proud to remember, Schubert's songs accurately and eloquently presented anguished states of the psyche, and their effects, long before Freud, and followers, struggled with scientific descriptions. From its beginnings psychiatry has depended upon the materials of the myth-makers, the artists, the "singers."

The need for cooperative research has been pointed out to us before. Leading laryngologists, like Levin and Brodnitz, have reminded us that speech and vocal therapy are forms of psychotherapy, and that teachers of singing, whether they know it or not, look for psychogenic symptoms. There is an urgent need for generalists in vocal studios, in vocal science laboratories, in laryngologists' and psychiatrists' offices, who might be able to translate and interpret among those disciplines. Jargon gaps must be ridged in the discussions of causes and cures. Symptoms we think "functional" may be "organic" to the laryngologist, and "neurotic" to the psychologist. The best possible outcome of combined research into all matters vocal-verbal, functional-organic, physical-psychological, would be a removal of the hyphens. We would ultimately agree that structure and function were indivisible, that their separation had been a linguistic convenience for the specialists involved.

Since Manuel Garcia invented the laryngoscope, teachers of singing have become more and more interested in vocal science, primarily in fields of physiology and acoustics. Many have joined with specialists in those fields, testing whether our practices and principles were consistent, or justifiably inconsistent, with objective findings in the natural sciences. With this increasing interest there has been a steady evolution of teaching terminology toward the "scientific." Now, in most discussions of vocalism it has become necessary to demonstrate our fluency in the current and evolving technical lingo.

But teachers of singing, everyday, deliberately and intentionally modify behavior, and so doing, modify personality. And this ought to generate an equal enthusiasm for as close a conference with those in the behavioral sciences when and wherever our interests in the complexities of language behavior converge.

Linguistic parochialisms are apparent when we consider that the causes of neuroses seem to depend very much upon the denomination of the psychiatrist: the Freudian attributions to instinct repression and childhood trauma, the Jungian to the splitting-off of thought and feeling, the Adlerian concerns for status and power, the Frommian struggles for validation, the behaviorists' simple conditioning, the humanists' drive toward peaks of actualization.

(Meanwhile, from other isolated specialties come newer descriptions of biochemical processes and structures, defects in which result in functional deficits which affect psychic health, but are not caused by it. Very likely the future fascination of vocal scientists will be the biochemistry of the vocal event, and the complexities of left-right brain involvement in the practice, performance, and appreciation.)

What is to be understood is that in all these descriptions, however varied, and in all the techniques derived for diagnosis and treatment, however justified, are wonderfully useful analogies for the teaching of singing. The parallels are illuminating and simply stated: The neurotic seeks out certain relationships and avoids others, mistaking the real nature of both according to his emotional needs. The student of singing "selects" certain sounds and avoids others, mistaking acoustical reality according to his expressive needs. Both involve distortions of perception.

The causes of bad singing are as variously attributed: Speech is unnatural, learned from careless models. Those responsible for our early schooling show a deplorable indifference to either vocal beauty or efficiency. Constellations of bad habits are formed by the imitation of peers and "significant others." There are pervasive examples of bad singing in the temporary enthusiasms for popular styles. There is an absence of good singing in most intermediate and secondary schools. There is minimal exposure to our artistic vocal heritage in the popular media. Premature exploitation of young singers is common. There are many inadequately trained and incompetent teachers. And there are more than a few

charlatans. And, added to this are all the negative effects of the
"given word" error; the naive ignorings of the larynx-word order,
the misconception that one is born with the voice he now
produces, the crucial identification of self with sound, and all the
compromises of freedom resulting from vocal-verbal role-play.
And all these modify aural perception.

By the time students arrive for their earliest lessons they will
have already acquired repertoires of psychomotor responses to
accommodate their particular distortion of perception; habits
automated at the lowest levels of the neural hierarchy, structured
into the neuro-chemistry of the brain. Their present concepts of
singing do not merely distort perception, but can prevent it. A kind
of selective "conceptual deafness" may keep them from "hearing"
a better sound. And like the neurotics, they will try to deny any
vocal experiences inconsistent with their present distortions. They
will justify and rationalize their interferences; interpreting as
consistent the acoustical results and tensions involved. They may
accept vocal fatigue as normal, and have become quite insensitive
to discomfort. They will rely of their present vocal behavior as the
neurotic does on his rigid emotional patterns; their "way of
singing" may be inefficient, even destructive and painful, but it
represents and in a profound sense is an internal "self." Vocal
abuses, thus, are frequently personality requirements. They need
their interferences, and the greater the need the greater the
resistance to the teaching.

An experienced teacher hears the distortions, and can see them
in action. But a more subtle test of his art is in intuiting the nature
and strength of the students' reliance on them. From these
intuitions come the first assessments of talent and trainability, the
earliest prognosis. Ah, there is an irony familiar to voice teacher
and therapist alike: People come wanting help and resist it with
powerful inertia.

Students should understand that voice teachers also may show
strong denominational preferences: There are mechanists, who
teach with constant reference to physiological function;
empiricists, who develop eclectic methods out of experience;
illusionists, who rely on poetic imagery approaching the mystics.
There are objectivists, who hesitate to say anything unsupported
by observable fact; and pragmatists, who don't care what they say

so long as it "works." There are even evangelists, to whom "the way" seems to have been revealed and who seek disciples rather than students. And there are reductionists, who attribute all vocal faults and ascribe all cures to "nothing but" some singularity of posture, breathing, pronunciation, or attitude. There are behaviorists, whose students labor under routines of operant conditioning, and vocal architects, who "build" voices. Most singing teachers, consciously or not, seem to move with remarkable freedom among these persuasions throughout their careers; the best and most successful being, it seems, ecumenicalists.

There are excellent books of vocal pedagogy on the wrong shelves in the library, with misleading titles: *The Theory of Psychoanalytic Technique* by Karl Menninger; *The Art of Existential Counselling,* by Adrian Van Kaam; *Confrontation in Psychotherapy,* by Gerald Adler; *Change Through Interaction,* by Strong and Claiborn. In these are illuminating descriptions of the dynamics of one-to-one and group relationships, the establishment of rapport, and of the healthy and not so healthy dependencies involved. With an average appreciation for analogy, and moderate skills for translating jargon, these become manuals for the teaching of singing – for the teaching of anything.

The translations need not be literal: we don't have to consider a neurotic compulsion and a vocal interference as identical, but we can be reminded of an important relationship. We need not assume that any vocal fault identifies a neurotic personality, but we can be aware of the striking similarity. And, indeed, some vocal-verbal symptoms seem to coincide with psychiatric syndromes, especially when we realize that both are some distance from spontaneity. We learn that training and treatment are not simply related, but inseparable. Thus, an equation – doctor is to teacher as patient is to student – applies to all aspects of our studio activity. Another equation is easily derived – analyst : group therapy = teacher : class voice.

Group therapy involves techniques for exploiting the interactions among a small number of patients. Its justification is that through a sharing of experience members of the group gain insights and perspectives which are helpful in overcoming, or coping with individual problems. It may be used as a supportive therapy for those who may be undergoing or have completed private analysis. It may be the treatment of choice for some who cannot afford the private sessions, or for those whose problems are not so critical as to require private attention.

Group therapy had a fortuitous beginning; a group of patients suffering from tuberculosis – incurable at the time – were brought together by a compassionate physician who hoped, having exhausted all medical resources in their treatment, that a sharing of experiences might at least provide emotional support. Very soon the obvious values of the group process were applied to psychoanalysis and therapy. Since, the process has had wide acceptance and a great variety of applications ranging from the problems of alcoholism, obesity, criminal rehabilitation, drug addiction, to the special problems of groups of parents whose children suffer similar disabilities. The technique has been popularized in forms of social encounter.

The group process is appreciated and has been exploited because it appears that nothing has greater power to comfort, or advise, or to bring one face to face with reality, as does the support offered by others who have lived through, or are living with one's own problems. The consolation is more authentic; the comfort, advice, and even the criticism is more acceptable coming from those who have "paid their dues," or are undergoing the same fearful night journeys. This empathy is more intense than the usual "feeling for"; this is a "feeling with," and more, a "coinciding with." The emotional support can be more effective than that offered by family members; the group becomes a "family" of members who can be trusted. And this form of interaction among members of a group sharing such an identification and mutual acceptance offers an unusually effective form of therapy – and a magnificent teaching opportunity.

Happier kinds of problems may be shared by members of a voice class, but they do share the same problems. The class has the same special power as those other support groups to help its members through trials as "real" to them. The impressive results of group therapy have convinced some psychiatrists that it should be the primary form of therapy. No voice teacher has yet asserted that class lessons ought to be the primary form of instruction, but the possibility ought to be carefully examined, not casually dismissed.

There have been no reported results from experiments with longer and more frequent than usual class sessions, which have been more of an economic than an instructional impracticality. We do know that many fine singers have reported that their most productive practice has been in the close company of other singers. And we might reexamine the evidence of the spectacular results of the day-long classes in the homes of the great masters in the early days of Bel Canto.

But nothing having to do with the values of group process had anything, intentionally, to do with the beginnings of class voice lessons in institutional teaching. The justification was frankly economic, with overtones of academic compromise offsetting the argument that voice teachers ought to earn their academic keep – not being scholars after all – by teaching their fair share of larger classes which might justify, in part at least, keeping them in the perceived luxury of private lessons. Class voice teaching was widely accepted as expedient, as "second best," giving it a bad name to begin with; one that persists in affecting opinion of its worth.

Most teachers of singing justify class lessons only as an addition to private study, as a kind of adjunctive activity. Many consider the teaching an onerous, unprofessional assignment, unworthy of artists, and useful only as a kind of purgatory for purifying the poorest singers into states of worthiness for acceptance into the blessed realm of the private lesson. Some think class lessons have little or no value at all. But these, surely, are among those without the experience and expertise to appreciate and exploit the unique values of the group setting.

There is an economy of effort in class lessons; the teacher is spared many repeatings of lectures on the common elements of the art – which is the reason why many teachers agree that it works well in addition to the private sessions and find it useful to get all their students together from time to time. And the class offers performance practice before a small audience, introducing young singers to the possibilities and problems of solo singing. Among such young singers are many who have enjoyed singing in school choirs and who have reason to think they should explore the interest. Some of these might not be quite ready to invest in private study and it is arguable that the class might be the "right" place for them. But this argument is too often used in the sense that only those truly committed are worthy of precious studio time – and also that students need not consider class study as important as private work.

It is argued that the class properly serves those who "minor" in music, or who "elect" some voice study while working at other major academic interests. But voice teachers ought to wonder why so many first-rank singers went through their early academic training as business, or English, or engineering students.

And some feel that the class is the best place for amateurs and dilettantes. This is true, but only if we remember that "amateur" has its proper connotation as "lover" of the art, and if "dilettante" refers to its earlier sense of "one who takes delight in." For indeed these, without any question, are among the most delightful to teach. These will be first among the passionate partisans for our art, our most appreciative audiences, the parents who will sing with their children at home, the loyal members of church choirs and community choruses, the semi-professional soloists in local and regional opera and oratorio productions, and, we may hope, members of school boards who are eager and equipped to argue for the values of the arts in our public schools.

To some, the values of the class are those of a music "appreciation" experience. Taste may be elevated by exposure to a variety of song literature; knowledge and understanding of the art broadened. Some see a purely practical purpose, the class as a means for instrumentalists and pianists to meet the minimal requirements thought to qualify them to teach vocal music in our schools. Alas.

Any of these academic and practical arguments is enough to justify the class as expedient. But beyond these is the often overlooked but incontravertable fact: class lessons have an intrinsic value in the dynamics of group interaction. And for the effective exploitation of this unique value the size of the class is critical. A group of four has an ideal symmetry, insuring that each student might receive an equal amount of attention, a half-hour a week, assuming that the class meets twice a week for one-hour sessions – the standard practice. But the class can still function well with six or eight, not quite so well with ten members, and after that the effectiveness falls off by the law of inverse squares.

A description of such a class in process can illustrate its values, but it must first be understood that the goals of the class are no different from those of private study: vocal freedom, technical proficiency, comprehensive musicianship, expressiveness, performance skills, and appreciation of style. Each student is to perform near as possible to his artistic potential. All are to experience and accept responsibility for their own talents. In sum, the class goals are a full use of the voice, the development of artistic resources, and, beyond the development of a dependable technique, the skills for self-teaching.

The teaching emphasis is to be *on* the individual *in* the group. Rarely will the intent be to teach the group all at once, except indirectly, and for basic generalizations and group vocalizations. The teacher's method will be more spontaneous than didactic, and he will not be the sole "teacher."

The teacher may employ the group process without mentioning the term, but some explanations of the similarities can be useful. Most students will have had some acquaintance with psychology, and young singers, particularly, will welcome its relevant applications – to themselves and to the interpretive art. They are well acquainted with studio stress and stage fright, acutely aware of self-doubts. It will not be hard for them to understand that misuse of the voice is often a role-playing compensation for such doubts. They already know and appreciate the level of artistic confidence that solo singing requires, and now can be made to understand that it must be acquired through the rigorous reality testing which this class is designed to offer and can uniquely provide. Most will have heard something about group therapy; some may have had personal experience with it and these will recognize the process and can help the others. Cooperation is easily enlisted when the process is described as a kind of laboratory activity in which all are to be experimenters and evaluators. Response to the novelty of the therapy metaphor can focus attention on the instruction, as will the realization that, in this class, everyone is to be a full-time participant.

Those who enroll will already be united by a common interest, as are members of any therapy group. And the teacher can exploit this interest in establishing personal relationships, and in creating an atmosphere of mutual confidence and trust which is to be the constant climate in this class. Preparing for the process requires some form of introductory lecture, describing the nature of the procedure, and introducing some of the basic elements of vocal theory as a foundation for understanding the teacher's particular approach.

The informality of this introductory "lecture" is intentional; it is to be presented in a manner which will be helpful in adjusting to this first meeting with strangers, and it will be intended to encourage questions, questions which, of course, will be early clues to readiness for, or resistance to instruction, as well as to individual attitudes and specific problems.

But where, actually, to begin? Perhaps thus: The teacher asks, "What are the functions of the vocal cords?" the plural being a deliberate hint, and the first responses are predictable.

"To speak with... to enable us to communicate." "Yes," says the teacher, "but what is their primary function?" And now a bright student, suspecting the question contains something less obvious, might reply,

"For self-preservation...for making sounds of alarm to call for help?"

"True," the teacher says, inflecting a comma rather than a period, implying that there is something more basic, prolonging the suspense for stimulating interest and dramatic effect, "but what else do those muscular folds we have come to call 'vocal cords' do?"

And this form of the question is likely to help someone remember something of the physiology and reply,

"They open and close!"

And the lecture is underway. Scarcely ever will anyone in the class know, or remember the answer without the leading questions.

"So, .what are the most basic survival functions of that laryngeal valve, of those muscular folds we call 'vocal cords'?" And this time he answers the question himself:

"Well, they close when we swallow, keeping foreign matter out of the windpipe. Survival value! They close when we cough, building up breath pressure that clears the respiratory tract when released. More survival value! The vocal cords close whenever we exert force against heavy objects, immobilizing the thorax for leverage while lifting. One would have depended on this closure to climb and swing through the trees, to jump to safety, to stand and fight, to roll a large stone against a cave opening, to accomplish most any physical labor. And, speaking of labor, that laryngeal valve closes to help power the pushings required during childbirth. And, of course, this closure helps coordinate and facilitate other basic functionings which, in deference to delicacy, we shall eliminate altogether or just note in passing."

(None of this is news. Everyone in the class remembers all this with the reminding, but at first the use of the term "vocal cords" seemed to make the question contain its own answer, and they had been caught off-guard by the ubiquitous "given word," the universal cultural necessity for speech which so overshadows all earlier laryngeal functions. But an awareness of these prior functions will be enormously important and helpful when we get around to the diagnosis, treatment, and cure of the vocal ills.)

So, the lecture continues: In the beginning was the Larynx, but in it a felicitous arrangement of muscular folds came to have a potential for a "secondary" function. With these folds as vibrators the air that passed through could be compressed into sound waves which resonated in the laryngeal and pharyngeal air spaces. And these sounds were modified by chewing mechanisms which could intermittently interrupt and alter the acoustical properties of the sounds. Man was a potential vocalist, and later, verbalist.

So, there are no primary organs of speech. Speech came in the form of a biological hitchhiker, catching an evolutionary ride, so to speak, on breathing and feeding mechanisms which were also subject to the laws of acoustics. An agnostic ought to have a proper reverence for this miracle, and anyone professing a religious faith ought never to require greater evidence of the miraculous than that of the human voice.

We don't know and may never know just how or when speech began, but the important thing for this class to remember is that the hitchhiker, very soon after catching the ride, ousted the host and took control of the vehicle, driving man to abstraction; you might say. The larynx continued performing its life-preserving duties while taking on this even more important, culturally speaking, survival value for the superorganism, mankind.

Language enabled man to define, describe, control, and enrich his life, adding enormous dimensions of freedom to instinct. Speech, you might say, became for man what the long neck was to the giraffe, or the plated deck to the turtle. Our greatest survival mechanism, interdependence, became a much greater success with this useful communication tool. Man could now preserve experience, create and transmit it. It was, and is, so effective a tool, so precious, so omnipresent, that we easily forget that it is only a tool, and it is this forgetting that we might call the "given word" error. We treat language as if it were utterly natural – as instinctive utterance. So, you should not be surprised that the first off-hand responses to the question were, "to speak with... to communicate..." Ask any of your friends the question. Ask the next person you meet and the responses will be the same.

We certainly have reason to wish that speech was instinctive; we might all be much better speakers. Instinct is dependable; we leap away before we can say "Snake!" Instinct is efficient, but when we need speech the most it often falters and fails. In emotional crises it is altogether inadequate and deserts us.

Instinct is all appropriateness; speech can be awkward and destructive. This is why the popular term "Adam's Apple" has had some profound implications. Folklore had it that the bite of forbidden fruit, that small bit of knowledge, stuck in Adam's throat. He was not ready or able properly to use the knowledge, and his guilt made it impossible to swallow. And if we think that the story means that he fell from innocence with the invention of language, the ability for abstracting which removed him from "nature," we can understand a great singing lesson from Genesis: Our speech and singing are often "stuck in the throat" because of our incomplete knowledge and the psychological problems that arise with self-consciousness.

What makes your present use of voice seem and feel natural is habit. Whatever effort seems to be required appears to be equal to the need, and this causes us to expect and to endure vocal fatigue, wear and tear. And it causes us to believe that we are stuck with our present usage. If it were "given," instinctive, it would be difficult, maybe impossible, to change. But what you are to understand is that the most severe limitations in your present use of voice are those imposed by habit, not by nature. Unbeautiful sounds, so common in our culture, are not necessarily the results of physiology, but of misconceptions about speech and singing which have become automated into reflex. Some of this began early in life as you were learning to talk. In the home and at school we learned from careless models who were not much concerned with beauty or efficiency, only in roughly understanding each other. We imitate role-models and peers, pick up localisms, impose personal styles. And since even the bad habits serve, they are preserved, feeling "natural."

But you should know that although the larynx may not have been originally designed for the purposes of speech and song – there being no early biological imperative – it turned out to be the prototype wind instrument; a length of pipe with a vibrator at one end and an amplifier on the other. And your "working faith" should be that every human vocal mechanism, excepting those with some organic deficiency or pathology, and those damaged by prolonged misuse, is capable of efficient and beautiful phonation. Rarely is something wrong with the equipment, but one can own a fine car and be a terrible driver. This means that a beautiful sound is built into the mechanism which can be discovered, if we can find the proper coordinations and adjustments, physical and psychological. You will notice that this is not to say that anyone can sing; singing requires much more than the perfected phonation. But it is to say something very close; anyone – almost anyone – can phonate a beautiful sound, when there is functional health.

As a "working faith" this conviction is to be much preferred over the popular notion that a fortunate few are "born with" beautiful voices. For a student to lack this faith may be to become discouraged too soon, failing to discover his or her vocal potential. For a teacher to lack this faith is to dismiss potential talent too soon, and a great deal of singing talent is buried under that misconception. In fact, this should be more than a mere article of faith; it is simply more accurate to assume that anyone is capable of beautiful phonation.

But there is another serious effect of the "given word." We accept the inefficiency and tension in our vocal and verbal habits because we identify that personal use with our psychological survival. Our vocal-verbal use is a precious part of out personal ego-construct; it represents a desired self to others. In a profound sense our sound is our self. Have you not noticed how demeaning and irritating it is, for instance, to have your grammar or usage criticized in public? And surely you know how difficult it is to sing if you do not think your voice is beautiful, how critical it is to the performance to have an audience think your sounds are beautiful. And the reasons for this are not all artistic ones.

Our vocal-verbal uses are, in a way, what we think we are, what we want and wish to be, or what we think others want us to be. So, no matter how unbeautiful the resultant sounds we resist change. We are likely to feel that criticism of that use is personal, insulting to a central self. You see, we sing not only for our suppers, but for our psychological well being. Remember, in this class, that when your singing is criticized we will not be commenting on your real or imagined shortcomings as persons, not on your character or morality. It will be because your singing-ego-construct is somewhere left or right of reality.

What you are to do in this class, insofar as possible, is to suspend your self-criticism, your ego-identification with your present personal style of singing and all aesthetic judgments based thereon, long enough to experiment with a variety of unfamiliar, perhaps threatening and symbolically dangerous, different sounds. These will be compared and analyzed for their ease and beauty, and you will be asked to note the physical sensations that accompany them. You must understand that, very likely, you have been hearing what you intended to sound like, not what you sound like to others; your vocal habits will have affected your aural perception. Your ego may fight all kinds of retreating actions in this class, but you will come to welcome radical changes, contribute to them, celebrate them, because we are going to exploit the ease and efficiency of those previous laryngeal functions as models of the coordination and freedom needed for expressing your own authentic artistic selves.

You are going to learn to say, "This is the way I have been using my voice," not "This is the only way I can use my voice." Limitations of range, flexibility, stamina, and beauty that have seemed natural are not so; a different use of the voice produces not just an improved voice, but a different voice.

All this is intended as an appeal to your optimism. You will be expected to progress, not by tedious increments, but by long discoveral leaps. We shall not dwell on present habits, hoping to develop them into better uses; we shall outwit and overleap them. Our first goal is not to begin "developing" your voice, but to "discover" it, exposing what may be beneath the habits when you are able, with the help of this class, to turn off self-defensive attitudes and silence your internal critics.

And when you hear fine singers perform, you are not to conclude that they do so merely because of great "gifts." If their singing appears to be easy you are not to think that it is only easy for them; you are to conclude that it is easy for them because singing is easy when it is well done, and it is supposed to be easy for you also. In fact, doing it easy is a most important part of doing it right. What is "given" is the physiology. Some are "given" flutes and others trombones, but the art is to be learned.

(End of lecture.)

*　*　*

Now the process begins, an interaction with peers in a manner obviously not possible in the private studio. The teacher asks the group for spontaneous reactions whenever any one member of the class has been the "subject" working in front of the others. They are to say whatever they wish about the performance; the sounds, the technical problems, musicianship, expressiveness, appearance, body language, anything. They are to react without much reflection, at first, with praise or criticism, with any suggestions they might have for improvement. And each student is also encouraged to offer perceptions of his or her own singing. The sharing of opinion will reduce the resistance of those who are hesitant at first, and in this interactive process they reveal themselves to the teacher who can begin devising strategies for the teaching.

The teacher knows that many of the students will not be "singing" so much as they will be defending themselves in the activity – there are, of course, teachers who do the same in the activity of teaching. Since most all vocal interferences will be justified by preference and habit they must be clearly displayed if they are to be treated properly; there is to be no restraint in the display. The atmosphere of this class must allow the students to be comfortable enough to show just what it is they do, in order to be shown what they might be able to do.

"Subjects" may know nothing about the causes of their problems, nor understand what "goes on" beneath their singing. Their interferences, seeming natural, have kept them unaware of choice. And, just as feelings are overlaid with defenses in the neurotic whose public persona masks a real self, the students' "real" voice is almost always layered over with defensive devices. So, the teaching of singing is a sculpting art; taking away and taking away until an authentic voice appears, confirmed by the teacher's ear and, here, reinforced by class enthusiasm. It is a simplifying process. We are to find a way of singing for each individual. A way of singing, not as many ways as there are pitches, vowels, songs, styles, or interferences. A way that solves all the student's technical problems. Vocal freedom is the singer's Pearl of Great Price. The singer's admonition: Seek ye first vocal freedom and all else shall be added unto it!

The teacher's observations follow and expand on those of the class, and these diagnoses, descriptions, and directives will have bearing and application to the performance of the "subject," who then repeats the effort. The class listens, comments, and the clarifications continue. The class is lead toward perceptions they may have missed, directing their attention, perhaps, to the physical causes of the faulty singing when the class comments dealt mostly with the aesthetics, or drawing attention to lack of expressiveness when theirs dealt only with the physical problems. The teacher sums up, clarifies, and relates all vague and disparate comment, leading the class to a subtler appreciation for a song's formal structure, or to the requirements of style, or subtler implications in the text.

A fundamental principle guides the teaching: the students' emotional, technical, and artistic levels determine the time, length, manner, and substance of the teaching. Students may be "hard of hearing" for some time, and no repetition of teaching cliches will force them to suspend their judgment of what is either beautiful or safe. Novelties of sound will rather upset than excite them, at first.

They will not be hearing with the teacher's ears, nor with each other's. They will not be hearing an accurate "present," nor an inferential "future" sound, as the teacher must be able to do. Teachers of this class must "locate" before they can lead, by trying to grasp each student's present perceptual reality and to teach "right at and just above" that level. When improvement is noted the teacher will reinforce it with a brief lesson and move on to the next level of the specific.

Since all vocal problems are directly related to a present ability to hear, the best and most effective "lessons" are created out of the spontaneous materials furnished by the performance, comments, and criticisms, and have greater force for being related to the "nowness" of the students' present realities. The teacher does not anticipate, pointing out before the "subject" sings, the many technical and artistic pitfalls which may be encountered. And, after the performance, his teaching is restricted to the student's "present." Anything said to students before they are capable of grasping its significance, according to information theory, is "noise."

Timing does the teaching if the teacher recognizes the readiness, sensing when a student is nearly perceiving a better use of voice, knowing when a student is nearly ready to stop justifying his preferences and defending his habits. Then the teacher clarifies, explains, interprets, defines, directs, reinforces — teaches. The exquisite timing required may be thought an intuitive gift of a few teachers, but it can be earned by experience and a proper regard for its importance.

Coherence in this group process is in the practice of relating all activities to the "nowness" of individual problems, not in the restrictions imposed by efforts to progress all at a rate. Generally, the teacher follows the class, waiting for their insights, not getting ahead, teaching "just at and just above," keeping the teaching at a bearable level, engaging students with just the nicest balance of pressure and support. Students are to be made just uncomfortable enough with their present vocalisms to welcome change. As they progress there will be an increase in their abilities to endure frustration; insights disturbing to them now will not be so later. But real distress caused by the teaching, now or later, is unproductive, always unnecessary.

Now, for instance, it will not help to tell students repeatedly, that their intonation is bad, that they sing "flat," that they must concentrate more and more on pitch. Driven deeper into their defensive distortions they will try harder, so anxious about pitch that the whole act of phonation is skewed off-balance, and the intonation likely worsens. The fact is that singers rarely hear themselves singing out of tune; they "hear" the very center of the pitch they intend to sing. Anyway, all singers will have occasional pitch problems. The instrument, being flesh, is subject to all the fleshy ills. They are to be forgiven their lapses, and must forgive themselves if they are to improve. Persistent problems with pitch are symptoms of inhibited and incorrect tone production, rarely a problem of the "ear." What helps are suggestions about attitudes toward singing, and descriptions leading to the discovery of the kind of production that corrects the intonation. Teaching is not a pointing out of faults; it is an overleaping of faults.

This does not mean that the students are not to be required to face their faults. They do so in the continuing criticism of the class, coming to realize that their interferences have recognizable patterns that only seemed to work in the past and which cannot solve present problems. Like neurotic symptoms, vocal interferences are outdated self-deceptions, as must be explained to discouraged students who often think they are regressing when, actually, their criticism is improving.

The class-group environment confers a deserved and necessary status on the students, a status easily overlooked in the unequal prestige relationship between them and the teacher. Here, students are encouraged to contribute to the teaching, their suggestions are valued. Teachers who feel uncomfortable sharing this "power" will not be so successful in this setting. They will be among those who deny the values of class work.

Some of the first comments may take a form that a student thinks the teacher "really" wants to hear. This is to be overcome by consistent assurances that the student is to use his own language of description, and state his own opinions. The teacher starts the process and restarts it when it halts, guiding it, not with adherence to a fixed, formal lesson plan. And the spontaneity transforms an enjoyable activity into a learning activity in which the real barriers that delay the progress of truly motivated students are more easily identified.

In a "good" class a family feeling emerges. It can become such a closely related group that a kind of "class language" develops, and the teacher must shift semantic gears when meeting the next group. In the flow of interactions what one may not see or hear, another does. The "subject" hears descriptions of his problems in a great variety of images, relevancies, and examples, many of which a teacher might never think to use. And this is to be celebrated because nothing so strengthens students' confidence as a confirming of the values of their own understandings. A class morale develops from the excitement of this collective self-improvement. Without personalizing the risks students can express themselves freely, as performers or critics, and are relieved to hear open and honest assessments of their work from their peers.

Peer relationships have prodigious power to teach. These students are identified and united in their artistic and emotional efforts. This trial by peers is authentic, and they know it. Teachers may be "parent" or "establishment" figures at a time when there is an urgent need for assertions of independence and individualisms, which can be dramatically illustrated in the class when, at times, the teacher is almost ignored in a heated discussion among the peerage.

The group may be much less threatening than an authority figure, and its approval has a power altogether different from any the teacher can offer. His title, alone, can stiffen defenses; there are times when the class is the more effective teacher. A "teacher" is "supposed to be" supportive and encouraging; his praise can be devalued. But when the "subject" can hear a teacher's meanings in the comments of his peers, the praise is an undeniable affirmation. The class does not offer unwarranted affection or rejection; over and over it offers "acceptable" corrective artistic experiences.

Those who doubt the values of class teaching ignore a mighty truism: Every act of criticism is one of self-revelation! The students' individual vocal, artistic, and emotional problems are revealed in the accuracy, originality, and validity of their criticisms. The teacher may not agree with the comments, nor approve of them at all, but they are solicited and accepted for what they reveal. A teacher hears, often, more than the students intended saying, getting answers to questions that need not be asked, making useful inferences from what the critics leave unsaid.

The students' opinions are based on standards developed out of their experiences, and the critics locate themselves by revealing what that experience has been. While attending a "subject" the teacher will make mental notes for later reference when the critics become the subjects, noting what it is that a critic values in his or her own voice, or what it is they think they already have in their own voices, from what they fault or praise. So it is that the teacher is not in any hurry to explain that their criticisms are self-references; that understanding will come later.

Some will try to turn criticism away from themselves with every device from plausible rationalization to purest fantasy, which, to the teacher, are further clues to the psychic weakness and habit strengths, as well as to artistic insights. When appropriate the teacher will bring this to the student's awareness, but often the class will do this for him.

Some who avoid speaking about themselves may project their problems onto the "subject," revealing themselves in this way. Some may misconstrue criticism as censure; some will accept no form of praise without disclaimers, and for some even massive doses of reassurance have minimal effect. These will be hard to reach, and teach, but are often more reachable in such a class than in the one-to-one studio sessions.

One may lie in the theoretical thickets and leap out at wrong notes or rhythms, at mispronunciations and memory slips, earning the respect of the class, if not the gentlest regard. The others will be alert when he sings.

Another's comments seem always intended to reflect a command of musicological minutiae, and unarguably do. Seizing on slight stylistic improprieties may be her specialty; she deflects others' criticism of her own tone production or inexpressive singing by justifying her stylistic intentions. She will need guidance toward a recognition of her intellectual compensations for her bad singing habits, and, with the help of the class, urged toward a confronting of the repressed emotions that make her interpretations so bland. It may be that the teacher's special concern for such a student reflects the memory of a failure with a former student, one who continued compensating with academic brilliance, becoming a respected and feared journalistic critic, wonderfully able to dazzle other critics with his intellectual footwork, but forever a frustrated performer, troubled by envy, and heartless in his judgments.

Some will make great efforts to keep their comments consistently positive, insuring approval but casting doubts on their levels of taste and understanding. Others may try as hard to be negative, seeking status while protecting their own suspected guilts. And some will be ambivalent, waiting to join in with stronger opinion, displaying a need for continued dependency. The quietest one in the class is likely to be the first to arrive and the last to leave, but the preference for vicarious experience is a poor promise for solo singing.

Among the innocently revealed defensive evasions will be appeals for sympathy, for approval, for love, which are hard to resist for a tender-hearted, or innocent teacher. And among the defensive evasions of instruction will be unconscious expectations of failure – almost overt appeals – by which students try to justify poor opinions of themselves, keeping themselves safe by keeping expectations low. And it will not be a typical class if there is not at least one display of "Prove I can sing!" – a challenge usually accompanied by distortions, not too deliberately deliberate, intended to demonstrate the teacher's ineffectiveness.

But there will be some who do not just repeat the teacher's language, who are comfortable with their own means of expression. These assume a more mature responsibility, showing strength enough to risk disagreement. They will be first to put their own interpretive stamp on the songs they sing, and can be pushed to greater accomplishments than those who are reluctant to choose their own words, distrusting their own thoughts and feelings, unwilling to risk.

So goes the process. While one is performing or commenting on the performance of others, all members of the class are listening, identifying, and, one hopes, learning. But all are to be kept in continuous practice whether as subject or critic. And any form of expressive behavior, any comment, any action by any student can set off multiple reactions which can reveal further distortions of perception which the teacher may interpret for the students' understanding. Perceptions are sharpened and discriminations refined by the requirement for constant attention and alert response.

The process becomes more and more one of self-teaching. This doesn't mean that the teacher abdicates responsibility. This class only appears, at times, to be more process than structure. Class interest is the teacher's control; maintaining the proper climate the constant concern. The teacher fills in the gaps in the students' perceptions, designing vocalises for specific problems, demonstrating by performing, deciding when to teach in objective modes and when to rely on metaphor and illusory language. And when the students are ready the teacher chooses song literature to suit individual instructional needs. Success in teaching this class depends upon an understanding of the students' personality and artistic needs, on the teacher's own psychological and artistic maturity, and, it must be emphasized, an ability and a willingness to adjust the teaching to the students' present realities.

It is a poor use of class time to have all members sing the same songs, but one or two "class songs" can increase the empathy with the "subject" and allow for useful comparisons in performance. But the first songs to be performed ought to be chosen by the students. The teacher must remember why these students are in the class and never deprive them of artistic satisfaction altogether. So, the first songs are to be in styles and idioms with which the students are comfortable; songs which can be performed with their own present artistic convictions. These will be indicators of present taste, and the "right" problems present themselves when the students are performing within the bounds of their familiar technique. Even later, the gap between student abilities and those required by an assigned song must not be so great as to reinforce interferences. Ah, voice teachers are wise to wonder, now and again, whether they want their students to learn to sing, or to learn how hard it is to learn to sing. The students' emerging technique will indicate the most proper time for a deeper immersion in the art's next subtleties.

"Subjects" come to accept the fact that their singing has a different reality for the class, and on the basis of this audience judgment they begin to redefine singing, and themselves-as-singers. They begin to suspend preconceived notions of control and beauty; the class makes these judgments for them, for now. They begin to understand that their effect on this audience – perhaps the most sympathetic they will ever have – is more important than holding on to old habits.

This class is *the* place to verify or invalidate their talents, their technique, and their intuitive expressiveness. It has a supportive atmosphere that allows them to concentrate, seeing and hearing their problems clearly, exampled by others, and not through a fog of personal doubts. This is a place where it will be safe for them to fall on their faces again and again, if they must; a place to splay their sounds all over the walls, if they must; a place to perform at great heights without a net, to do their worst in order to discover something of their best. Again and again they are asked to compare their perceptions with those of the others in the class. "What did you feel?" "What did you do?" "What did you hear?" And the comparisons do much of the teaching.

Typically: A "subject" might be asked to slur up and down on an interval of a fifth, on a specific vowel. Perhaps the teacher is interested in illustrating and deconditioning a common vocal interference, an arbitrary adjustment of the sublingual muscles with the change of pitch. Or perhaps the subject has been told to try to vocalize without moving his larynx up and down with the slur and to notice what happens. And perhaps the subject is more successful in this effort than before. The class notices the improvement and praises the greater ease, but the subject says, "But that sounded so bad!"

Asked how a certain sound "felt," a subject replies, "It was so out of control!"

Told that a particular sound was "beautiful," another responds, "It felt as if it had no support!"

Asked to concentrate only on keeping the particular shade of the pronunciation of a certain phoneme constant throughout a legato exercise, another says, "It went really flat, didn't it?"

Asked if a particular sound was "comfortable" while singing a high pitch softly, one says, "It was so weak, falsetto?"

Someone tells a singer that her phrasing had improved with a posture that seemed to allow a better use of breath, and she replies, "But I just hate that brassy sound!"

Or, where the class may have heard an improved "placement," another complains, "It was so shrill." Or, where the class remarks on a clarity and brilliance of tone, a young tenor thinks the tone was "too nasal," or "too thin," or too fill-in-the-blank. But all such inappropriate responses identify the problems.

The young tenor who thought the sound he had sung was "weak, falsetto" was expressing a common misjudgment of young singers, more often male, when first experiencing a greater ease in singing into the higher ranges, reflecting a desire for a more "dramatic" voice. And this although one of the critics may have said the sound was "comfortable and easier to listen to," aware of his own hypertension. Another thought the sound was clear and "brilliant," with an acute ear for quality. And it is enormously helpful when a beautiful young lady says, "I liked it, I really did," with implications of approval and inflections of interest in more than the singing.

Yet another found it "warm and beautiful," an immediate emotional response.

Four judgments, attitudes, descriptions, and contexts, and now the teacher explains the relevance of each to the reality he hears, to the meaning of what he may have been trying to say. A teacher's work is easy when the class comments are so specific and deal with differing aspects of the singer's affect. Now it can be explained that the tenor has been mistaking effort for control, that he "misses" the familiar tensions required by his old habit of forcing the "heavy mechanism" too high, that he "hears" a richness in mature tenor voices he has admired, and has been trying to do what he had thought those singers must be "doing" to produce those glorious sounds. To him, the muscle tension had been an insuring of control, a trusted confirmation that he is "doing" it.

Many singers think they need only to get "stronger" in order to achieve the sounds they want; this is implied in the common concepts of "voice building." But now, our tenor is to understand that he will not really be able to sing those higher pitches at all without giving up the association with sheer strength. He will be directed to practice with the faith that "comfort" is a far more desirable goal than "getting there." The class has told him that his "weak" sound actually had a greater acoustical efficiency than his old sound; everyone in the class responded with some form of positive praise. One even said his voice was "beautiful" – the sweetest music of all to the ear of any singer. Now he has a new set of terms to try out in his practice, significant clues to vocal freedom.

The class is all the more inspired by those for whom all songs are "Songs of Innocence," who love the songs they sing, for whom the most beautiful song on earth is the latest one they are learning. Their delight in singing is so fresh and unrestrained, their devotion to the music so pure and complete, their intuitions so accurate that indeed we can "weep with joy to hear."

But such a loving regard for musical phrasing, such an emotional identification with a text, such rapture in a melodic line can so envelop these young artists in the personal aesthetics of making music that their vocal faults become part and proof, to them, of their expressiveness. In an eagerness to be worthy of the songs they sing they must force their voices to do what they know in their hearts the music requires of them. Beautiful singing is going on "inside," but everyone in the class can hear and see that these singers hear their intents instead of their results.

A high price may be paid for so precious an intuitive artistry; slower progress at vocal technique. Often, those less sensitive will have fewer technical problems with the mechanics of vocal production, but for these there is an even greater price: We may admire their singing, but not "weep with joy to hear."

Some of the most often repeated teaching phrases of an experienced teacher: "What you just did is what I meant," or, "You have just done what the class has been trying to describe. Now, you describe it. Tell us anything you can about that sound." Or, when something goes well, "Because of what you have just done and felt you now know from actual experience everything anyone 'knows' about 'head voice' (or 'placement,' or 'support') because you have just found it. All my descriptions and those of the class, and those in all the books about singing were meant only to describe what you have just experienced. Now, what was it to you? Remember how it sounded and felt. Wish it, will it, want it again, but don't 'make' it, and try to find those sensations again."

So much for the limits of the Word, but if a student like the "brassy" soprano can be made to understand what the teacher and class want from her, she may be able to suspend her older judgment and try again, or, in the case of the young tenor, try not to try so hard again. Students should know they have made a long perceptual leap forward when they begin to hear the sounds of their favorite famous singers with "new" ears and a new empathy. Their frozen concepts are beginning to melt.

However stubborn the interferences, a "subject" cannot long deny the obvious effects of his best efforts on the others. And with enough of this correcting of perceptions the properly coordinated complex response in producing the sound begins to be called up by progressively smaller and smaller portions of the whole activity, until, the teacher hopes, the singer can "turn on" the act of singing with a simple, trustworthy, single sense datum. This trusted specific serves as a reduced cue, a blessed mantra for the singer, wonderfully useful as a pious utterance when in need, a telling-of-the-beads before a performance. It might be a silent, to-the-self reminder that "The vocal cords are an automatic pitch making device." Or, "think posture," or, "feel fat and breath low," or any other small specific, even one of attitude.

What makes the discovery of such reduced cues even more valuable is another discovery that generally follows: Singing is not going to be a tedious mastering of a more and more complex activity; it is going to become simpler – properly meaning indivisible – and simpler until that small, single sense datum comes to "stand for" the whole act of phonation. Then the singer is freed to attend to the musical and expressive values of the art, with the voice as slave, not as master.

But teachers must never decide what the reduced cues are to be for the student singers; they can only help the singers to find one for themselves; theirs seldom are and may never be quite the same as the teacher's, but all singers will appreciate the aptness of others' cues, after finding their own. Ah, every day, experienced teachers remind themselves that singing probably cannot be taught. The consolation is that it can be learned. Voice teaching is midwifery to discovery.

Teachers may describe the desired coordinations, sounds, and sensations leading toward the discovery of reduced cues from a vocabulary of adjectives and images collected throughout a career. But "describe" is the significant word. Before students have authentic perceptions of the "right" sound, teachers must use theirs as descriptions, not as directives. Afterward, teachers need to study "studentese" for translating student terms into their own. Once the students have conditional adjectives of their own, a teacher can use them to call up the desired activity. Once students can describe the changes in their voices, in their own terms, the improved perceptions can be brought "into repeatable focus." Self-teaching truly begins.

Meanwhile, a teacher can explain just how a student's terminology relates to his own, to that of other singers and other teachers, to the whole glossary of the art. This is important because students must begin to acquire the means for evaluating and cooperating with the efforts of future teachers. The class can help prepare them for the time, which will come, when practically anything said about singing makes perfect sense to a singer. Once something is known it can be recognized in an amazing variety of descriptions.

The division of class time for individual attention is to be flexible. A routine rotation through the class roster is neither necessary nor desirable. The teacher will soon know which student will learn more by performing at a particular session, and which will learn more by listening and analyzing.

Sometimes it will be most valuable to keep one student as "subject" for most of a session, with the entire class giving an intense lesson. This must be done with no overtones of favoritism, and there should be none if the proper class attitude is maintained. It should be apparent to all that this particular "subject" is on the verge of an important discovery; everyone is alerted for the quantum leap. Clock time is an abstraction; this drama is in real time and to be a witness is to understand the possibility for all. A flexible order will be accepted as the class progresses, so long as it does not appear to be establishing a pecking order.

Still, there will be forms of competition for attention, and these are added to the materials for the teacher's interpretation. There may be students who truly feel that they cannot be helped in a situation where they do not have the teacher all to themselves. The class work may not be helpful for someone with so great a dependent need, and, after a fair attempt at adjusting, the teacher may suggest private study. Class time is to be spent only in productive interactions.

The flexible division of time will identify the frequent volunteer, which may be an indication of talent – as is the degree of active participation in the critiques. Students whose focus blurs while they are not the "subjects" give poor promise for progress in their own performance. There is always an unmistakable glint in the eyes of the truly talented.

When an aggressively talented student is too often first to volunteer, or a timid one too reluctant, the teacher will suggest whose turn it is, not being arbitrary about the choice. One student might beg off by saying that he thinks it best to listen, that he has not been doing so well in practice today. The experienced teacher knows an excuse from an evasion and without hesitation selects another. It is not likely to be productive to face a student with an evasion in front of the class, or later, perhaps not at all. If it has been an evasion the teacher's non-judgmental passing on to the next student is a much better motivating device than an insistence on a proper order. Those with significant talents will never sit passively for long, knowing they will not get attention without showing a desire for it. When they do they are eminently teachable.

It might be thought that class sessions are more effective when all members of the group are fairly near the same levels of ability and experience. But the practice does not confirm this. Being "on the same level" can imply a loss of individuality, as does the practice of having the students all sing the same songs, or spending too much time on group vocalizings. In the mixed class there will be less of a feeling of competition, each is more strikingly individual, working on individual problems and song literature, while observing a wide range of problems and solutions. A homogeneous group does not reflect the realities of the art, of an audience, of life. And a relative beginner often progresses faster by having better examples against which to judge his own work. And the more advanced student often gets helpful insights for refining his technique, by hearing and seeing his own problems in more obvious forms. The beginner senses "where" he is and where the training is to take him; the advanced student is often able to make the most helpful comments about the singing of others, becoming more articulate in the art, a crucial requirement if later he or she is to become a teacher. Nothing so clarifies the thinking as does a requirement for explaining to another "just exactly what is it I do?"

Sessions usually begin with a group "warm-up," best used for reviewing the basic coordinate skills needed by all singers. Whenever possible it is best to require students to arrive already warmed-up. But when the warm-up, or any group vocalizing, is done it is most effective with all members of the class standing around the piano in a kind of "sing-along" formation, making it easy for the teacher to observe each student, and each to observe the others.

Revealing attitudes are reflected in the students' choices of position in this standing arrangement. One stands close on the teacher's right, perhaps even joining him on the piano bench, obstensibly to turn pages when songs are studied, a kind of "teacher's helper," self-appointed. Another will stand on the other side; perhaps the teacher has made her feel somehow favored.

One will stand behind the teacher, trying to remain out of sight. One will take the position opposite the teacher, at the far end of the piano, in the "prove I can sing" position. Another may be reluctant to join the group, the last to take a position, another form of resistance. And in a very few sessions these positions will become favored and fixed and should be altered from time to time, with or without explanations.

The group warm-up can easily degenerate into a mechanical repetition of basic exercises, implying a faith no voice teacher should ever espouse in the efficacy of sheer repetition. If there is any fundamental principle to be made clear to students it is: Nothing, absolutely nothing *inherent* in any vocalise will improve anyone's singing! Improvement does not come from vocalizing; it comes only while vocalizing with an understanding of why one is doing the vocalise, precisely how it is to be done, clearly what it is supposed to do for the singer, and exactly how singers can tell whether or not it is "doing it." Intelligent practice away from the teacher is a primary goal of all instruction. The singer, about to choose a teacher, ought to understand that nothing in the teacher's art is more important than an ability to make clear what and how to practice. Any vagueness about this is poor teaching indeed.

The group-process nature of the class is more effective when the teacher can accompany at the piano. Just as in the private session attention can be held at a tighter focus when the rhythm of the teaching is not disturbed by another party to the interaction. At first, an accompanist is most valuable for practice and coaching outside the class; later an absolute necessity when assigned songs have been memorized for performance in the class. Then, the teacher observes, teaching from the critic's distance.

Then, during the final sessions, the teacher and class become an authentic audience while each student performs a group of songs, applying what he or she can of what they have learned. Judgments are based on a sense of how far each has progressed from the earliest sessions. Teachers will know they have created and kept the proper atmosphere if the class never fails to applaud each best effort.

Singers are hardly expected to pass written examinations, but, for such a class, there is one of inexpressible value for the inexperienced teacher – and for those who doubt the values of class lessons. Let each student write a few unsigned paragraphs on the topic, "What has happened to my concept of singing as a result of this class."

Let the doubters learn what a superlative teacher the class can be.

Chapter Six

Class Lessons: Coda

> *Singers have resonance where*
> *their brains ought to be.*
>
> – Unknown

Part of the popular mythology of the art has it that singers need not be burdened with much learning, but the aphorism above is wittier than intended. It perfectly describes one of the most trusted confirmations that singers are singing well; their heads are as alive with noisy vibrations as a church belfry on a Sunday morning. It is a sharp reminder that overintellectualizing is death to the art. And it is even flattering, implying that singing can be so artful as to appear artless.

It might even be wise to have it needle-pointed as a sampler, framed, and hung on the wall of the voice teacher's studio, for it could have been inspired by a profound teaching-truth: the more intelligent students often have greater difficulty with vocal technique. Being more conscious they can be more self-conscious. Having thought more about singing they will have acquired a greater number of misconceptions. Having listened more intently to other singers their singing is likely to be layered over with eclectic imitations. Having stronger personal preferences they are more likely to have misclassified their own voices. Knowing what ought to be done with a musical phrase they "make" their voices do what the music requires. They will have developed personal styles rather than vocal freedom. And the aesthetic deprivations in technical practice may be much more painful for them; they prefer to perform, and even while practicing they perform for an internal critic who never nods.

The ratio of resonance to brains can affect the teacher's assessment of talent in subtle ways. A bright student will handle the teacher's conceptualese quickly and with apparent understanding. And this, because it flatters, can be mistaken for talent. Or, for some time, the internal critic may be so resistant to instruction that the teacher makes a premature judgment of a lack of talent. Conversely, the more "innocent" student's early technical progress may be impressive, and the teacher may infer a talent greater than proves justified when, later, expressive limitations become apparent.

Singers themselves contribute to the notion of an imbalance between resonance and brains. Some are not at all articulate in discussing their art, and most of them are not nearly so articulate as they ought to be, not just in the studio but at meetings of school boards and curriculum committees, where they should be arguing that vocal music in our schools must be something much more than an innocuous activity.

Some students, not yet overburdened with learning, may rationalize that there are great singers now performing – and that surely there were many great ones in the past – who sing magnificently with very little knowledge of how and what they do. But this is true only insofar as there are always extraordinarily able performers, in every field, who are not particularly skillful at explanations. Many fine singers discover this when they begin teaching after retiring from active performing careers. These may be uncomfortable with students who ask difficult questions, and impatient when their convictions are challenged. They are most likely to be selective in accepting students, thinking, in one sense, that those most worthy of teaching are those who need it least. And that contributes to a decline of interest and participation in the art.

But some singers sincerely and legitimately believe that discussing their art might disturb their hard-earned and reliable "reduced cue," that in dissecting their technique they might lose the total feel that has served so well. There is a very useful moral, for voice teachers, in the old story of the centipede who was unable to move at all after an incredulous ant asked him to explain the order in which he moved all those legs. The fear of losing the "feel" is an understandable reason why some fine singers dislike teaching – besides the obvious fact that teaching takes so much energy away from what is needed for performance.

Others are hesitant to talk much about their singing for fear of revealing an ignorance of the most recent researches in vocal science. Perhaps these remember how some great performers of the past have been mercilessly ridiculed for the innocent subjectivity of their explanations – though everything singers say to each other about singing makes useful sense. It may have been that apparent lack of scientific precision, mistaken for ignorance, that inspired the aphorism. But singers understand the precision of poetry.

Because they use their whole bodies, not just the neocortex, singers are more interested in sensations and perceptions than in definitions and concepts. No one should expect their talents to include an unusual patience with academic lectures or theoretical discussions. Nor, for that matter, should anyone expect them to believe that their singing will be much improved by reading books on the subject. They are naturally and properly concerned that any academic approach to the art might dispel the magic. But the voice teacher must be alert to recognize that this attitude may also be a rationalizing of a subtle and stubborn resistance to the teaching. Teachers must remember that students like the way they sing *now*. This is what brought them to the teacher and what continues to motivate the study. One of the more delicate difficulties in teaching requires that we do not deprive students of this feeling while, at the same time, leading them toward discovering that the feeling is neither reliable nor realistic.

In truth, there is an enormous body of knowledge to be absorbed along with polishing the skill. The singer obviously needs to know enough about the physiology of the vocal apparatus and the science of sound for maintaining vocal health and a durable technique. But more than this, there must be a rich appreciation for the evolution of vocal traditions and styles. There must be the training required for independent musicianship: music theory, harmony, ear training, sight-singing. And language study, not merely for the requirements for proper phonetic renderings of several languages, but for a useful facility, along with a study of literature for assimilating something of the zeitgeist in which the great vocal literature was composed. It is clear that the singer with a lot of resonance and a little knowledge is in no danger of maturing in the art, or of ever becoming an effective teacher.

But the economic realities of present educational policy and practice are such that almost all elements of the vocal art, not immediately related to technique, are left for the student singers to acquire as they may. Of course they may enroll in classes in theory, history, aesthetics, but these are almost always designed either for the general student or for the theoretical specialist, not for singers. And, such subjects are generally presented in lecture form, seldom by singers, and rarely in relation to performance.

There is not enough time in the private lesson for more than the barest exposure to all the requisites. Studio time is spent scrambling for discovery, with an intense focus on vocal particulars, punctuated by the teacher's comments, criticisms, descriptions and demonstrations, followed by the student's renewed efforts at refinements. So, the lesson is primarily a form of guided practice; it can often be no more than a supervised preparation for the next performance. This means that lectures in the studio, if they may be called such, are offered in bits and pieces, clarifying, correcting, answering questions, firming up faltering faiths, integrating earlier teaching with present efforts, tightening up the semantic slippage, and generally preparing the students for new perceptions.

It is a constant test of the teacher's ingenuity to keep these bits and pieces from being a confusion of disconnected particulars. Too many such ad hoc specifics and the student may just stand there in the crook of the piano, snowblinded in a blizzard of details, while the music goes off and leaves him behind. Of course these mini-lectures are intended as open-ended and partial introductions to the particulars of the art which the teacher assumes, or hopes, will somehow, in time, fuse into a gestalt which will enable student to appreciate the basis of the teacher's aesthetics and musicianship, and to grasp the ultimate logic of the methodological approach. But in practice this can mean that a student must stay with a particular teacher for a number of years, or carry away an incomplete understanding which makes the next teacher's approach all the more mysterious.

All this argues for a special teaching opportunity that class voice sessions might provide, other than those aforementioned. This might be a once-a-week meeting in which the voice teacher has the time to approach the formal lecture and lead general discussions. This would supplement the technical and artistic work done in the studio and in the regular class voice meetings, but would not be a duplication of a course in vocal pedagogy – which properly presents careful comparisons of teaching techniques for those who anticipate teaching careers. In this class all the related and neglected aspects of the art might be more adequately and certainly more leisurely presented: linguistics, acoustics, vocal literature, repertoire building, program planning, reviews of current writings on technique, aesthetics, criticism, career management, preparation for auditions, psychology of performance, body movement, and the bases for persuasive argument for equal time for the arts, particularly vocal music, at every level of general education.

The breadth of subject matter may range beyond the voice teacher's expertise, but guest lecturers might be invited. The voice teacher, however, would make certain that, in this class, everything discussed would relate directly to the students' present needs and performance realities. Ideally, every lecturer ought also be a singer. Singers listen to other singers.

Ideally, but breathes there a voice teacher with psyche so scarred who never to himself has mused about the "old days" of Bel Canto, when the student came to live in the master's home, vocalized four or five hours a day for five years, never out of the master's hearing, before even attempting performance. According to Mazzocchi: One hour a day on difficult pieces, one on trills, one on passages, one in front of a mirror, and one on ornaments. And when not vocalizing: one hour on theory, one on composition, and the rest of the day on keyboard.

Ideal. But alas, the scarring of the voice teacher's tender psyche is now the result of living in a culture where talent is economically defined, where voices are recognized by earliest possible commercial success, enhanced by technology, unencumbered by taste. And for this there seems to be no minimum requirement for either resonance or brains.

Chapter Seven

Two Teachers

> *To sing well one must*
> *sing the Good.*
>
> – Plato

Most teachers of singing consider their methods to be logical procedures, guided by a set of principles. But most would find it difficult to defend those guiding principles as being inter-related, without internal contradictions, and rooted in a fundamental premise justifying their application. The fact is that most voice teachers find themselves applying contradictory principles, often in the same lesson. The most common of these imply that vocal technique is attainable through various kinds of volitional control, as heard in such directives as "open the throat," or, "support the tone," or "place the sound forward," when all the time we know – or ought to know – that the student cannot "do" any of these things. It is just that these phrases are such wonderful descriptions of what seems to happen with good singing that we forget that they are useless as directives.

In casual exchanges among singers are heard such assertions as "posture is everything," or, "it is all a matter of breath control," or, "the whole secret is in singing 'pure' vowels." And sometimes these are actually intended, offered, and heard as fundamental premises. Of course they are not. At best they are reduced cues; at worst the simplistic shibboleths of reductionist teachers.

Training in logical skills, for a critical analysis of just what premise might be implied in a particular practice, is not part of voice teachers' usual pedagogical preparation. No one expects them to talk like philosophers. And, being artists, they have a general, and reciprocal, disdain for logicians who are fond of thinking that singers have resonance where their brains ought to be. It is true that no logician could approve of the slippery language in a voice teacher's studio where the terms have a uniquely accurate ambiguity. And, being neither theorists nor logicians, most voice teachers, most of the time, teach in an artistic unawareness of any such thing as a philosophic premise for their work.

This may be because our most influential teacher, or teachers, never disclosed such a premise, if indeed holding one. Or, holding one, had not the time or inclination to trace the specific principles being applied to us to their source in some unifying premise. Anyway, impressionable students are not likely to have the wisdom or temerity to inquire into the teacher's philosophical principles. It is usually only after considerable experience, singing or teaching, that we come to realize that those applications were far more flexible than we supposed. We understood, or thought we did, the applications of the method to ourselves, but may have carried away "principles" that later proved to be only unrelated devices.

The prospective teacher usually has little opportunity for observing the best teachers working with other students, and so can fail to understand the bases for their methods. A few observations at an occasional "master class" offered by a highly reputed teacher is not enough to grasp the master's fundamental premise. Neither are the seasonal observings of "demonstration lessons" offered by teachers at workshops or conventions. The "students" at such events are usually those who present the fewest teaching problems – singing teachers feeling themselves to be judged, supply their most talented students as "guinea pigs" for the demonstrations, which limits the observable range of the teacher's pedagogical command.

A much greater part of the time of the teacher-to-be ought to be spent observing the best teachers as they work with many students of all vocal categories and in all stages of artistic and technical maturity. Nothing at master classes or at workshop demonstrations, and nothing taught in vocal pedagogy classes can equal the values of that kind of experience.

There are, of course, teachers who can lecture at length – or write at length – on their particular "philosophic" orientation, but these, over a period of time, may have neglected periodic re-examination of its validity. In practice, there are fascinating drifts, over the length of careers, from premise to premise; some almost imperceptible, some dramatic as sudden spiritual conversion – the mechanist becomes an empiricist, the empiricist a vocal scientist.

All this means that singing teachers should always remain within consulting distance with their avowed principles, comparing what they do with what they say they do, keeping a clear, conscious reference to some unifying basic principle – such as our opening axiom – as a guide for even the most improvisatory of their teaching strategies.

Some effects of an unconscious premise on actual teaching practices can be illustrated in a comparison of two teachers of singing whose "philosophies" are poles apart; one a Platonic "idealist," the other a Bergsonian "realist." In the flesh the two might smile at being so labeled, but the terms apply; the examples that follow are barely exaggerated composites of familiar teaching types.

But the comparison requires a short prelude: Plato had a bias which persists as an influential part of the inherited "common sense" of Western culture. Philosophically troubled by the instability of all breathing life, by the eruptings and erodings of nature, he longed for permanence and for truths that endured, and found them only in the realm of ideas. It was here that began the reverence for theory above practice. Experiment was unnecessary; intellectual activity needed no testing; the really "real" was outside our perception. "Being" was real; "becoming" was an illusion. And for Plato it followed that our most noble human endeavors ought to be in the contemplation of timeless ideals in their essential, archetypal forms, which existed, not on earth, somewhere in a kind of heavenly realm. Mundane things, ourselves included, were only imperfect imitations of those perfect ideals.

So, Plato believed that artists were not creators, but imitators, and could only do this because they must have remembered something of those perfect ideals which they may have encountered in the wandering of souls during transmigration. But more that this, artists were potentially dangerous and perhaps ought to be excluded from an ideal state because they might entice the young away from the contemplation of the divine ideals. At least, the artists' works ought to be kept under official control and devoted entirely to the service of the state.

Since Plato's time, the history of philosophy might be summed up as cycles of trust and distrust in either our intellect or our

intuition. But the notion of permanence as the only "reality" was
most dramatically upended, inverted, by Henri Bergson (1849-
1941). Change, he was first to say, is the true "Reality," the only
constant. Becoming, which he termed "duration," is the real, and
can be experienced in the "nowness" of things, as revealed by a
direct intuition of an immediate present. "Everything is but a
vibration of vibrations," he said, lecturing at Oxford University in
1912, anticipating time-lapse photography and the later revelations
of subatomic physicists. Reality is an "uninterrupted upsurge of
novelty." (Can there be a better description of a phrase of Bach's
music?) And the perception of this reality cannot be the exclusive
property of singular intellectual abilities; it is available, as the
authentic experience of the "real," to anyone capable of sensitive
intuition.

For this, Bergson has been considered a romantic turncoat by
the logical positivists, but for singers he deserves the status of
patron saint. He told us that those with the profoundest grasp of
reality are the artists, because of their superior intuition.
Intellectual analysis, he reminded us, can only take us to any one
of an infinite number of points around the object or event being
analyzed, and will always have to depend on the points of view
and the apparatus being used for the observation. But through
sensitive intuition we are able to "insert ourselves directly into the
'duration' of the object and 'coincide' with it." Thus, if our
perceptions were pure enough there would be no need for
analysis, for abstractions, generalizations, conceptual thinking,
categorizing, or, for that matter, philosophy.

Our "reality," Bergson described as an "uninterrupted melody
of self" to which the artist listens more intently than most. Stop
the flow, for the sake of analysis, and the melody ceases to be a
melody, and that is something every singer knows; it refers to the
indivisible musical "line" they strive to perfect and reveal. Singing
is not a series of discrete events, divisible, juxtaposed in time,
controlled in sequence; it is an indivisible, simple, flowing whole.
Plunket Greene said it simply: "Never stop the march of the
song."

No two bases for an understanding of "reality," or for the
teaching of singing could be further apart. For the Platonic idealist
talent for singing would require an unusual conceptual ability. For

the Bergsonian realist talent would be an unusual perceptual ability. The idealist will rely more on routine and repetitious vocalises, reflecting a faith in behavioristic conditioning, reinforced by authority. There would be high expectations for the adequacy and efficacy of his precise terminology – there can be, after all, only one true meaning in Platonic terms. The realist will rely less on precise definitions, reinventing the teaching terminology daily, hourly, translating terms into whatever the language of a particular student. For the idealist, learning to sing is a developmental process; for the realist, it is discovery.

The Platonist intends to lead students toward an ideal sound, conceived in his mind as nearest to that singular perfection. But that ideal exists only in the mind, an unreachable perfection not to be realized in the flesh. The student imitates. There can be psychic damage as well as artistic inhibition in imitation and comparisons with an ideal, as there may be in comparisons with others of similar vocal classification who seem to be nearer the teacher's conceived ideal. Yet, students are mightily attracted to ideals, particularly young students for whom the sacrifice of self for an ideal seems not only nobler but certainly easier than the difficult, daily disciplines of self-fulfillment. But then singers might easily understand why Plato is still so persuasive; many of the songs we sing remind us, and our audience, that the ideal of perfect love seems often superior to its imperfect earthy instances.

The idealist's method appeals to those students who seek the comfort of absolute authority. To the undiscerning the realist's method appears to be less disciplined and concrete; it will be more of an experimental guiding of students toward their individual best, seeking precisely the uniqueness in each. The realist believes that striving for one's own best may be an even more demanding goal than striving toward an ideal, but that it is also more humane, and it is achievable.

The idealist will be anxious to "alter concepts of tone," relying on definitions and directives, in the belief that a better tone is the automatic result of an improved concept. But improved concepts follow improved percepts, and the idealist's practice may be merely an intellectual exercise; student's concepts may be altered, which is to say that they might "understand" and still be unable to "do." By itself, an altered concept cannot guarantee an improved sound; it may not affect the present interfering habits. And abstractions can be traded between teacher and student without any sensory experience at all.

The realist will spend much studio time establishing such conditions as might alter the student's perception of tone, working toward a kind of controlled spontaneity – not at all a contradiction in terms – trying to get students to produce freer sounds by a heavier reliance on description, with a particular interest in sensitizing students to their own sensations and feelings. Rather than working, primarily, for improved concepts which might help a student do well on a written test this teacher believes that students need purer perceptions of what their sounds actually are, trusting that old interfering concepts will melt in the intense personal experiences.

With the idealist, indoctrination into vocal styles may precede technical facility; interpretive refinements may be introduced which are beyond present experience and understanding. Only an idealist, for instance, would assign Dowland's Lute Songs to a tense young soprano, or to most any beginner, as perfect examples of stylistic purity, feeling it an artistic duty to illustrate how far present taste, technique, and interpretive abilities are from ideal, and believing that such comparisons "teach."

The Bergsonians begin with the raw materials of such talent as they intuit, and with vocal literature within the students' present taste, technique, and performance abilities. They will listen, for the thousandth time, if needed, to the most banal song because it represents personal taste and makes assessments of talent and the diagnosing of vocal problems more reliable. Platonists may not be able to endure the musical cliches; the Bergsonians trust the talented to outgrow them.

Students of a Platonic teacher may sound noticeably alike, and those of the same vocal classifications very much so. They will interpret a particular song in much the same manner – there can be but one ideal interpretation. The Bergsonian's students will not sound at all as if they studied with the same teacher, and their interpretations will be offered from, and in, differing contexts, always with elements of novelty.

Platonists plan, predict, and carefully prepare, in order to control the lesson. Comfortable with the feel of substance and structure their approaches have the greater academic respectability. But adherence to plans may cause them to fail to take advantage of ad hoc opportunities in the lessons. They will maintain a fairly wide prestige gap between themselves and their students. They are less likely to recognize, and may disregard transference effects.

Bergsonians improvise more often, creating spontaneous lessons out of the materials and problems of an immediate present. They may appear to be anti-structure and to have pragmatic methods. They will be less comfortably suited to academic environments, and, consciously or intuitively, consider transference roles important.

The disparity extends into the teachers' choral practices. Having conceived and contemplated an ideal choral tone, the Platonist, in auditioning voices for his choir, will choose those he believes can best be led toward the conceived ideal. The realist will pick voices he likes best, for whatever reasons, making mental notes about what may be done to improve each singer's efforts toward the best individual sound. This teacher will wait to hear just what kind of composite choral sound the choir will have, knowing only that it will sound like no other.

The idealist requires each of the singers to strive toward an ideal composite choral sound, and since each may be singing artificially, there often may be difficulties with blend and intonation. In fact, idealists generally assume that hard work will need to be done to achieve accurate intonation and satisfactory blend – the work to be done being proof of the distance from the actual to the ideal. They are likely to begin all rehearsals with vocalises intended to improve intonation and purity of blend, even the first meeting, before the singing gives real evidence of pitch problems. A matched vibrato may be desired, or for the sake of an ideal purity, none at all. Singers in an "ideal" choir are often hypertense and likely to overcontrol; their joy in performance will be literally confined.

The realist will assume less trouble with either blend or intonation, building on the concrete possibilities of a natural composite tone, believing that the desired blend and intonation are related to and will improve with the proper relaxation, vocal ease, and authentic joy in performance. Where the Platonic conductor believes these goals are to be "earned," the Bergsonian finds them to be the natural results of his practice, and the less it becomes necessary to say about blend and intonation the better.

The idealist's artificial practice can interfere with and undermine the individual solo techniques. For this teacher there are "soloists" and "choristers." He may not wish to have "solo" voices in the choir. The realist expects choral singing to reinforce the soloist's singing, convinced that when all the voices are singing freely the "solo" voice will not disturb the balance.

Idealists equate conducting with controlling, seeking the ideal performance, the perfect tone, tempo, dynamics, and definitive interpretation. Performances are measured against sets of preconceived values and standards. Working in clock-time they tend to ignore the novelties of the evening, the hall, and the particular audience.

Realists lead, but an important part of their conducting will be a constant reporting to the choir of how things are going and how they might now take advantage of the evening's possibilities. They will exploit the best of the present, working in an internally perceived time, existentially, and their interpretations evolve through performances.

For the idealist, beauty need not necessarily be healthy; students may come away from rehearsals or performances with voices roughened from artificial strivings toward perfection. And in such cases the students generally blame themselves for failures to reach the ideal. The roughened voices can be a kind of reassuring proof that they tried. For the realist, vocal health is a prime element of beauty; students coming out of a rehearsal with some hoarseness indicate a need for individual help. They are hurting themselves and the composite.

The idealists might well show preferences for the vocal literature of the Baroque and Classical periods; the distance from an existential present makes it easier to abstract the essence of "pure" performance practice. They may also show great interest in the works of the Avant-Garde, for much the same reasons; its values can also be distant enough from the present that the works can be idealized. Music of the Romantic period will be lower in the hierarchy of ideal values, having its expressive emphasis on individual experience, affectivity, and intuition.

Realists will be less likely to think in terms of a hierarchy of musical values. They will choose those works which they feel will have an authentic immediacy and relevance for singers and audience, regardless of period. But they will be attracted to the vocal literature of the Romantics.

Not much introspection is needed to discover that most of us have not been immune to the influence, positive or negative, of these powerful teaching types. So, one moral of this not altogether hypothetical comparison might be: Whenever teachers of singing begin to suspect that they possess some absolute truth about voice teaching, they should immediately declare a holiday, dismantle their methods, if only for the artistic refreshment of discovering newer and wider applications for them. Methods should never become static. We may not stop the march of reality either.

A more profound moral can be offered in a Bergsonian sentence: "It is so easy to confine oneself to the notions stored up in language."

*   *   *

Years ago I was invited by my teacher to attend a regional meeting of a newly forming professional association of singing teachers. The organizational meeting was to be followed by an afternoon recital and an early evening banquet. Two things have kept the events of that day memorable: first, the flattery felt as a young student to have been asked to accompany my teacher, a man whose integrity and musicianship had earned him the respect of all in attendance as the de facto elder statesman; second, an unforgettable lesson in vocal pedagogy.

At dinner I sat at my teacher's right, sharing the table with two other voice teachers. Soon the conversation turned from organizational matters to a critique of the song recital. And at some point the teacher on my right spoke about the pianissimo with which the young tenor had ended the final song, remarking that it had been a perfect example of "pharyngeal falsetto." But the teacher opposite immediately protested that it had been "labial falsetto," not "pharyngeal."

A heated discussion ensued on vocal technique and physiology from which, with characteristic dignity, my teacher refrained as it degenerated from debate into argument. And soon the argument escalated into an increasingly vehement exchange of doubts about each other's educational background, vocal training, and teaching methods, climaxing when one declared, con brio, "What an ear! You couldn't hear a door slam!" To which the other responded with a two-word negative inference about paternity.

There was an exciting likelihood that we were to be treated to a bare-knuckle exhibition between two fairly well matched voice teachers. But just then one of the near-combatants appealed for arbitration, turning to my teacher with, "Well, sir, what did you think it was?"

There was a brief and intense silence, reputations resting on the definitive judgment of the respected master. Then, without disturbing the rhythm of his knife and fork, he said, "I thought it was beautiful."

Chapter Eight

Singing in Our Schools

Doubt young David and be wrong,
Philistines are slain by song.

— Jones

To sing or not to sing? That is a question for a culture to ponder, but one that does not often occur to singers themselves.

Most will have been singing from an early age, perhaps having grown up in homes in which music was an important part of the family environment. Many will have taken piano lessons as children, or played an instrument in a school band – directed by a music teacher too busy tuning instruments, chasing notes and fingerings, fixing embouchures, to find time for discussing aesthetic values. Those who sang in high school choirs performed among the persuaded. And, for the rest, most will have reached the age of 18 to 20 before becoming aware of an interest and potential in the art; these will have had no particular reason to have wondered about its values.

Later, attending music schools, conservatories, or private studios, they study with artist-teachers whose early experiences were very like their own. Now, they devote full time to acquiring the necessary technique and learning the required vocal literature, moving in a like-minded comraderie, a kind of exclusive artistic cult. So, except for their own obvious love for the art, little in the singers' training prepares them for more than a superficial justification for the art's reason for being; its values are assumed. And in that assumption is a tacit acceptance of a cultural bias against the arts in education, a denigration of affective experience favoring quantifiable, measurable, objective subject matters.

Teachers of singing spend little time questioning the values of singing, beyond those directly concerned with performance. At best they are too busy; at worst, unaware of any need. But this silence surely appears to be assent, an acquiescence to the cultural bias as a fact of the artistic life. Rarely is any form of the question raised in vocal pedagogy classes, or discussed at voice teachers' conventions, or even speculated on in professional journals.

118

Some voice teachers seem to feel that such questions are "beneath" them; one should not have to explain the values of one's art. Others feel that such questions might be "above" them; better left to the philosophers. The trouble with the latter is that our most influential philosophers have been great distrusters of the senses, and most of them able to hear only the sensuous half of song.

But artist-teachers, beneath or above the question, ought to sense a cultural obligation for preparing their student-artists for a literate and persuasive defense of the values of their art; offering their students a fairer acquaintance with the nature and function of the aesthetic mode of experience, identifying the sources of the educational bias and preparing them with materials for rebuttal – with greater fluency in "educationalese."

So, one of the primary goals of the special voice class described earlier (see Chapter Six) should be to dramatize the need and means for this preparation. And there, the question might be posed in a form most likely to get and keep the students' attention: "What makes you think that you, or your most talented future students, will ever be able to make a decent living at the art?"

Class members might assume the roles of would-be-public school teachers about to apply for a position in an excellent school, one able to afford a national search for just the "right" person, and willing to support the aspirations of its faculty. The teacher might assume the role of the school's principal who tells the applicants that he will base his comparisons on their answers to this form of the question: "Why should we teach music at all? Convince me and I will give your application serious consideration."

"Well," says an applicant, "Music is a wonderful means of self-expression."

"I know that," says the principal, "I played trumpet in my high school marching band, years ago, and kept it up for a while in college. But I had to give it up to prepare myself for a job in the 'real' world. Self-expression is insufficient reason when we have to emphasize the 'basics' like math and science."

"Well, " says the applicant, "Singing or playing in an ensemble is great for teaching teamwork and discipline, valuable social skills."

"Surely those things are important," the principal says, "but we already have a very expensive sports program, very popular with the parents I might add, which probably teaches those things just as well, if not better."

"But proficiency in musical performance or appreciation provides an excellent use of leisure!"

"Exactly," says the principal, "just my point. How can I justify spending precious time and taxpayers' money to teach a few musically gifted students the skills they might use for enjoying their leisure – a leisure they won't have anyway unless they are prepared for life's practicalities? Besides, I should tell you that we already have a fine music program here. Our choral group meets during lunchtime, our jazz band practices after school, and we have, I think, the best marching band in this district. All this takes a full-time faculty position; well, almost, our music teacher also teaches two sections of English. And, so far, you have not convinced me that the program should be expanded."

And if the "applicants' " persuasive powers have brought them to this point, their arguments are likely to have been exhausted here. It might be worse; the administrator might have had no background at all in the art. Applicants frequently need, and are unable, to frame their arguments in the language of those they must convince, as is often the case when appealing to school board policy committees, or curriculum committees, whose members are most likely to feel that their primary responsibility is for budget and fiscal matters rather than for educational philosophy.

The would-be teacher must understand, and acquire the rhetorical powers to convince those who do not, that music education has values far more important than those of superficial self-expression, social disciplining, or the pleasant use of leisure. It must be understood that the aesthetic experience involved in the creation or appreciation of music – in any of the arts – has an overriding value, the profoundest and most practical of all human values: Survival Value!

Understanding this, an "applicant's" response to the "principal's" challenge might be much more eloquent:

"Indeed, I can tell you why we should teach music in your school, in every school at every level, and why you should be eager to expand your present program. But it cannot be a simple answer; your patience must permit perhaps an hour to make my case. Agreed?"

Two primary and powerful influences have directed and distinguished "Western culture"; first, an artificial split between intellect and intuition, the dominant dichotomy of contemporary common sense, and second, a long tradition of belief in individual worth.

The first, the troubling division between thought and feeling, has been widened by the dramatic and diverting "practical" successes of technology, even though many such successes turn out to be suicidal just because we tolerate the separation. As Tom Lerher sings:

> once the rockets are up
> who cares where they come down?
> That's not my department!
> Says Werner Von Braun.

And where this division runs deepest an arrogance implicit in concepts of "pure knowledge" persists, anarchies of sensation are offered as artistic norms, versions are defended as verities, style passes for substance, the sense of community dulls and declines, and diseases of the spirit become epidemic.

This means that a general education, aware of its social responsibilities, ought to be designed to close up – not further widen – all these self-inflicted wounds of dualism. We should at least present the cognitive-affective modes of experience as polar rather than as schizoid, unrelated, opposed. We should remember that poles are, after all, parts of the same thing.

For example: If an artist is to share his intuitions they must be disciplined into shareable forms; a logical, technical, and intellectual achievement. And the scientific method begins with an intuitive desire for aptness, unity, harmony, for "beauty" in choosing a hypothesis. And the findings of science must be imaginatively interpreted for general understanding, an artistic achievement. The two modes interact, interconnect, co-exist. Cognition evolved through the affective, but ought never to replace it. Properly, they fuse.

And this "fusion" surely is a happier symbol for human values, whether it is the fusion of hydrogen into helium – where "It" all began – of previously separated ideas, materials, arrangements, in science, philosophy, or the arts, or that of lovers in the creation of new life. How much nobler and truly more natural a symbol for health than "fission," whether of atoms, societies, or the internal and expressive lives of individuals. "Fusion" represents the healing of the artificial split, and, for this, educational policy ought to require equal time for the expressive arts, prominent among them, music.

And as to our regard for individual worth; most contemporary humanistic thinkers, psychologists, and theologians, seem to be telling us that evolutions' arrow points in the direction of expanding awareness and widening contexts. I take this to mean that once physical survival is minimally assured the basic drive for it transforms into an exploratory, discovery drive, expressed as a primary need for a more and more effective creative expression of a unique self. And this drive ought to be harnessed in the service of the arts as well as the sciences. It is a drive that cannot be satisfied in passivity; it requires active participation in the creative-appreciative process. So, education must not only be concerned with the technical skills for physical survival; it must also be concerned with the means for psychic survival. It should not be just for the material but for the meaningful; not just for existence, but for expressiveness. Evolution's goal is "significant survival"; education's ought to be the same.

"Significant Survival" requires striving to become fully human as possible; we move in that direction through involvement in the arts. As for widening contexts: I cannot be female, but through the poems of Edna St. Vincent Millay I can better understand what it might be to be a woman in love and loss.

Renoir's eye compensates for my visual illiteracy. Chekov reveals the dark and lighter aspects of my nature. Obvious? Yes, but the point is that only through our efforts at personal expressiveness can we be prepared to recognize in others the expressiveness that verifies, expands, and validates our own humanity. Anyway, "culture" means a receptiveness to beauty in every form. Music offers a means for all.

We should be aware of some of the sources of the educational bias against the arts, for genius-level thought of the long past has a way of becoming the unexamined "common sense" of the present – and the basis for present educational policy:

Begin with Pythagoras, who believed music to be an expression of universal harmony (surely if there was such a thing, music should be its symbol). His was an early intuitive grasp of the expressive power and importance of music; he believed it had a therapeutic effect on the human spirit, but, of course, being a mathematician, he assumed that any qualitative differences in music, as in all Nature, depended upon and were controlled by mathematical ratio.

But a primary source of the bias is found in the writings of Plato (see Chapter Seven). The purpose of music, and all art, was to assist in the perfecting and ideal functioning of the state and its citizens. Certain musical forms and materials had certain ethical effects, good or bad, on those who heard – and this "doctrine of ethos" has been with us ever since; some believed that the Jazz of the 1920s was responsible for the carefree "roaring" life-styles of the times, and many now believe that the aberrant behavior among teenagers is caused by the current popular music. Plato seems to have anticipated by several centuries some current psychological theories about conditioning. But, in any case, it is probably because Plato was so persuaded, and persuasive, that we are having this interview. It was he who argued that artists might constitute a real danger to an ideal republic, and that their best works were imitative and in no way comparable in value to the abstract disciplines. Theory was all; practice was unnecessary. And this is an attitude toward the arts that still dominates far too much of educational practice.

There followed Plotinus, who, struggling unsuccessfully with the difficulties of explaining music's values, came to fear its powers to affect listeners; it seemed a power mysterious, occult. His was another important contribution to the long-held popular conviction that musicians, like other artists, were strange, antisocial beings.

But worse, Boethius, who believed that only the intellect was truly human. Philosophy was all. Ah, how much nobler to "know" what one did than it was to "do" it. (Some great universities cling to that conviction.) Performers cannot even judge their own music, he thought, having no rational powers of understanding, being incapable of thought. Musicians were merely motivated by some "natural" process – he was right about something. Like many present formulators of educational policy, he would have been hard to convince that with music the emotions can function "cognitively," that art works convey meanings that words cannot.

Or Hegel, who said that rationality, only, included all other modes of thought. And corruptions of this notion have led many to feel that subject matter is more important than the student, that a curriculum defines the study rather than the student's needs, putting a twist on an old adage: The proof of the pudding is in the recipe!

And among the present day detractors have been the behaviorists, that school of psychologists which holds that quantifiable methods for conditioning pigeons and rats to various behaviors – behaviors never required of them in their natural environments – may be preferred methods for teaching children, or rather, for conditioning them to certain desired behaviors. Arthur Koestler called this view "Ratamorphic." Being at a loss to account for intuition, insight, or creativity – which are unexplainable by conditioning – behaviorists simply have insisted they cannot exist. A lovely example of the "Given Word;" what cannot be explained in my terms cannot be. Behaviorists forget to add, "for me."

But there have been eloquent and expert witnesses for the defense:

Schiller, who insisted that any dogmatic method based only on logical assumptions had to be suspect. Poets, he thought, were the authentic philosophers; philosophers were caricatures of poets. Reason may implant social principles, but only "beauty" can confer a social character on man; the perception of the beautiful makes us whole.

Or, Henri Bergson (see Chapter Seven) who argued that if only our perceptions were keen enough there would be no need for abstractions and generalities which are, after all, only conveniences we use to fill in the gaps in our senses. And whose perceptions are the keenest, most valuable, most reliable in revealing reality? The artists!

And Immanuel Kant, who believed that the works of artistic genius were not explainable in language, which accounts for the fact that the arts are devalued in any culture which assumes there are no ineffables. But a singer knows that the expressiveness of song exceeds that of language.

Karl Jaspers felt that the worst assumption of contemporary thought was that everything, anything, could be reduced to perfect order by reason alone, and that the arts do not submit to exact treatment because there are no logical tools adequate for the treatment.

And Jacob Bronowski told us that we did great harm to our children by getting them used to the idea that reason was somehow separable from imagination, just for the school's convenience. We ought not think that "imagination" is confined to fantasy. We must prize it, and train for it because our nature and freedom depend upon it. Music is a means.

Alfred North Whitehead said it simplest: "Facts keep like fish!"

Man's earliest thoughts about the power and place of music were properly reverent and humanly accurate; all nine Muses were singers. And singing was an indispensable part of the ancient Apollonian rites; it was believed that music eased the soul and purified the body – an early understanding of the indivisibility of thought and feeling. It was no accidental association that made Apollo the god of music and medicine. And we can still insist that music cures when those present sicknesses and impurities are caused by a denial of the primary expressive drive, or the psychic anguish of the "split," or the somatic sequelae of boredom, depression, disillusionment, skepticism, nihilism, and fears for the future. An educational program ought to address these ills, and can do so through music.

At least, a reasonable program of music education might balance the effects of some contemporary Dionysian, overamplified, ear-damaging, painful assaults on soma and psyche that isolate, overpower, and prevent thought, while latter-day Dionysian priests in ecstatic display, perform rites of rampant technological hubris, innoculating massive young audiences against good taste. You ought not judge any art only by its temporary, disposable forms.

Among the early references are those in the Old Testament, wherein we learn that Saul was soothed and made sane by David's music. And wherein we find exhortations for the use of music for divine praise; a precious insight, music as the worthiest means of praise. Later, its power seemed so dangerously great that Pope Clement revised history: Orpheus was a fraud! Christ was the true Orpheus!

Fortunately, artists have generally been disposed to ignore cultural labels applied to them and their works, and most of the intellectual efforts to explain them. In fact, most often it has been the artists who have proved to be the clearest prophets, being extraordinarily sensitive to their present they have been more accurate in their visions of the future. Indeed, artists have been the sources of most new intellectual movements.

But so ingrained is the cultural bias in favor of the rational, the tangible, measurable, quantifiable, that there are phrases frozen in our language characterizing unimportant things as those that "don't count," or "don't matter," being "immaterial." So great is the educational overemphasis on intellect that you use the term "first things first" to describe the "last thing" in our development. "First things first" has a satisfying, righteous ring and may have ended many an argument about the allocation of educational budgets, but it does not reflect the realities of the evolution of the species or the individual. Cognition came last, and comes last. Expressive behavior precedes thoughtful behavior.

This doesn't meant that expressive behavior is infantile and that an education should serve to put it behind us and get on with abstracting. Rather, it means that expressive behavior comes first because it is a more fundamental human need, having come before all those things that "count" as survival aids. An education ought not to ignore or extinguish it, but sensitize it, give it greater range, means, and opportunity. We should seek it out, recognize and reward it, prize it. And to do this is to insist that music becomes a "solid" subject.

There is increasing evidence that the optimum development of conceptual skills depends upon an early and continuing development of perceptual skills, making it clearer than ever that the divisions between reasoning and feeling are artificial, unjustified. In *The Art of Growing,* Robert Nixon tells us that before the young can acquire and apply their "cognitive gains" in a humane and healthy manner, they must first deal successfully with the problems of being physical entities, feeling entities, sexual entities, and expressive entities, and that later things, the conceptual powers, may not develop to mature capacity if the truly first things are neglected, stifled, inhibited, carried over unresolved into adulthood. You should not be surprised to find a positive correlation between involvement in the creative-appreciative processes in music and academic success. Talent for music is a measure of intelligence.

Jung often noted that consciousness was a very recent acquisition, referring to its "frail and fallible" nature. An implication was that educational policies which overemphasize it can cause us to cease listening to that internal melody of self. We then suffer what primitives have called a "loss of soul."

Suppressing that part of our nature becomes a prime cause of neuroses – our less poetic term for the loss of soul. Psychic health implies a balance between intuition and intellect: the very requirement, incidentally, for the composition and performance of song.

The assumption that intellectual exercise is somehow a more "basic" human pursuit than is affective expressiveness – which some have considered only diverting – has meant that the "purer" the academic substance the greater its respectability. There are great universities – great in all respects but this – which offer academic credit for "knowing" about music but not for "doing" it. And from this has come one of the most irritating and misleading bits of terminology in all of academic practice: "Applied Music," a terrible term, as if the performer does something unpleasant to an audience, against its will.

The term comes, of course, from the distinction traditionally made in the sciences where theoretical disciplines are to be kept separate and distinct from the lesser concerns for how any "knowing" is to be "applied." So, performance classes in music are credited toward graduation as if they were laboratory sessions; a student gets three units of credit, say, for attending academic lectures each week, but only one unit of credit for five hours of "lab." And with that as a university model it cannot be surprising that high schools, and elementary schools, have neglected the study of performance skills in music.

Consistent with that university model is the fact that musicians who teach performing skills are required to have more "student contact hours" – they teach longer hours in order to earn the same faculty work load credit as their academic colleagues whose work is credited on a lecture formula. The usual justification for this is that the musician-teacher has no papers to correct and grade, no theses to read and evaluate, no obligation to publish, no requirements for research, and because they have been "gifted" with talents which took no great academic effort to acquire. Ah, musicians are entitled to wonder why they must re-earn their "gifts" with a daily discipline of practice – to say nothing of the long and uncredited rehearsal hours and the constant need for researching the literature of their specialties.

Alas, how common and how damaging to the art is the notion that its expression is merely the outpouring of the "gift." It is never so; it is the result of long preparation. The fact is that a fine technique conceals the effort. And this misunderstanding is more than a "commonsense" notion; it is formalized in current psychological dictionaries which define intuition as "the sudden apprehension of a concept without prior investigation, or without prolonged reflection." Such is the naive conclusion of those unable to explain the apparent spontaneity of the completed song or poem, or the immediate aptness of performance. It ignores the testimony of our greatest poets, composers, painters, performers, and more, that of our greatest mathematicians and scientists, all of whom have testified that the "sudden apprehension" is the result of long incubation, of lifetimes of total immersion in the materials of their particular disciplines.

But there is a much more down-to-earth reason for the separation of "pure" from "applied" activities in the teaching of the arts, at all levels; it has been an effective means for vested-interest academicians to maintain their traditionally largest share of educational budgets. And among the effects of such vested interest has been that the earliest college and university degrees offered in "music" were not for performance but in musicology and music history, both perceived academic in nature. Later, degrees were

granted in music theory and later still, in music education –
conceived as a theoretical study of "how" to teach music. But in
most cases special degree designations were created to justify the
coexistence, but not the equality with the more prestigious Ph.D.
Still, in many universities, no "creative" work is acceptable in
place of a traditional thesis: the composition of a symphony, for
example, not being considered an effort equal to that of a doctoral
dissertation – though anyone holding this conviction can not have
read a large number of such dissertations, in which
straightforward "Skinnerian" studies, form and procedures are
valued above the significance of the topic. And still, candidates for
advance degrees in music performance are required to submit
theses, and to perform not just recitals, but "lecture-recitals." It is
doubtful that any graduate degrees would have been granted, to
this day, if it had not been for those theorists who happened also
to be performing musicians who established beachheads in
academia, and the Trojan-horse infiltrations of performing
musicologists.

But to other arguments: From what we are learning about the
functioning of our two-part brain we must understand that
whatever inhibits imagination also cripples the intellect. It appears
that the "right brain" generates the ideas, imagery, and materials
for the "left brain" to analyze. But the two parts are compatible,
complementary, functioning in a holistic manner. It seems clear
that "meaning" is a function of the whole brain; specific controls
and functions may be centralized, but understanding is not.

It appears that symbols are processed by the right ear (the left
brain) and melody by the left ear (the right brain). And there are
shifts of dominance while listening to music, or performing it.
There appears to be a left-ear superiority for recognizing melody,
and a right-ear superiority for analyzing it. This may indicate that
some forms of musical talent are associated with hemispheric
dominance, perhaps as in the case of the "right-brained" young
musician who plays an instrument "by ear," or who can sing a
second part, "harmonizing" with a melody. Some of these perform
without training or reference to musical symbols at all, and
perhaps increase the involvement of the left brain as they learn
more about musical abstractions.

This gives us important reasons for respecting the "right-brained" youngster's early need for artistic training. It means that if we do not cultivate that part of the brain's capacity for generating expressive ideas, for creating novel relationships, in a manner that only appears like "play," there might be far fewer ideas and materials for the analytical left brain to exploit. Einstein always insisted that imagery came first with him, and that symbols were only useful for trying to explain the imagery to others. So, imagination is not only the basis for knowledge, it is the most productive means for "applying" it.

You must know from experience how very difficult it is to teach language and literacy, or any "cognitive" to those who were not properly exposed during an earlier readiness. They seem to suffer an almost irremedial reduction of left-brain potential. Yet, right-brained youngsters are routinely neglected in typical public school programs, suffering a similar atrophy of their imaginative capacities.

Educational policy ought to be guided by the no-longer-to-be-argued fact that a rich environment actually stimulates brain growth. How could it be that any educator believed that we need to use only half a brain? How can it be argued that the other half would have evolved without a crucial survival function? Should educators maintain that their responsibility is only to train the analytical half? Should we admit to educating half-wits?

"First things first" has become the simplistic slogan of educators who follow rather than lead the superficial thinking of parents who accept the old bias. Many such parents demand "discipline" in the schools – a term which seems to mean passive obedience from all students. Many seem to imagine their own early educational experiences to have been the norm; a dull atmosphere, the drudgery of rote, being regimented like prisoners in buildings resembling correctional institutions – a result of having to accept the lowest possible bid – where creativity is thwarted and conformity rewarded. One cannot help wondering if this may not be a kind of "getting even," making their children suffer what they had to endure. This kind of "discipline" is an unimaginative substitute for the creation of authentic student interest, a crude and ineffective means for treating the memory slippage educators and parents have come to accept as normal –

though the "slippage" generally results from attempts to teach abstract concepts detached from experiential meanings. Ah, so much time and energy wasted that might be devoted to the art of music.

The truly first "first things" are expressiveness and experience, providing the materials and the need for analytical skills which are all the more readily learned when understood as needs. Conceptions are useful, practical, important tools for formulating knowledge into general propositions, but they are not ends. Generalities, taught without reference to experience can only prevent fresh and alert observation. It is the aesthetic mode of experience that is immediate, a revelation of reality beyond and surpassing all conceptual ability. Propositions impose particular definitions on reality with a narrowing of focus. Music, and the other arts, broaden contexts. Knowledge and understanding depend upon perception and may be limited to it. Surely we ought to educate for it.

And isn't it ironic that in the very schools where the values of the arts are almost ignored that there are classes in the history of western civilization in which students discover that what we truly know about earlier civilizations we learn from their surviving arts? Those arts tell us who they were, where we came from, what it meant and what it means to be human. How can we judge the successes of previous cultures by their artistic accomplishments and think of music as a "last thing"?

"Nihil est in intellectu non prius fuerit in sensu!" Nothing is in the intellect that was not first in the senses. That old Latin phrase inspires a digression – with a point. Years ago the study of Latin was required in many high schools in this country, but by the late 1930s the study was discontinued in most public schools. It had been included in the curricula for some "wrong" reasons, and was later removed for the same. It had long been considered a necessary part of a classic education in British schools, after which many of ours were modeled. But here, where the "classic" education was neither so traditional nor so respected, educators found that they had to justify the inclusion of Latin as a kind of "mental discipline." It was argued as obvious, and widely accepted as true, that anyone who was successful wrestling with Latin declensions would, as a result, become a disciplined, reliable, dependable member of a society that valued restraint, courtesy, and custom.

But with the progressive psychological insights of the 1930s it became apparent that a "discipline" employed in one activity did not necessarily carry over into another; there seemed to be no such thing as a "transfer of training." One might be a decent Latin student and an outright sociopath. It became more and more difficult to justify the requirement in a pragmatic culture.

There were not enough teachers of Latin, apparently, who were able to persuade curriculum committees of the true values of their discipline, at least not in English. Not enough argued effectively for the teaching of Latin for the "right" reasons: as the basis for the study of other languages, or for understanding and appreciating the great range of Latin stems and word-cells in our own language through which so many unfamiliar words flow into the mind with a flood of meaning.

The point of this digression is in the fact that music education has had a similar history; it was often introduced into public school programs, and later removed, for similar "wrong" reasons. The study of music theory and performance practice could be argued as mental and social disciplines; there was, and still is, a kind of specious merit in the argument; every musician knows the determination and concentration that practice requires, and everyone understands the values of "team play" in ensemble work, subduing individuality for the greater good of the art. But we can only guess at how great a disservice has been done the art, and general educational values, by the attempts to justify the teaching of music in our schools by those superficialities. For that matter, we can only guess how much the deleting of Latin has contributed to a lowering respect for language and literacy in our culture, by lowering our resistance, so to say, to linguistic entropy. But still, today, music teachers must often justify their positions and their specialties as contributions to socialization, their teaching as adjuncts to an otherwise "practical" educational program. What is worse, many actually believe it.

The term "education" comes from the Latin "educe," meaning to "draw out," or "to lead forth." But the practice is more of a "pumping in," which can be quantified, and the results measured, which makes the teaching of the "rational" disciplines seem much more substantial educational activities. But for artists, for singers, there is a painful irony in our corruption of the Latin "expressus," for it implied a "squeezing out," a long forgotten insight into the fact that artistic expressiveness requires a discipline strict as any of the rational derivatives of the old "Three Rs."

The Latin term "fine," as in the fine arts, is a clear indication of an early recognition of the primary human need for expressive behavior. "Fine" does not relate to precision, or to intricacy, or to the technically admirable. It meant, and ought to mean, "end," both as the goal of a process and/or involvement in the process, because it is involvement in the arts that defines us as human beings. Evolution's arrow comes through instinct to expressiveness toward intellect, and finally to Art.

When this perception is clear it will be commonly understood that art is the "complete culmination of nature," and that science is properly the "handmaiden," serving the arts, as John Dewey asserted early in this century in *Art as Experience*. He could not abide dualisms in any form.

And how should we go about the teaching? By following evolution's arrow! "First things" in the study of music – as should be the first things in all early schooling – would be the exploration and expression of feelings, for locating that essential "I-ness," the regard for creativity and originality from which naturally flows the understanding and appreciation for the expressiveness of others. Music making, dance, drama, are all proper activities to be combined in the exploring. Young children should be given all manner of materials and the freedom with which to make music: drums, penny whistles, wooden instruments, tape recorders, synthesizers, anything they might use, and the class time and encouragement they need to "compose" their own songs, to set their own poems to their own music and to perform them. Singing would naturally be emphasized; everyone has an instrument.

Doing this, the time naturally comes when the students sense the need for more and better means, more subtle and sophisticated techniques, and principles, in order to express themselves satisfactorily. They will become eager to learn the next necessary steps and skills, eager to see their songs written out so that next year's class might sing them, so that they might be sent to friends in other schools, or even published in a whole book of songs.

Then it is when the cognitive needs are apparent to them, for learning the theoretical elements of the art which ought never to be taught apart from their application to the making of music. Performance generates intellectual needs. It might be an instructional educational experiment, somewhere, sometime, in some school, to wait until much later than is the current practice to introduce any of the rational, misleadingly termed "basics."

There would be no news is this approach; Dewey lectured constantly about the values of "learning by doing" in the early 1900s. And, ah, if such a program of music education had been everywhere applied since then we would have, by now, generated a great singing culture, great audiences for our best performers. But we might start from here and now.

You mentioned a "fine music program" here in your school. But you cannot be justified in thinking you have a fine program when your vocal group meets during lunchtime, and your band after school, in order not to interfere with "regular" class work. Nor can you think you have a fine program if you do not have a vocal specialist, a singer, directing your choruses. Voice teachers spend careers repairing the vocal damage done to young singers from misconceptions about vocal use learned under incompetent, untrained leadership. Surely, you would not expect, say, a journalism graduate to teach drama just because both involved language skills?

You cannot have a justifiable pride in a music program if your students must seek out training with private teachers; you would think yourself derelict if you had to send students "outside" for lessons in reading or computing.

You can't have a fine program if there are no classes in musical literacy, in theory and sight-singing. Nor if your students move on to high school and college without experience in singing some of the standard choral literature in three or four parts. Nor if your students have no understanding of the physiology of the vocal equipment. As it is, do your classes in public speaking include a concern for either the beauty or mechanical efficiency of vocal-verbal use?

You can't have a fine program if your students are surprised, even embarrassed, to hear their "real" singing voices, nor if their concepts of singing have been formed by hearing only some of the excruciating vocalisms of many "pop" singers. You cannot have a fine program without a fine preparatory program in those elementary schools that feed students into your school. Have you not seen, and heard, something like this? Little first graders with the instinctive good taste to be embarrassed by having small triangular pieces of red paper stuck to their small noses for a performance of "Rudolph the Red-Nosed Reindeer" at what was presented as a concert of Christmas music? While the classroom teacher who led the singing, herself a non-singer, encouraged the blatant, shouted use of their "playground" voices? They could have sung beautiful music, beautifully. You and your students' parents must not think that the singers in the Vienna Boys Choir, for example, are all little geniuses. They are not. They are ordinary boys who have come to love music and have learned with "fine" instruction, how to use their voices properly.

You cannot think you have a fine program if only those who already show some unusual facility in singing are in your choral group, while all others are considered as non-singers. Of course one might make the same criticism of most high school athletic programs in which limited resources are concentrated for the benefit of the most obviously talented athletes.

You can't think you have a fine program if potential is not sought out, identified, encouraged, and given opportunity for training. You might be amazed at the prevalence of musical talent, if actively seeking it out. But how can it show itself without an opportunity to function in a musical environment?

You ought not to think you have even an adequate music program if your students later become interested in musical study and arrive at college with years of remedial work to do. Ah, if that happened year after year to math and science students, school boards would search for other administrators.

Finally, you may not think you have a fine program if you permit your students to believe that music's primary functions are providing background for formal ceremonies, assemblies, scholarship and awards presentations, graduation marches, for entertaining at P.T.A. gatherings, or for pumping up school spirit, and surely not for invoking the favor of the gods for the home team on Saturday afternoons. No. It must be treated and taught as an "end" art, a means of expression otherwise inexpressible.

A fine program? Let me cite an example, one that puts "progress" in sad perspective:

Fifty years ago in a typical small town in upstate New York, students did not graduate from intermediate schools into high school without some facility in sight-singing and basic music theory. Singing was taught from first grade up by vocal specialists who traveled from school to school. High school choral and glee clubs had the prestige of varsity sport teams. Annual homecoming concerts honored all past members, many of whom attended yearly and joined the current singing groups on stage for some of the closing familiar songs. These were singing reunions, festival celebrations, as joyful as a Welsh Eistedfodd. Typically, more than half the enrolled students were in one or another of the school's singing groups. There were "concert tours" through neighboring towns.

That program was the result of the work of two individuals; Hollis Dann, who had spent forty years developing a general program of music education for the schools of the state, and one particular high school teacher who followed Dann's work with forty devoted years in this particular town. By the late 1930s the high school had three more full-time music teachers; one who taught music appreciation, theory, and history; a violinist who taught small string classes and conducted the school symphony orchestra, and a clarinetist who taught classes of woodwinds and brasses and conducted a concert and a marching band. That was a fine program. And you could be credited with beginning such a tradition, here in this school, at the small cost of one full-time faculty position.

You used the term "practical," implying that the study of music was not. True, it has been thought, along with the other arts, not serious, the surplus energy of a culture, a decoration on an otherwise useful education, a hedonistic, pleasant, entertaining activity, and, at best, a means of emotional catharsis.

And all these have been cited as sufficient cause for pushing music, along with the other arts, out of the educational mainstream. And all can be summed up in the frightening adage: "art for art's sake!"

Art for its own sake? Nothing could be more damaging to, or more distant from the truth. The arts are not decorations on an otherwise "practical" life; life would be barren, unshareable, utterly material without them. Sharing in the creative-appreciative processes in the arts raises the individual out of his limited context into that of the species. Music, like all other arts, has not an ordinary utility, it has a noble one: describing, defining, distinguishing, sharing, and preserving our humanity.

This transcendent utility is of utmost importance in this era of increasingly complex technology; a technology, alas, truly for its own sake, which offers speed of communication, mobility, convenience, but contributes nothing to a significant use of any of these, nothing to assure us of a distinctive personal life. Technology's ethic: If it can be done, let's do it! And if we survive that hubris it may be only a greater sensitivity, learned from exposure to and experience in the arts, that preserved us.

Artists have been thought antisocial, but what ever has there been in the artists' grossest arrogance to match the shortsighted applications of technology? Surely, singers are never likely to be seated at coffee discussing the assembly of a device that just might strip all atmosphere from the earth. We would be wise to remember that intellect, that "latest thing" in our evolution, is still unproven as a successful survival mechanism. Ignoring our affective, expressive needs expresses an attitude that is fundamentally anti-feeling, anti-sensuous, anti-emotion, anti-moral, anti-life, and certainly anti-song. And this is thought "practical"? It is crucial for our culture to expand our definition of "practicality" to include the most basic needs of the human spirit.

What else could Shakespeare have meant by "He that hath no music in himself," meaning one unable to create or perform it, and "Nor is not moved by the concourse of sweet sound," meaning unable to appreciate it in others? Indeed, no such man is to be trusted, "fit for treasons, stratagems, and spoils."

Is not the practical purpose of science the reduction of an otherwise unendurable chaos to a manageable order? And the same to be said for theology? It must be considered so for the art of music. But your science classes are required of all, as if everyone was going to be a scientist; more, the subject matter is usually taught out of books, usually without reference to either experience or ethical values. Our music classes will not be taught as if all were to become professional musicians, but only to allow all to participate to the limit of interest and talent, and not out of books, but in the actual making of music. And, because of the nature and substance of the art, with constant reference to human values.

If your patience permits, three brief and final arguments; first, the philosophical: Education should be aimed at evolution's target, a more abundantly perceptive life. This has led us to prize originality and creativity. Instinct, intuition, affectivity, and responsiveness to expressive utterance preserved our species long before the advent of logic. This means that the aesthetic mode of experience is the root of all philosophy, not an isolated branch. We know this by realizing that the premise upon which any philosophy rests must have an aptness, a "poetic justice," that satisfies the aesthetic sense of its founder. It has to "feel" right. Thus, in truth, subjectivity is the starting point for all rationality, because existence can only be individually experienced. Our expressive selves can be said to be the only existential realities. By this we should understand and affirm that the primary purpose of intellect – of all your "basics" – is to permit us a more complete and eloquent expression of our perceptions.

All scientific inquiry that later proves productive begins in an aesthetic mode, in kinds of "play." Why, then, should "play" have a generally pejorative flavor, as "not serious," as applied to musicians who "play" an instrument or in an orchestra? The term properly has the sense of exploration, of discovery, of joy, but not frivolity.

A philosopher's premise and a scientist's hypothesis are akin, emotionally identical to an artist's "inspiration." And the philosopher's "Q.E.D." and the scientist's "Eureka," express an aesthetic satisfaction on the same emotional wavelength, so to say, as that of an appreciative audience listening to a Schubert song cycle.

An ontological argument: Proof of music's values is apparent in its universal practice. Science, too, is practiced everywhere, whatever the degree of its sophistication. Why educate for one and not the other? What have the "basics" that is more humanizing than training in the arts, in music? If we truly and solemnly meant "first things first," we would shatter the entire sorry scheme of educational practice to bits, and remold it much nearer to the singer's heart's desire.

Since I approach evangelism, a theological argument: In every culture the two primary attributes of deity are creativity and omniscient wisdom, the two attributes humans value most – creativity and ultimate appreciation. If, then, we are in any, even allegorical, sense "in the image made," it can only be insofar as we display these attributes on a human level.

And why singing? Because music began with singing. Because the voice is the original and only truly human instrument. Because everyone has a voice. It is an art available to all.

But I can sum up all previous arguments with a question of my own: Have you ever met anyone who did not wish to be a good singer? There are not many, and they are not well.

*   *   *   *

At a service club luncheon a few years ago, I happened to be seated between two high school principals whose schools were on adjacent edges of two towns within the same school district. The two schools had carried on an intense football rivalry since living memory.

Having been introduced as a musician, I soon learned that both principals, coincidentally, were interviewing applicants for music teaching positions at their schools. Both were searching for band directors with proven success in entertaining alumni and fans with half-time maneuvers, a critical element in the rivalry. Both were thinking ahead to the climactic Thanksgiving Day "big game."

With what seemed like a stroke of sanity I suggested that one hire a highly qualified marching band director and the other a vocal specialist, assigning each to half-day schedules at each school. That way, both would have the benefits of two specialists.

But it was not too much of a surprise to learn later that both had hired band directors who, when not planning derring-do for half-times, also directed the schools' choral groups. One of their annual concerts featured a medley of television "sit-com" themes, for which the young singers had been coached to belt out an artificially mature sound.

One might wonder what would happen if the varsity football team played a game against the Cleveland Browns. So much for "first things."

Chapter Nine

Perfect Singing

> *One's self I sing,*
> *A simple, separate person.*
>
> — Walt Whitman

Most singers remember their first conscious experience of exhilaration in performance. For one, it might have been while singing *Silent Night,* as a boy soprano, for a Christmas gathering of family and friends, and seeing tears in the eyes of elderly aunts. Whether the tears had been from the beauty of the singing or a sentimental overflow of holiday emotion he might never know; but at the time he sensed something of the magic of singing, and the singer's power to affect the hearts of an audience. It had a special status, being a singer.

Another might remember having been singled out for a solo at an elementary school concert, or for a special church service. Or, joy of joys, having been chosen for the leading role in a high school musical production. How indescribable the delight in that first "real" performance, and how inconsolable a sadness to see the curtain fall on the final performance.

Some may have sung in a high school choir, led by an inspiring director, and remember performances during which they knew themselves to be a part of a perfection as absolutely pure and joyful as only heaven might be.

And what is so striking about such memories is that the remembered exhilaration is not diminished by realizing, now, that the aesthetic judgment, then, was unsophisticated. The joy in performance may have been a childlike thing, but it is never to be put behind the singer as the songs of innocence become those of experience. We are to graft a maturing technique on that innocent expressiveness.

Such memories are not to be dismissed as nostalgic, nor disregarded as naive. Rather, they should remind the mature artist-teachers that the joy they now feel, in their most satisfying work, may differ in degree but absolutely not in kind from the present joy that young singers bring to their first lessons. It is the promise

141

of that shared joy that forms the empathic bond between teacher and student, so necessary for the study. The delight in making music is the fundamental motivator; it is at the heart of all discussion and the essence of all writing about the art. It is the art's reason for being; the Canto, Ergo Sum.

But often with the beginnings of the study there comes an abrupt and disconcerting end of innocence. It can be very disturbing for young students who have been the best singers in their schools or communities suddenly to find themselves among many whom they think sing so much better.

It is enough to realize that pianists and instrumentalists, their age, have already achieved impressive techniques, are much more experienced in performance, more skillful at sight-reading, and who may not even think of singers as "musicians." It is enough to discover that there may be few performance opportunities, and more than enough to find that every aspect of what had been a spontaneous and happy form of self-expression is subject to excruciating forms of critical disapproval. But, after all this, to infer from teaching attitudes and approaches that they are to undergo a protracted, painful, purification process before becoming "real" performers; then, present taste and talent may be severely challenged, blighted beyond revival. So, often in the early stages of formal study comes disillusionment, despair, and a high dropout rate, even among those who have seemed to show exceptional promise. Many, many who ought not to be, are lost to the art.

A significant part of this loss is the result of an assumption common among voice teachers that "talent" for singing must include an extraordinary will for surviving the training. Teachers, so convinced, may also assume that this early discouragement explains why so many of those students who do survive seem to progress so much slower than they might.

"If a student can be discouraged at all, he ought not to study at all!" So goes a high-sounding old premise, ostensibly a defense of artistic standards. But it permits voice teachers to rationalize the dropout rate, and to accept the lagging progress, by begging the question of talent. We are powerfully tempted to believe that students lack talent when they do not readily respond to our particular methods. This calms the teaching conscience, but evades responsibility to the art. And it is unwise; discouragement can be an indication of a talented student's own high standards.

Some teachers avoid the emotional unpleasantness, the musical dissatisfactions, and the pedagogical risks, by accepting only those students whose obvious talents seem likely to make them easiest and most gratifying to teach. But there is more than a tinge of irony in teaching those who, in a sense, need it least, while attributing successes to the teaching method.

It can't be argued that all will become great singers, but many more might become good singers, many more than do. And we need the good "local" soloists and semi-professional singers fully as much as we need those few of international acclaim whose rarest abilities allow them to perform in the world's great opera houses.

For the aesthetic welfare of our culture – to say nothing of the economics of voice teaching – teachers of singing ought to encourage a much broader interest and a much wider appreciation for the art, catering to the least interest in it and cultivating it where dormant. Otherwise, we add professional credence to the popular conviction that only a favored few can really sing, contributing to a decline of interest in the art.

So, there ought to be compelling reasons for the early dismissal of students who, at first, appear untalented or who seem to become too easily discouraged. All early judgments ought to be made in favor of the students; where they are not the students ought to seek other opinion, always being entitled to wonder if that first opinion might not have reflected the teacher's limits of skill and patience. Experienced teachers will remember many "late bloomers" who became very good singers. But there is no way to know how many others might have bloomed had they not been too early and too violently pruned.

But how to reconcile the need to cater to all levels of interest with faithfulness to high standards? How? With a teaching premise of quite a different kind: one that justifies the joy young students bring to their first lessons and exploits that joy throughout the study; one that keeps students aware of their present limitations while encouraging improvement; one worthy of our sincerest reverence for the art; a premise applicable to the entire range of abilities within it. Stated so: Perfection in singing is the best of the existential present.

And this, of course, is another of those simple sentences that require lots more sentences by way of explanation, beginning with a brief description of the voice teaching process.

In *The Art of Growing,* Robert Nixon describes a sequence of stages in the process of learning, or in progress toward maturity, as: experimentation, discovery, and mastery. And these perfectly apply to the singer's growth toward artistic maturity. But these "stages" have an even greater application to the study of singing if one earlier stage is added, and a later one interpolated, so that the sequence becomes: disinhibition, experimentation, discovery, identification, and mastery.

There is not to be an insistence on an absolute sequential order for these stages; they are only describable aspects teased out of an indivisible process for convenient consideration. The actual process is holistic, and effective teachers, regardless of method, reveal the inter-relatings from the earliest lessons. But, keeping in mind this "wholeness," it is clear that disinhibition must be first considered; the inhibition of inhibitions, so to say. This means achieving a freedom from physical and psychological restraints that prevent or suppress ease and expressiveness in singing. We might think of these interferences as "functional"; the poorly coordinated mechanical action of the vocal apparatus resulting from poor concepts of singing. Or, we might think the improper concepts are the results of the inhibiting habits. But whichever we think, the first teaching requirement is the out-witting, undoing, setting aside, or "overleaping" of habits and attitudes which prevent or delay a student's readiness and willingness for experimentation.

Students must be made to feel psychologically and artistically "safe," comfortable enough to experiment with something so precious and personal as their present way of singing. But with the teachers' guidance and encouragement, they must experiment with sounds new to them, sounds they may never have thought they could or should make; sounds they might not have found without their teachers' reassurances: whines, wails, moans, yawns, sighs; all manner of joyful and lugubrious animal noises. They must experiment with new physical adjustments, new sensations, descriptions, perceptions. For only through experimenting can they arrive at discovery.

Discoveries are to be made of the possibilities of a much more versatile instrument, capable of a greater variety of colors and textures, of greater range and flexibility. Particular sensations will accompany specific discoveries, and these the student begins to incorporate into a general, personal "feel" for producing better and better sounds. And each new sound and sensation opens new areas for further experimentation.

Often, in the experimental mode, a student will produce a sound on a particular pitch and vowel, or as a part of some vocalise, or a phrase of a song, so easily, so beautifully, so dramatically "right," that it simply cannot be explained in terms of "vocal development," where the semantic flavor of that term is one of muscle development, like weight-lifting. Such a sound, the student realizes, was not "developed," but discovered. It is, therefore, a present possibility, available "now," repeatable "today," if only it can be "found." Singers all learn that the "right" sounds are much harder to find than to "do," once found.

In such discoveries the teacher hears where the voice "will be" when this kind of sound is routinely the least good sound the student makes. And students, trusting their teachers' ears, if not yet their own, begin to understand that they may not have to fight their way "through" all their vocal problems; many of them can be overleaped, leaving a bad habit behind. One such sound can completely revolutionize a student's perception of his or her voice.

These novel discernments, "Ah Ha!" experiences, are prime teaching opportunities. And they can be integrated into the total technique as part of a coherent whole, being models for the modifications needed in the coordinated functionings of the vocal apparatus. The teaching becomes a progressive correcting of students' assumptions, a continuing reorganization into an emerging whole.

If a voice teacher must have an ideal in mind, it ought to be: One eureka experience per student per lesson! And, in fact, such discoveries can be commonplace if they are expected and prepared for in a studio atmosphere encouraging freedom and flexibility of behavior, without self-consciousness in the presence of the teacher, or a platonic ideal.

So, guiding the students toward a discovery is generally not difficult; convincing them to accept it is another matter, a severe test of the teacher's skill in the early lessons. And the length of time it can take to overcome the students' resistance to accepting a novel perception has led many voice teachers to over-value such concepts as "vocal development," and "voice building." These, we ought to remember, put all emphasis on the teacher and the teaching method. "Discovery" puts the emphasis where it has greater effect: on the students and their unique perceptions.

For some time, students may have difficulty "finding" the right sounds in the practice room where old habits reassert. Or there, they may find the sounds, but without their teachers' confirming ears, distrust them. So now, the substance of the lessons, testing the teacher's eloquence and empathy, is in encouraging them toward an identification with the most promising of the discoveries – some of these, of course, will prove to be dead ends, but the most promising will be clear indications of proper directions toward improvement. For with these the students have more than any generality, abstraction, or any intellectual concept can offer; they have personal perceptions from actual experience. And the teacher will adjust descriptions and directives to bring these into repeatable focus, until they are no longer radically new but routinely, spontaneously theirs, describable in their own terms, confirmable in their own sensations.

Practice is often unproductive and may even be counter-productive prior to the discovery stage. But after, the students know, or begin to know, exactly what and how to practice, adding each new perception to an emerging technique which they may now begin to automate into mastery, such mastery as their physical and artistic resources will allow.

Such is the process. Now to return to our premise, to be considered as a teaching definition: Perfection in singing is the best of an existential present.

It is apparent that if the words "in singing" are deleted the definition applies to any art, to all life. But for voice teachers it is intended to mean that perfection in singing is not to be conceived as a distant goal, an ideal to be grasped only conceptually, intellectually, not realizable as a possibility for perhaps many years. That is a concept likely to keep "perfection" forever at an unreachable distance, a denial of present joy.

"The best of the existential present" does not mean that students are to be permitted to remain in their present innocence, nor that they are to regress to earlier concepts which seemed to serve them in the past. Old concepts are to fade as new perceptions occur. Young students should know that an ideal can be used to justify a fundamentalistic faith in a no longer questioned method of teaching. Our definition aims at the possible. Striving toward a conceived ideal a student swings between efforts to sing into an unknowable future, and falling back to old lines of defensive habit. Both limit awareness in the present. The frustrated thrashings about which result from these polar swings make up the student singer's syndrome. The student's goal should be constant, though constantly changing: the best that can be done in an existential present.

"Existential," here, refers to the meaning of events to individual students, with a focus on their immediate experience. It means that their real nature consists of conscious, decisive actions. It means their awareness of their position and possibilities, now, an awareness of being, functioning, in present time. They are to practice in a perceivable now; their technique emerges as they study and perform with a present, relevant reference. There is no principle with a more important application to the teaching of singing, of any art.

Comparing one's present performance with conceptualized abstract ideals can deceive and defeat, enough to stifle any art, enough to fairly strangle a struggling student singer – or to attract only the masochistic to the study. And the fact is that it is very common for students to assume that their particular interferences are proofs, confirmations, that they are indeed striving their best toward an ideal. And this prevents perception in a present; this kind of striving is a particularly pernicious form of self-deception, causing and ingraining poor vocal results.

"The best of the existential present" cautions a teacher to be very careful not to teach "outside" a student's present, trusting sheer repetition, assigning song literature beyond a student's present ability and understanding. Students must not only love the songs they sing – the talented always do – but they must have reasonable hopes for singing them well. The instruction is to be based on efforts to improve what they now do best. Teachers who teach from their own present may be asking students to sing toward a present impossibility. Instead, students are to be required to sing "up to" the level of their emerging technique, their emerging "perfection," and that is challenge enough. In any case, it is or ought to be a sobering realization for all voice teachers that many of the students' problems will be cured only by age and experience, often in spite of earlier instruction.

Idealistic comparisons have another common, negative effect: they intensify the sensitive young students' feelings of unworthiness for the vocal masterworks. Those formidable names, held in an almost sacred awe, can almost paralyze a young performer. Our definition is a caution against presenting any vocal literature as sacred relics, either by intent or inference. Students rarely need reminding of their present unworthiness. Sometimes they need reminding that Bach liked beer, and that Brahms loved Clara Schumann.

Pursuing the art of singing is an ideal way to spend one's efforts, if insisting on unattainable goals. Any performance might have been "better," or "different," or "better next time," or "not so good as so-and-so's." Singers may never be certain they have achieved their full potential as artists. Whatever they do, even when they think they have done well, they fear they may not do so well next time, and what state their voice will be in on performance nights. The singers' can be a manic-depressive life. The "best of the present" is an indicated cure.

It does not justify exhibitionism, arrogance, or artistic pretentiousness, nor any evasions into eccentricity. It justifies only authentic efforts in an actual present. It stipulates the students' worthiness for the same sense of fulfillment as that of the mature artists, when they are doing their present best. It permits them to practice the confidence they must have for performance as they mature, for to acquire that artistic confidence the student's "present," whatever its state, must afford musical and artistic satisfaction. It is this satisfaction that alerts students to the need for constant improvement, for greater satisfaction. And that need is the basis for the most effective teaching; open-ended, flexible, opportunistic teaching.

Furthermore, "the best of the present" can reduce all abnormal stress. The teaching of singing ought to be done in situations as free from stress as possible; no method can justify its creation. Some may argue that it is "good for the student's character. They will all have to face it in 'real' life!" But studio stress can only reinforce their inhibitions; it shields them from present reality.

Some argue that students need a symbolic representation of future attainment, that an ideal is a kind of functional goal, justifying the stress involved. But stress always results in forms of disorganized behavior, altering the student's reality. And this alters the teacher's reality; a teacher may find himself criticizing vocal technique when the problem, really, is one of anxiety. "The best of the present" is to be interpreted to mean that students practice the "feel" and the attitudes of artistry from the first, and as their techniques emerge, becoming more and more secure, anxiety is transformed into an artistic and professional excitement, into the exhilaration with which it all began.

Some may fault the definition as being only "relative." The rebuttal is indeed, "Indeed!" Einstein, who played the violin not really well, surely would not mind a paraphrase: Our perception of perfection depends upon the artistic position of the perceiver, and that position has constantly changing frames of reference. Teaching directives and definitions are relevant only to "present" understandings.

There may be no adequate definition of perfection in any art other than such a relative one. It allows us to consider performances of the same work by different artists as equally beautiful, perfect, while different. Performances of Schumann's *Dichterliebe,* for example, by Fischer-Dieskau, and Fritz Wunderlich can each be thought perfect though certainly different. To be consistent, holders of ideal definitions must choose one or the other for being nearer the ideal perfection – whatever it may be.

And, when a mature singer performs this Schumann song cycle it is clear that he cannot sing, convincingly, from the point of view of a young man's delight and despair with first love and loss. He can't really solicit sympathy from an audience; it is clear that he did not die of unrequited love, nor reject the world, forever, because of it. Ah, but he can remember the experience and can evoke that memory in others, expressing with authentic pathos the sadder and wiser resignation that maturity brings. And when we listen to a young mezzo sing the *Frauenliebe und Leben,* the beauty we hear is a reflection of the innocent understandings in her portrayal of the experiences a woman's life might bring. Songs are always sung in a different "present." There can be no "ideal" interpretation of the great songs; only authentic or imitative ones. That is part proof of their greatness.

Ultimately, all ideals reduce to preferential taste, and the teacher's taste is not to be imposed, only presented as an illustration of the possible to be tested against the students' present comprehensions. When the students' interpretations have been imposed, not really theirs, the performance may have, for them, no existential present at all – and the audience will know it.

"The best of the present" can relieve much of the artificial tension which makes so much of first formal performance more of an ordeal than a happy opportunity. And the end-of-term testing of student singers, in academic settings, is often more a test of psychic strength than of musicianship and vocal artistry. A common term to this test of nerve is "Vocal Juries." Students are tried, not by a jury of their peers – who ought to be present – but by committees of voice teachers in an otherwise empty hall, engaged in sotto-voce discussions of the students' artistic futures. They are not likely to be hearing the best evidence.

There are subtle and serious implications in this "ideal" testing in which stress is artificially created and rationalized as a constructive element in the learning process. Might it be that teachers think it natural to allow their students to endure such stress because they, themselves, once had to do so? Under powerful and dominating teachers? Must students "pay their dues" thus? In a revengeful getting even with old teachers? Tamino kept waiting at the door indefinitely? To preserve the priesthood? An unconscious envy of young students' gifts? Playing the authoritarian role to keep the student dependent? Resisting the Oedipal overthrow? Keeping an antiseptic distance between the teacher's and students' personal and emotional lives?

Such motives may easily be inferred, and their effects are all the more serious when the teachers are unconscious of intents. A student, now on the short end of the prestige relationship, may suppress the humiliation and one day get even with her students. There is a great need for researching the implications of "counter-transferences" (see Chapter Four). "The best of the present" offers a useful starting point for introspection. It allows and encourages students to bring, consciously, whatever they now have to the studio and to their performances. So, diagnosis is made easier and more accurate. The lag between practice and performance is narrowed, and because the students are practicing the possible they grow more rapidly toward a self-directed maturity, toward an ability to make confident artistic decisions. Defensive inhibitions fall away; they approach a childlike spontaneity, enjoying and exploiting the artistic risks. The training is not just to be endured, but authentically experienced.

And years after a particular present, one of our students may audition at one of the world's great opera houses and be accepted. And on that day her definition of perfection will be the best of that existential present.

Chapter Ten

The Spontaneous Cure

Beauty is not caused;
It is.

— Emily Dickinson

For several sets of reasons, in keeping with our opening axiom, we do not begin the teaching of singing with the Word. There are evolutionary reasons, cited earlier: The most useful physical models for the coordinated workings of the vocal equipment are in the conscious experiencing of its prevocal and preverbal functionings. The teaching Word, directive or descriptive, comes later, confirming the sensations associated with perfected use. The student's spoken Word is likely to be encrusted with habits that override the biological efficiency of the earlier functions – the experienced teacher keeps an unspoken axiom in mind: The vocal equipment works perfectly except when communication is the goal – and even where motor habits of speech are reasonably efficient the Word is split off from feeling, having a narrow range of expressiveness, and being very vulnerable to disturbances.

There are psychological reasons: mastering and maintaining a responsive technique requires the identification and removal of all the restrictive results of the assumption that the spoken Word is natural. These include all degrees of hypo/hyper functionings, extraneous muscle effort, the mistaking of functional abuse for organic limitation, the misclassification of voices based on faulty tone production, and the common, crippling assumption that "singing seems so easy for others and so hard for me," all appearing in constantly varying permutations. Not only do students think they are doing what their voices require, but what they think and do are usually precious features of well-defended egos, self-images not likely to be altogether conscious and sure to be, for some time, unaffected by any intellectual approach.

And there are semantic and pedagogical reasons: We must not bewilder the beginner with abstractions, the Word in its categorical forms. There is no need, for that matter, to engage even the more experienced students with over-elaborate expositions of method. Students come to the studio to learn to produce the sounds needed to serve their artistic abilities and expressive intents. And only the most stubbornly antisemantic teachers can ignore the differences in context between themselves and their students which distort both their intentions and the students' understandings. Jargon is always incomprehensible to the uninitiated.

We must, of course, carefully attend to the students' Word. We must understand their present logical grasp of the activity, and the terminology which has helped to fix their aural environments. Just what is it they think they do in order to do what they think needs doing? Knowing this we can provide them with perceptual experiences to displace their present concepts and prepare them for clearer perceptions of acoustical and artistic realities.

So, we ought to begin by reacquainting the students with their vocal and verbal inheritance, as illustrated in the spontaneous activities of their own vocal equipment, identifying the first functions of the breathing and feeding mechanisms, and illustrating the manner in which the most primitive forms of phonation are grafted onto those early functions, and, later, how traditional kinds of vocalises used to explore vocal freedom have been derived from and are dependent on that primitive efficiency.

This guided rediscovery is less difficult in the doing than in the saying – certainly in the writing – but the principle is simple: Lead students to conscious experiences of vocal freedom before representing it by symbol. Percept before concept. Insight before intellectualism. And no premise serves this process so well as one that sounds, on the tongue of a singer, much better in French: Reculer Pour Mieux Sauter.

"Drawing back in order to leap farther forward" is a principle discussed at length by Arthur Koestler in *The Act of Creation* – another of those books on vocal pedagogy kept on the wrong shelf in the library – as operant on all levels of physical, psychological, and intellectual life, from the single-celled organism to the most highly complex.

Examples: The tissue around the stump of an amputated leg of a salamander "regresses" to the unspecialized nature of embryonic tissue in order to respecialize as a new leg. Higher levels of organization, like ours, don't allow for such regeneration, but there are illustrations of the Reculeur in our rest and sleep as preparations for renewed efforts, in our withdrawing to forms of infantilism under stress or during illness when we want bland foods and maternal care. The Reculeur appears in those forms of meditation not meant for escapes from reality but for recharging the energies for greater accomplishment.

The Reculeur is everywhere preserved in fairy tale and folklore; the hero undergoes severe testing, physical and spiritual, in order to win a princess and kingdom, at times descending into actual death and returning victoriously. The Reculeur is the essence of mystical initiation, of baptismal rites. It is profoundly illustrated in the great allegories: Buddha under the tree of enlightenment, Jonah in the belly of the whale, Joseph in the well, Jesus in the desert, in the tomb. It appears in all the archetypal themes of darkness followed by light, night and day, withdrawal and return, death and resurrection, all of which ought to remind the discouraged that the seeds of greatest victory may be sown in the sloughs of despond.

The Reculeur is operant in the creative and intellectual lives: a poet, composer, or scientist may wrestle with a seemingly impossible problem; blocked, baffled, because it will not yield to any of the usual techniques, procedures, vocabularies, or methods. So, the problem "draws back," incubates for months, for years, until a solution may present itself in some surprising eureka experience. Incidentally, it is the failure to appreciate the nature and need for this incubation period which has led so many – many in positions of responsibility for educational policy, for instance – to assume that the sonnet, the song, or the solution is the result of a sudden flash of "inspiration" which makes creative expression appear to be some special kind of "gift." But all such "gifts" are earned; inspiration strikes those prepared by immersion in the methods and materials of their art until they achieve the spontaneous vocabulary of maturity.

The Reculeur is the basis for most psychiatric analytical techniques: "Shall we start at the beginning?" Patients are "regressed" in order to discover the origins, and later the extinction, of those blocks which have prevented spontaneity and freedom of action – just what we seek for the singer.

There are everyday examples: the pitcher's wind-up, the golfer's backswing, the archer's full draw. Even the Lord, in

Marc Connelley's *Green Pastures,* has to "rear back" to pass a miracle.

Intuitively, and sensibly, voice teachers generally begin the teaching with ad hoc forms of the Reculeur, regressing the students, by whatever the method, in order to diagnose the problems and devise a teaching strategy for treatment. But as a conscious discipline, the Reculeur can clarify this process, enabling teachers to judge the proper regression "distance," at which a particular student's technical study and practice needs to be concentrated.

Earlier, as a teaching device, five stages were suggested for keeping in mind the evolutionary progression from larynx to Word: The "Five S's:" silence, sound, signal, symbol, and their final fusion into song. (See Chapter Three). These stages can be helpful guideposts for the applications of the Reculeur. At the first meeting an experienced teacher will note particular interferences which indicate the proper depth for the "withdrawal," by listening and looking for faults in the tone production, and their physical causes or effects, apparent in the student's speech habits. What idiocyncracies of speech are carried over into song?

And if there are phonating problems associated with habits of speech, the teacher will "regress" the students to the next more primitive mode, to signal, encouraging them to note the sound and feel of greater spontaneity, by hearing themselves moan, sigh, wail, whine, drawing their attention to the greater ease of production and the extension of the range; the art and the challenge being the making of such sounds without their original biological or emotional necessity, but students can be alerted to pay closer attention to these sounds next time they are naturally called up.

Where the problems persist the students will be regressed still further, back to the sound mode, which almost always proves the best place to begin a daily warm-up routine for any singer. Now, students are to listen and feel for the sensations and sounds accompanying chewing, yammering, yawning, sighing, near as possible to the biological real thing, further disengaging their phonating habits from cultural accretions. This regression takes them back to the phylogenic functioning, to find and establish a personal, verifiable, repeatable feel for free phonation; to an understanding of the connections of artistic singing with the biological ease which is to become the automated basis for their technique; "free" just because these meaningless sounds are not, originally, intended for communication.

There is this caution: Any of the "old" sounds may be used for kinds of non-verbal communication. We can cough self-consciously, laugh nervously or socially, grunt in grudging disapproval, irritation, non committally. And when any of these mannerisms serve an ego-image they are not likely to be useful as phonating models. We must be sure that the "recoiling" takes us back beyond intentional communication, back beyond all vocal habits, beyond judgments of beauty or control, back to the egoless, thoughtless, non-critical yammerings upon which intentional sounds will later be grafted, while maintaining the original spontaneous mechanical efficiency.

If stubborn difficulties persist, it may well be time to regress a student to silence, at least temporarily, consulting with a laryngologist to discover whether the symptoms have an organic origin. After which, we begin the return, the "leaping farther forward," the overleaping of interferences, retracing the evolutionary sequence, now, to sound, signal, symbol, and song. We recapitulate in formal vocal exercises the entire evolution of our vocal and verbal acquisitions.

This never means that all the other elements of the study are to be ignored; except in the cases where silence is indicated, students must practice and perform. But they are to be guided by the insights provided by the Reculeur. They learn to apply the principle to self-study, preparing for the day when they leave their teachers, able to judge the validity of other teaching, and prepared to find their own ways out of vocal difficulties throughout a performing or teaching career.

But for now, at the beginning and throughout the early lessons, students are not so much being "told" how to sing as they are being encouraged, permitted , to discover their own vocal solutions, after which they may be told how they did it.

Better still, they can "tell" how they did it. For with each discovery the Reculeur brings, the students are to be asked to describe the physical and acoustical experiences in their own words; the teacher can relate these to his own. And thus it is, after the fact, that the Word may be used to clarify, condense, reinforce, and fix in the students' evolving understandings of what they do to sing well, and what they must learn to do to sing better. Following are some examples of vocal exercises used in the Reculeur process, "regressing" the singer back to the silent and sound stages. These are illustrative only and do not constitute a "method"; variations are numberless as the particular needs.

I. The Chew and Hum

Have the student place a forefinger laterally across the top of the "notch" in the upper edge of the thyroid cartilage – the Adam's Apple – and swallow. The cartilage will want to "climb" up and over the finger, rising as a part of the swallowing reflex. With a few repeatings have the student become familiar with the action.

Now, have the student place the finger, or a thumb, slightly more forward, pressing gently up into the sublingual muscles, into that soft area behind the point of the chin. Again, have the student swallow, calling attention to the strong contraction of muscles pressing down against the finger. The same can be felt by thrusting the tongue forward against the front teeth. Have the student repeat this becoming familiar with the muscles' action.

This is one of the simplest means for identifying one of the most prevalent interferences to free phonation, common in speech and singing; the tense contracting of sublingual muscles required for swallowing but which are not to be involved in vocalism.

Why are these muscles involved? We might as well ask why not? One can speculate that an ancient partnership may be involved; the vocal folds close when we swallow, their primary function. Now, for singing, when the folds must close, it may be that this "artificial" closure calls up an accompanying action of the muscles that have always cooperated and still "want" to do so. But there might be an even simpler explanation: Everyone knows "where" his voice is, right "there" in the throat. Speech and singing are intentional, and the only muscles in that area over which we have voluntary control are those swallowing muscles which can be easily associated, by proximity, with intentional phonating. In any case, we are to help the student separate these associated functions, coaxing the sublingual, swallowing muscles to remain relaxed while, at the same time, closing the vocal folds for singing.

Now, with a finger alternately across the top of the "Adam's Apple," or pressing up into the sublingual area, have the students speak a vigorous "He! He! He!" The EEE sound exaggerates the sublingual effort – in most cases – where this interference is at all present. Have the students notice the strength of the "bunching up" of the swallowing muscles, again and again, for familiarization.

Now, have them sing a slur on the vowel E, up and down an interval of a fifth or octave, again with finger or thumb alternating in the positions suggested before. Such slurs are invaluable diagnostic devices for the teacher; the interference will be dramatically increased in the wide slurs, bringing to the students' attention, too, the obvious interfering reflex of which they may have been totally unaware. The exaggerated tension is feelable, hearable, and best of all, undeniable. Students will have positively identified an enemy of vocal freedom, one of the worst, and now have incontrovertible, personal evidence of a primary interference. They are to discover that they can speak, attack a given pitch, slur up and down anywhere in their phonating ranges without calling up that swallowing reflex.

How? We begin with a silent chewing, a comfortable, uninhibited chewing, with a finger or thumb exploring the sublingual area once more. They will notice that those sublinguals will be soft, relaxed, uninvolved in the action of chewing. So, they have been given a personal example of the reciprocal innervation of muscle opponent-partners – the cooperation of flexors and extensors during which one set relaxes while the other activates. As, for instance, when lifting an arm, fist closed, bending an elbow to "make a muscle," the biceps contract and the triceps relax; the reverse when the arm is lowered.

The opponent-partners of the interfering sublingual muscles are the chewing muscles. Ah ha! One cannot chew and swallow at the same time. The interfering swallowing muscles must relax while we chew. Students can experience the feeling of freedom from the swallowing interference, sensing, at very least, how those muscles ought to feel while phonating – though just now it is the feel minus the sound.

Now the students are to "graft" a humming sound onto the activity of chewing, humming without interrupting the chewing action. They are not to stop chewing, start the hum, and then resume chewing. They are to make the chewing a continuous activity, for the time being more important than the sound. It is to be a HUMMMMmmmmmmming sound, much like one expressive of the deliciousness of whatever is being chewed.

The audible humming is to be pitched at or near a comfortable speaking level, probably around A, B, or C, in the proper octave for male or female voices. But it is not important, now, that the pitch is arbitrary or remains at a certain level; it may be gently inflected within the conversational range. The important thing now is that a resonant hum is to be produced without activating the swallowing muscles.

This "primitive" vocalise is based on a discovery independently made by laryngologists and singing teachers, both of whom noticed that the "twin functions" – chew and hum – might be exploited with therapeutic effect on abused voices while affording a useful sensation of "free" phonation. It is an exercise that, by itself, after voice rest, silence, can "cure" pathologies on the leading edges of vocal folds damaged by abuse. The gentle hum encourages the folds to meet in a complete closure at mid-line with the gentlest possible approximation. Properly practiced, this illuminates the "target" for the desired "placement" of the speaking voice, and for the singing voice once phonation is resumed after rest. There is no single exercise more effective in giving a student such a clear, comfortable, easy-to-find model for healthy phonation.

Next, the Chew and Hum might be given specific pitches, and perhaps a sustained four or six beat duration. If this goes well the student should try moving the pitch up and down, diatonically, perhaps first on three note scales, 1-2-3-2-1, or five notes, 1-2-3-4-5-4-3-2-1, and later progressing to small skips, ending with a slur, 1-3-5-1, a very good test of the exercise's effect in outwitting the sublingual tension. And while slurring, it should be noticed that the larynx is not to rise and lower with the pitch.

Chew and hum, chew and hummmmmmmmmmm, chew
before humming and all during the humming. And what are the
students to be thinking while doing it? They are to notice, in order
to be able to describe it later, whatever sense of vibrational
"location" the chew and hum produces. Where is that sound?
Where do they feel the center of the vibration? And almost all will
respond that it was felt, sensed, in the front of the face, around the
nose, the sinuses, the front teeth, the bony hard palate; in short,
"Forward," where it belongs.

But is the vibration only in the frontal bones of the face? Place a
hand on the upper chest, over the sternum, and feel the vibration
there. Put a hand on the top of the head, and feel the skull
vibrating like a hi-fi tweeter. Cultivate a loving acquaintance with
the specific and general locations of that vibrant feel. Can the
intensity of the vibrations be increased somewhat, without calling
up the sublingual interference? Continue the humming until there
is a sensation almost like that of warmth in that frontal area of
most intense vibration. You are sensing the target and the
confirmation of "proper placement." Do you notice a sense of
increasing vibration in the upper chest as you hum on the lowest
pitches? An increase in the vibrations in the head as the pitch rises?
In both cases you should feel that you are adding dimensions of
intensity to the sound without detracting from the feel of
"forwardness" in the face.

This simple Chew and Hum is an indispensable exercise for
any singer, or speaker. Not only is it the happiest way to begin the
phonating day, it is the most helpful reconditioning exercise to
return to after a day of vocal fatigue or careless usage. It needs no
reference to particular pitches. It can be done anywhere, anytime;
walking along, driving a car, warming up backstage without being
heard out front. And applied as a model "locator" for the
placement of spoken sounds, it can turn everyday conversation
into singing practice. Every sound in spontaneous conversation
can, and should, afford the same bony "buzz" as the chew and
hum. Singers, lacking in technique, often report that their voices
are "lower" in the mornings and "higher" later in the day, and
while this may be an effect of individual biological and circadian
rhythms, this is usually a certain sign of overuse, or inefficient use
of the voice on the previous day, or a failure to speak near an

optimal frequency. The chew and hum can alleviate the symptoms of such misuse. Students confirm the value of the chew and hum by discovering that they need less and less time for "warm-up" before singing. The exercise cannot be overdone.

II. Yeh Yeh Yeh Yeh Yeh

Say this, don't *sing* it, rapidly on a conversational pitch. Notice that the repetitious sound requires the "chewing" motion of the jaw. There is to be no movement of the tongue, which just goes along for the ride. Make this a loose, comfortable, rapid, chewing movement; All jaw, No tongue! Notice that this seems also to "place" the sound in the same general, bright, resonant location of the chew and hum.

Now – all jaw and no tongue – try this Yehyehyehyehing on a five-note scale, ascending and descending, 1-2-3-4-5-4-3-2-1. If this goes well repeat the top note, 1-2-3-4-5-5-5-5-5-4-3-2-1, or an an arpeggio, 1-3-5-8-5-3-1, or, 1-3-5-8-8-8-8-5-3-1. There will be a sense of increasing vehemence – not loudness – as the pitches rise. But notice, does the jaw stiffen in the approach to the higher pitches? Does it seem to become difficult to maintain the rapid "chew?" If so, a specific interference is identified, the common up and out-thrusting of the lower jaw that pulls the larynx up, creating the sublingual tension we are trying to eliminate.

This exercise is meant to be a means for preventing the stiffening of the jaw, so again the concentration is on the easy chewing movement rather than the sound. Do this in front of a mirror; if the tension persists you will see the interference, perhaps the tongue "wants" to be involved. Properly done, this is one exercise that can facilitate a smooth adjustment into the "head register," the voice may easily just sail right through the "passagio" with a kind of natural modification in the character of the sound, without any increase in sublingual tension or thrusting of the lower jaw. And this can reinforce a prime singing principle for the students: The voice will, and should, feel, seem, and sound smaller to the singer as it approaches the higher pitches;

smaller to the singer, not to the listener, as if the voice were cone-shaped with a larger circumference at bottom and a smaller one toward the top.

With this exercise, as with the chew and hum, there is to be no concern whatsoever for "beauty," nor for "control," no worrying about intonation, absolutely no self-criticism. It is to be done with all concentration on the simple mechanical activity of natural chewing, noticing that the vocal equipment produces sounds seemingly focused "forward" without any raising or lowering of the larynx and without any arbitrary, feelable, visible muscular movement in the sublingual area being associated with changes of pitch. Those sublingual muscles ought never to know the difference between high and low notes.

III. The Yawn and Sigh

Take a slow, deep, complete breath as if about to yawn, change your mind and sigh through that opening. The throat naturally opens in the act of inhaling, and in approaching a yawn, and can remain in that position for the exercise. There is no better model for sensing the singer's desired "open throat." However, the approach must not become a real yawn, remembering the quite considerable jaw tension required by the real thing. Just approach the yawn, and instead, sigh. Sigh a high, aspirate Hhhaaah – it can be on an indefinite pitch – perhaps with the arms stretched out and up, as if rising from bed, feeling exuberant, and yawn-sighing out an "AAaaaaahhhhaah, what a great day!"

The sigh is to be "weightless," high, "falsetto" if you wish, but it is to be light, easy, with a loose lower jaw and no tension in the throat in starting the sound. Now, start the sound somewhere near a high A^b – higher if comfortable – then slur downward with a smooth, unbroken portamento into the conversational range.

If the lower jaw persists in its "reaching" for the starting pitch, place the hands, heel upwards, between the jaws, fingers pointing back toward the ears – not covering the ears – and gently hold the lower jaw down and slightly back; not forced down with tension, but loosely down as if at the bottom of a comfortable bite. Try the Yawn-Sigh again, watching in a mirror to be certain that the tongue remains relaxed – it may want to tense compensating for the relaxed jaw. Gently immobilizing the lower jaw in this manner often results in an immediate, dramatic ease of production. Ah, sometimes a singing teacher believes we all might sing so easily if only we didn't own a lower jaw.

There is another "handy" device: Using one hand, thumb and forefinger curved around the chin, pressing the lower jaw gently – gently – down and back; again repeat the Yawn-Sigh before the mirror, remembering that the hand is there only as an "observer," not as a "doer."

The yawn-sigh can lead to important discoveries: how easy it can be to pick high pianissimo sounds right out of the air without the usual tense preparation. How utterly weightless the sound can seem, this beginning of the body's unconscious association of height with ease – never minding the sound for now. And, especially with the use of the hands as suggested, the Yawn-Sigh coaxes the vocal equipment into a position for the freest, most efficient tone-production, it indicates the direction toward the most beautiful sounds to come. Students can learn that "where" they sense this sound is precisely "where" they are going to sense their legitimate and mature "head voices." They learn that, so, habitual interferences can indeed be "overleaped."

The Yawn-Sigh provides students with a conscious awareness of a widening of the pharyngeal and supraglottic resonators, often giving them their first experience of phonating without constriction in the throat. And an even greater freedom can be modeled if they use the high, soft sigh as an expression of sorrow, or of relief. Just as with the Chew and Hum, and the YehYehYehYeh, the Yawn-Sigh may afford the first authentic experience of a "non-volitional control" of the vocal folds. The students can identify, by ear and sensation, with the functional efficiency that results, that precise functional freedom which will be essential for the sensitive and immediate adjustments from emotional color to color required for persuasive song

But little progress will be made until the lower jaw is loose and sublingual tension is removed. The proper attitude, for now, is one of suspended criticism, careful listening and comparison of sensations, and perceptions of "placement." Not yet should the student decide how it should sound. Functional freedom first! And chewing, humming, yammering, yawning, and sighing are truly natural, functionally free activities. We do not now worry about beauty; it will come. The proper progression is yawn-sigh-sing.

IV. The Huh! Huh! Huh! Huh!

To prepare: Place the hands on the sides of the body, pressing into that soft area between the lowest ribs and the pelvic wings. Now, make a gentle cough. Gentle! Notice the outward reflexive muscle movement against the indenting hands.

Press the fingers deep into the lower abdomen, well below the navel. Now, make the gentle cough, noticing the outward muscle movement against the fingers.

Press the fingers into the soft triangular area just below the sternum, into the epigastrum, and again make a gentle cough. Notice the outward reflex against the fingers.

Now, with a finger across the notch of the Adam's Apple, or with a thumb pressed up into the sublingual area, as with the chew and hum, puff a vigorous, short, sharp, staccato: Huh! Huh! Huh! Huh! Notice that this sound can be made without any "feelable" activity in the sublingual muscles. Confirm this using the thumb and forefinger, like pincers, just above the top sides of the thyroid cartilage, with the lower jaw "a-dangly-down-o." Now there is to be no muscular pressure outward against the finger and thumb.

Next, try all of the hand positions while making a gentle clearing of the throat. Gentle! Notice the resistant outward muscle movement in the abdomen. This outward movement is part of the body's reflexive response whenever there is an activity requiring a closure of the vocal folds, compressing the air beneath; it clearly illustrates the direction of the dynamic "support" reflex we want to associate with singing.

This reflex is easy to find, to observe in one's own body; lie back in a comfortable chair, or stretched out on a sofa, belly muscles relaxed, in an attitude of thankfulness for the end of a trying day, sink the fingers deep into the abdomen and puff a sudden, sharp HUH! You will find that the appropriate reflex – our "breath support" reflex – can hardly be prevented.

The reflex can easily be tested in other simple Reculeur experiments: Next time you feel a cough, sneeze, grunt, or a laugh approaching, press your fingers in any of the locations suggested and sense what the body does when the resistance is naturally required. Fortunately for us, all these actions are truly natural; if in each instance each of these actions had to be analyzed to establish the precise levels of need and the exact degrees of response there would be little time for other forms of consciousness, for anything else in life. "Breath support" does not have to be learned – not in the sense traditionally presented to young singers – it is already "there" to be discovered. The singer only needs to learn to prepare for it, and to trust it; a preparation and trust that experience will automate into mastery. Vocal technique is based on a conscious preparation and a willful permitting of the necessary physical responses. There is such a thing as "controlled spontaneity."

And now, if you can imagine these dynamic responses, complex as they are, as being in a kind of "slow-motion," you will have an inkling of what the term "breath support" means when applied to sustained phrases in singing. This outward resistance is just what almost all the writings about "support" are meant to describe; the critical "hook-up" between tone and breath. The preparation involves setting up the proper conditions for its appropriate occurrence: a comfortable posture, a full breath – "belly breathing," as distance runners describe it – and a conscious resistance to immediate collapse of the upper chest when starting the tone. There must never be a deliberate "pushing out," and never, never, a deliberate "pulling in" of the abdominal muscles – the most common and deceiving, seemingly natural volitional action. In nature, action determines the response.

"Breath control" may be the most inhibiting term ever associated with the study of singing. "Control" implies deliberate action, effort, muscle contraction, interfering with the need to "let the body sing," or run, or swim, or dance. We don't always need a complete inhalation for singing, but the abdomen must be free to expand downward and outward – "the singer must feel fat in order to sing." But where there is deliberate control the singer will have difficulty relaxing the abdominal muscles quickly, as is necessary for properly inhaling a singing breath. Better to say, "Feel fat!" or, "Let your belly just hang from the ribs!" There must be a resistance to "collapse" and just the right pressure from beneath the vocal folds, but whatever the resistance may be it must be "unhooked" for the next breath. So, when proper, "support" is less of a transitive verb, implying the need for some specific, deliberate action; it becomes much more of a "something" singers allow to happen. It cannot be precisely defined, measured, or controlled; it takes whatever it takes, as each singer must discover for himself.

The experienced teacher finds himself more and more reluctant, in most cases, to launch into any detailed description of the "breath support" process with beginning students; at this point the more emphasis on it the stronger is the desire to "do" something about it. Often it is best approached by some form of analogy: Let's say you are going to pick up objects of differing weights, perhaps a light book or a heavy chair. Generally, we don't decide in advance just what such objects weigh, or just how much effort will be needed to carry them across a room. We simply exert against the object, against gravity, whatever it takes to lift it, an appropriate and balanced muscle effort, with an efficiency and even a natural grace. We don't act as if the chair is fifty pounds heavier than it may be, unless we are unusually clumsy and uncoordinated. We don't "white-knuckle" a grip on the book, just "what it takes." And, just as these objects existentially increase in weight the longer we hold them up, so does the sustained tone in singing. So, the body must be permitted flexibility of response to the varying requirements of pitch, duration, and intensity.

But it is common for untrained singers to decide, or guess, in advance just how much lifting effort a sound will require and crank in the vocal tension even before attacking the sound – the term "attack" does little to prevent this. And most often this will result in a "pulling in" of the abdominal muscles, this being the most natural volitional response, as if the sound was a dollop of toothpaste to be squeezed out of a tube.

Almost any description of "breath support," or of the desired "diaphragmatic-intercostal breathing," makes perfect sense to singers *after* they learn what it is by actually doing it. But before that personal perception all the writings, lectures, and descriptions are apt to be misleading, simply because "control" denotes volition. Ah, there should be a special voice class in Hell for all the non-singing choral directors who shout at their singers, "From the diaphragm! From The Diaphragm! Sing It From Down Here!" punching themselves in their own midriffs. The young singers obediently contemplate their navel areas, tighten their belly muscles, and "support" for all they are worth.

Once students have identified the spontaneous "support" reflex, the short, sharp, staccato Huh! Huh! Huh! Huh! may be done on specific pitches, on an arpeggio – 1-3-5-8-5-3-1 and later – 1-3-5-8-8-8-5-3-1, during which they may take their breath wherever needed. Again, they are to be reminded that accuracy, beauty, and control are not, now, to be important considerations in the efforts, only a familiarizing with the elegantly appropriate natural responses of the body.

The greatest difficulty in describing "breath support" and/or directing students to "support the tone," is that each particular pitch, at each particular level of intensity, for each singer, requires a precise resistance and rate of air flow. And no teacher can tell any student exactly what this resistance and rate should be. The Reculeur discoveries can.

V. The Slurred Signal

This is another primitive, useful device for finding the feel of "support" in its dynamic variations as it adjusts to vocal demands: With the hands once more alternating in the positions suggested for the earlier exercises, begin a sound in the conversational range – an "EH" works well – and slur rapidly up and down at an interval of about an octave. Not a "singing" sound, just a widely inflected, elegant "sirening" sound. Feel the body supply the needed resistant support – the outward resistance increasing as the pitch rises and decreasing as it lowers. Again, use the hand positions to monitor and assure the desired relaxation of the sublingual muscles, the absence of jaw-thrust, the still tongue, and a larynx that does not move with the pitch. "Siren" up and down, up and down, in vigorous legato waves, through a throat that feels like a simple stand-pipe.

If this goes well, the slur may be attempted on various phonemes and on specific pitches, at intervals of a fifth or octave. Now the students' attention may be directed to any change in the quality of the phoneme as the pitch changes – any interference will alter this quality. Students are to try to keep exactly the same shade of pronunciation throughout: "Sing the very same 'AH' from bottom to top." Maintaining the identical phonemic character keeps the instrument in the proper alignment. Students may now begin to hear that they have been singing each different pitch with a "different instrument," now judging the effect of the exercise by ear as well as by feel.

Even slight changes in their basic sounds, resulting from the Reculeur exercises, can make immense differences for the student singers, providing them with crucial insights. For however slight, any change alters the entire configuration of the vocal equipment, and it is this that alters the old "men'al concept" of tone. No methodological jargon can accomplish this; students cannot "think" their way out of problems in tone production. They must perceive their way out, by experiencing it.

The Reculeur exercises can be daily confirmations that the voice is "there," ready, placed, supported for the best open-throated use. The suggested use of the hands is not to become a vocalizing crutch by extended use, but it can have immediately positive effects because sounds made in this manner are not connected with any form of tone production in the students' experience. With an entirely new set of kinesthetic associations, which the students can easily recreate in their practice, old habits are "overleaped," often resulting in immediately more beautiful vocal sounds. And even where the "cure" is not yet permanent, the "handy" devices can be a constant reminder of the precise nature and strength of their bad habits.

Every change of pitch may formerly have been associated with and accompanied by some arbitrary and unnecessary adjustment of sublingual muscles. And the association may be of such strength and long-standing that it will accomplish little to tell students that the vocal folds, alone, can be trusted to make the pitches. Whatever their talent, interest, and motivation may be, they may, for some time, "need" the familiar confirmation of that "control"; many, at first, are unable even to imagine singing without it. Teachers may give them pitches to phonate, without telling them what the pitch may be, but their habits know, their bodies remember, and the associated "controls" assert. The Reculeur approach permits the teacher to arrange purposeful accidents in tone production.

A teacher may point out that a student's jaw is thrust forward and stiff, but even some of the most diligent and intelligent students can stand in front of a mirror and not "see" the jaw move, or the larynx rise, or the sublinguals tense, simply because these have been inseparable parts of the action. This apparent denial can frustrate an inexperienced teacher, but it must be understood that "letting go" of such interferences can mean, to the students, an inconceivable, unforgivable loss of control.

But the "handy" devices can make the efforts more experiment than performance, in which control can be made to seem less important. Now, students may notice, for the first time, that the sublingual tension sets in before the sound is started; anticipation being part of the habit. They may notice that they stop the tone with a contracting of those muscles, closing off the pharynx, pulling up the larynx, instead of "lifting the breath away from the tone" – like a bow from a violin string.

The Reculeur process is effective because it involves perceptual reorganization, requiring students to deal with authentic vocal experiences in a new system of relationships, a new framework and context, well apart from their own or their teachers' verbalized concepts which too often dominate the teaching and the study. Nothing is so ineffective in influencing vocal behavior as intellectualizing.

Improvement comes with a revision of concepts, which can only occur with fresh perceptual experience. Where the student's old associations have clouded perception, the Reculeur clarifies, sharpening the student's awareness of the internal events of phonation which elude the subtlest descriptions – until after the actual experience. A "total feel" is experienced without splintering

the attention on bits of the action. Definitions and directives
follow, with an evolving language for the individual's study.

The Reculeur exercises fix the students' attention on natural
activities their bodies perform dutifully, dependably, and countless
times daily. These are to be applied as models for intentional
phonation, while the teacher says, "Did you hear that? Did you
notice that? How did that feel? Where was that sound?" Or, "That
is what I meant by what I said a moment ago."

And the experienced teacher will not be surprised to hear a
student use a descriptive term that he, the teacher, might never
have thought to use. And it simply does not matter, for now, if the
student's sensations and impressions do not seem to square with
the physiological or acoustical facts. What is to be understood is
that nothing is so accurate for the singers as is their clear, personal
perception of the internal sensations which accompany their
phonating. These provide the only accuracy there can be, for
them, for now.

"Getting there" has been an unconscious imperative, but is not
now the goal. How one gets there is the Reculeur lesson. And the
Reculeur exercises enable the students to make sharper distinctions
among the sensations and sounds within their internal landscapes;
they gain a new set of interpretations of their own neural-
sensorial, auditory, tactile "feed-back." Any sound at all – no
sound at all – is to be preferred to any produced with the old
habits. We are just identifying the enemy.

This is why it is unwise to begin the training with the
presumably "easiest" of the traditional, graded vocalises which
"progress" from slow five-note scales to more rapid and extended
ones, and from those to arpeggios throughout the range, and
finally to intricate flexibility exercises. Rather, even the "easiest"
of these should be delayed until the student has experienced some
sense of the vocal freedom which can be maintained in later
vocalizings. Probably, we ought to avoid altogether the concept of
"progressing toward increasing difficulty." The truth is that an
ability to perform these vocalises is a proof of a perfected
technique; they are not necessarily a preparation for it. Singers
soon learn that, in a very real sense, singing is either easy or
impossible. In a profound sense one can say that a perfected vocal
technique consists in noticing that things are going well.

Once a sense of authentic vocal freedom has been experienced, through experiments at the proper Reculeur "depth," young singers can begin their progress, by quantum leaps, toward the ultimate confirmation of their vocalizing skills: a perfectly smooth portamento, an elegant legato, the easy "picking out of the air" rather than "attacking," and, finally, the Messa Voce, the limpid, fluent swelling of the sound from soft to loud and back to soft, on any pitch in the vocalizing range. Ah, when singers can truly do these things there is no longer much need for the teacher.

Since it is the "will to phonate" that causes the vocal folds to adjust to the required tension, length, and mass, then that "will" must be clear, intentional, unequivocal, without reservation. Any ambivalence destroys the coordination. But teachers can easily forget that the student's problem may not be one of technique.

Asked to sing a mezzo-piano "high" G, on the vowel "AH," a young soprano may make several unsatisfactory attempts. The teacher, thinking "technique," and knowing the student is certainly vocally equipped to do this, says, "Take a breath through an open throat." Or, "You are letting your body collapse; think of your posture." Or, "That was breathy; next time support the tone." Or, "Try to think of a purer vowel." Or fill-in-the-blank.

But the soprano's real problem has been a cumulus of cloudy thoughts: "Let's see, she wants me to sing a 'high' G but that's a little high for me... I couldn't do it in the practice room today... that's always been my hardest vowel anyway... I don't think I can sing it as soft as she wants... I remember my voice breaking when I tried it in my lesson last week... It probably will go out of control again... Oh, I hope not... I wonder if she really likes my voice... I wonder if she thinks I am really talented at all... Someone is listening outside the studio door... I wish my voice was more beautiful." And on and on, down the Freudian ladder to the unconscious, "I wish I was more beautiful... I wish everyone loved me." So, diffusing the energy, destroying the intent.

Psychological health and personality integration are important elements of singing talent because the intention to sing must be absolute. One can "tell" the vocal cords to sing... but maybe not. And this is why the "pour mieux sauter," properly understood, can be enormously helpful in simplifying the intent. "Technique" is its goal, but it is approached by creating an uncritical attitude

and a risk-free atmosphere of experimentation in which the student
will be much less troubled by indecision, freer to make the
necessarily clear distinctions among the sounds and sensations.
Technical progress comes with a leaping forward over old
"performing" habits and negative thinking.

But this "overleaping" will not be expected, and so, not
encouraged, prepared for, and perhaps not even recognized by a
teacher whose method reflects a "Gestalt" or "Behavioristic"
premise. The gestaltist offers the student an inventory of the
elements of phonation and waits for a "synthesis" of
understanding and application. The behaviorist may just wait for
his conditioning to take effect. Neither can explain an
"overleaping." The gestaltist believes that the synthesis – when all
the elements fall into proper order and effect – is the result of an
awareness of, and a concentration on all the discretes in the
singing act. Early quantum leaps seem unlikely. The behaviorist
believes that all bad habits, and attitudes, have been "conditioned,"
and begins a strategy of deconditioning and reconditioning,
depending more heavily on routine, rote, and repetition, rather
than exploration and experiment. Neither is likely to recognize
readiness. One assumes technique must be gradually acquired; the
other overloads the student with details. But the Reculeur alerts
the teacher to expect the overleaping to begin at the first lesson.

So, then, the Reculeur prepares for the mieux sauter, from the
indicated silent or sound levels to where the pre-conscious
presentational pathos of the signal provides models for authentic
artistic expressiveness. We move from the natural physical bases
for the "meaningless" sounds in the Chew and Hum, the Yawn-
Sigh, to the natural origins of the significant signal – the sound-
bondings of the species. These range beyond the "civilized,"
acculturated, role-playing restraints of common conversation.

One needs only to remember that when we are truly
overwhelmed by actual pain, grief, or greatly exhilarated by joy,
we care very little who hears. And it is the urgency, the "color,"
the quality of these sounds that has the emotional accuracy the
singer needs to "move" an audience. In this sense, signal and
"quality" are synonymous terms, though we keep in mind that the
term "basic quality," as used by voice teachers, is the result of a

particular anatomical structure which determines a distribution of overtones and formants which makes each voice distinctive.

All this confirms the value of some of the insights we have inherited from earlier, empirical masters; oversimplified, but very useful: When singing in the lowest ranges think of a moan; for the middle range, a sigh; for the highest, the wail or whine. Of course, these are to be tamed into technical recall and artistic refinement, guided by a Reculeur process which, at the same time, allows students to discover the physiological limits of their vocal instruments and their proper classifications.

And at last, the overleaping brings us to the symbol, the mechanical and expressive models brought to the service of the text. The Word, finally, must be sung. But not exactly the Word, and never the Word as spoken. The demands of pitch are far beyond that of speech; the duration and intensity range beyond even the most dramatic declamation.

Some earlier teachers were fond of saying, "We do not sing words at all! When we sustain a 'tone' we are sustaining a vowel. Vowel and tone are synonymous terms." Singers understand and appreciate this generality, but it needs qualifying. We don't always sing vowels either. More often we sustain parts of a vowel, phonemes, the indivisible atomic sound units which comprise the molecular vowels.

The vowel in the word "I," for instance, used to be thought a "diphthong," a two-part vowel – AH-EE. But closer attention has revealed "quarks" of sound which make the word more of a "quintiphthong," starting with the initial AH and gliding through EH to A to ĭ to EE. The singer's problem is to decide which phoneme should get all or what part of a tone's duration.

This is the primary caution against advising students to "Sing as you speak!" Gliding through complex sequences of phonemes is acceptable in conversation, barely noticed given the rate of speech. But in singing, the "right" phoneme – which seems to be what is often meant by the term "pure vowel" – is to be sustained. The best general advice is that the "dominant" phoneme gets all the duration; the rest of the diphthong, triphthong, quadriphthong, gets only the brief duration of a final consonant. Usually, the initial phoneme is "dominant," but not always; EE, in the word

"You," glides swiftly into the dominant U except, of course, by the authentic folk-singer and the not so authentic "pop" stylist.

For example: if the word "I" is to be sung on a two-beat note, singers sustain their best pronounced and properly expressive phoneme "AH" for the full two beats, ending with an almost instantaneous glide through the remaining phonemes. Merely recognizing the proper dominant phoneme and locating its best placement are problems enough for student singers to make it understandable why we do not approach the teaching of singing from the Word. They must rediscover both their best "placement" and their "Word" through practicing toward preverbal, "pure" phonemes.

The choice of phoneme is often not obvious to the student singers, particularly when singing in English, with its incredible non-phonetic spelling. How can one argue with a child who wants to write "nif," for "knife," spelling by ear? Or with George Bernard Shaw who suggested that the spelling of any language ought to be reformed when a word like "fish," can be spelled "ghoti!" (*Gh* as in rou*gh*, *o* as in w*o*men, and *ti* as in na*ti*on.)

The words how, heart, height, might, mound, bye, buy, barn, all share the dominant phoneme "AH," which can be spelled using any of the letter symbols for vowels. Singers must learn to look at these words and see "AH."

Or, the words bed, bay, debt, death, met, maid, are all to be sung on the dominant phoneme "EH," the Italian E. How lucky the Italian children, who can spell correctly for the rest of their lives after three lessons.

The singers' practice is to sing the dominant phoneme as if it was the intent to prevent the listener from knowing just what the word is to be, day or death, bind or bound, for the tone's duration, until the ending dipthong or consonant identifies it. Though criticisms of the clarity of diction are generally aimed at a lack of "clear, clipping consonants," more often what passes for admirable diction in singing is a reference to the phonemic purity; the fact is that a listener identifies words from the general context of what is being said or sung, rather than from an emphasis on consonants. Audiences, thus, supply much of the singer's elegant "diction."

But the dominant phoneme must be produced in its "purest" form, unaffected by carry-over traces of initial consonants or phonemes, and it is not to drift into an anticipation of a later phoneme or final consonant, like the "pop" singer's treatment of "Day" as DEHeeeeeeeeeee.

The "purity" of vowels and phonemes depends upon a tone production that facilitates their reinforcement by "formants" – partials resonating in a relatively narrow band in the vocal tract which are independent of and do not duplicate the "natural" overtones of the fundamental pitches being sung. Adjustments of the vocal tract – the supraglottic airspaces – alter these formant frequencies giving the vowels and phonemes their distinctive acoustical character, critical for the listener's recognition of the intended sounds. But singers sense wide variations within the range required for that recognition. (Some linguists have theorized that we might speak all our lives without ever repeating two identical "Ahs").

Familiar or not with acoustical facts, singers are all too familiar with a seemingly infinite range of choices for phonemic color and shading; they want to know which are best. What they will need to know is how to use that range of choices for artistic, emotionally accurate interpretive effect. Meanwhile, their study of fundamental technique is primarily an exploration of the possibilities for their individual best sounds. Their technical goal is "A" way of producing a distinctive, unique, "basic" voice from which they may deviate for effect and to which they can comfortably return as their familiar, trusted, consistent "basic voice." And for finding the "purest" phonemes – "the" way for producing that basic sound – Reculeur exercises can be used as "phonemic locaters."

VI. The Chew and Glide Phoneme Locaters

I. Yay Yay Yay Yay Yay – Say or sing these slowly, listening for the phonemes to "glide" past: E EH A i E. Notice that this requires only a chewing movement; the mouth is not held in one

position with the tongue rising and falling to and from a thin, tight
E. "All jaw and no tongue."

II. Yow Yow Yow Yow Yow – Do likewise with this and
listen to the gliding phonemes: E EH AH AW Ŏ Ō ŎŌ OO.
Repeated, this requires another chewing movement, with a
rounding of the lips for the final OO.

III. Why Why Why Why Why – Repeat, gliding slowly,
listening for the OO UH AH EH ĭ E, experienced as a chewing-
yawning movement, after the rounding of the lips for the initial
OO.

One of the commonest "placement" problems among young
singers is their concern, conscious or unconscious, for "vowel
discrimination," in the interest, they may think, of clear diction for
singing. But the concept of "clear diction" may be culturally
based, relating to English as a non-phonetic language. The concept
may have been formed by careless parental models, by superficial
instruction in high school public-speaking classes, or by
misguided efforts to imitate what the great singers "do." Or it may
have deeper roots, back in our grammar school days when an
eager teacher, anxious to teach proper spelling, concentrated on
lesson plans for "phonic discrimination," pursing her lips to a tiny
opening, forehead furrowed, eyebrows drawn tightly together,
saying, "This is an oooo, children," pointing to an ŏŏ on the
blackboard. "An ooooo," tongue depressed down and back,
larynx lowered in the throat. And, "This is an EEEEE," pointing
to the E on the board, "An EEEEE," teeth clamped closed, an ear
to ear grimace, tongue plastered against the roof of the mouth. So,
we may have learned "vowel discrimination," but ease and beauty
were not usually parts of the "desired outcomes" of the lesson
plan.

Whatever the cause, the students' concerns for proper diction,
for the "purity" of their vowels, often causes them to conceive of
phonemes as not just discretes, but as "muscularly" partitioned-off
from one another, as if each sound was to be produced with a very
different vocal instrument. But these same phonemes simply
"arrived at," stopping short of muscle "closures" on the desired
phoneme in the slow glide, will not call up such arbitrary muscular
associations. There are to be no partitionings; the best models can
be located with minimum efforts, and an experienced teacher will

hear the "purest," most promising phonemes and encourage students to relate their feel, location, and "basic sound" to all the others.

What may be consoling for student singers is the fact that there are not really many sounds to be "found," a relatively few serve an entire language. A glide through the words "I," and "OW" takes them through nearly all the sounds to be sung in English, and these are to be closely related in quality and "feel." As an old master-teacher has said, "We must reduce the physical and acoustical differences between the ever-changing sequence of vowels." No one has said it better.

The word "we" can offer students a convincing example of the closer-than-expected relationship between separated phonemes. Begin with an oo and glide into the final E; these are ordinarily considered phonetic extremes, but if the word is repeated slowly the oo to E glide is heard without any adjustment of jaw or tongue, only a rounding and spreading of the lips. A close acoustical relationship is apparent when the E is not "pinched" and the oo is not "throaty."

Finding the desired phonemic purity is a prime reason for having young singers begin the study with old Italian songs and arias. For these, students must learn to produce sounds unencumbered by conversational distortions. And once learned, this purity is transferable back into their native English, and the principle can be applied to other languages as well. More than this, none of the traditional vocalises are more effective than the Italian song literature for practicing one-at-a-time "pure" phonemes on long legato lines of evergreen melodic beauty.

The simplest exercises and the more formal ones will always be more effective if the teacher can improvise piano accompaniments. Doing so, the teacher can control the pace and tempo of the exercises, modulating up and down by half-steps during the singer's breathing sequences; a rhythmic breath preparation which all singers must master is practiced without awareness, becoming an unconscious reflex.

Later, the teacher should begin to vary the accompanying patterns, rather than merely doubling the singer's line, adding thicker harmonies and occasional dissonance, accustoming students to the need for singing against more complex textures and tonalities – an incidental form of valuable ear-training. Students can relax into prepared tonalities, relieved of an unnecessary conceptual effort, for now. Concerns about intonation can revive all the old habitual tensions. Students learn, in time, that intonation is less a function of conscious effort than of efficient phonation. But, for now, they are to be free as possible to concentrate on specific goals and desired outcomes for the vocalises, practicing practice, not performance.

Every young would-be voice teacher ought to acquire as much piano technique as possible; sight-reading is a daily requirement. The added color and texture make the vocalises into much more interesting musical experiences. And more important, teacher and student are both involved in the practice, closely associated in a relationship needed to give the student the confidence and trust so necessary for the study.

The Reculeur can also be the indicated antidote to one of the most prevalent and insidious preventatives of good singing: Coping! Coping with the voice! Singers are abnormally dependent for their sense of well being, personal and professional, upon the muscular and vibrational "feedback" that accompanies and confirms their trusted tone production. Every singer knows that the first indication of practically any oncoming infirmity or infection – and the last to disappear after any illness – will be a vocal symptom. It is hardly an exaggeration to say that if singers ever should break a leg while skiing they will be more concerned about how it affects their voices than their gaits.

This obsessive alertness, part of the necessary narcissism, makes them worry about the slightest abnormality in the "feedback." The differences may only be the results of differing acoustical environments, some lively, some dull. But whenever anything disturbs the "feel" singers are almost irresistibly tempted to "cope." They may compensate with greater force, or try to relax. They make conscious efforts to "fix" or to "place" the sound; they imitate their best, by adjusting their resonators; anything to get an approximation of the sensations they rely on and cannot find for the moment, or the day, or an agonizing week. They cope, simply have to do something to sing around, through, or above the difficulty. And this is particularly true when the timing of an important performance is out of "synch" with the singer's biochemical neural processes.

"Coping" is very often the fundamental problem, interfering with the teacher's efforts to lead a student to the discovery of a consistent, dependable basic sound. It can be a major cause of organic abnormality. Somehow, the teacher must convince students to trust those internal confirmations, plus or minus the variables resulting from a living vulnerability to irritations, emotional upsets, and alien acoustical environments. Singers cannot hope for more than a technique that enables them to sing acceptably on their worst days. This is why they need *a* way of singing; not as many ways as occasions. *A* way, not a collection of expedient ways.

The Reculeur helps find the way because the more nearly singers can identify with the feel and sound of the primitive functionings of the vocal apparatus, the more likely it will be that the associated motor behavior will be naturally applied to the singing, and the more the singing will have the emotional authenticity of the signal. From this comes the beginnings of an ability for a conscious outwitting of tensions, the deliberate overleaping of personal problems and inhibiting habits, the awareness of mistaken preferences for sound, and the "copings." Discovering that the sound can be produced with an animal ease is the technical foundation of the art. The study of vocal technique always refers back to the phylogenic facts, not only for the beginner but also for any mature artist who loses the "way."

Further, because it is an experience-first approach, the Reculeur can help students avoid the many confusing misapplications of our teaching terminology. When the "Word" precedes the experience it is meant to describe, many of our terms, in casual and common use, create or reinforce inhibiting imagery in the student's mind. But an even greater problem with this is that so many of the terms that have become attached to the art of singing have been borrowed from other disciplines, calling up prior references and connotations.

There are "high" and "low" notes with spatial representations "up" and "down," "above" and "below," "top" and "bottom." And while spatial representation is necessary for the scoring of music, all children know that going "up" anything is harder than sliding "down." And when they begin to think about "high" notes they naturally will, for some time, make that familiar association, reaching up for high notes with the larynx, lifting the shoulders, stretching the neck, rising on tiptoe. And they will pull the larynx down for the low notes. Watching a typical untrained singer, while wearing earplugs, one could take melodic dictation just by following the up and down directions of the singer's chin. "High" and "low" make vocal problems out of visual ones. And by the time students meet their first teacher these associations are reflex.

It is often hard for singers, beginning or mature, to ignore an apparent relationship between their visual perception of distance to their need to "project" their voices, as if the sound was a material object to be thrown. Standing downstage playing catch with an audience, the singer would need only a gentle toss of a softball to reach those in the front row and a greater wind-up energy for a side-arm sling to the middle rows, and for the balcony, a powerful overhand. Distance calls up this kinesthetic feel, and this has probably been reinforced by a drama or speech teacher – or, may the art forbid, a voice teacher – who says,"Project! You are not projecting your voice!" Ah, it can take a long time and much patience to convince students that acoustics is an altogether separate branch of physics; that what we need is to become more efficient resonators, not more powerful launchers of vocal projectiles.

We speak of "light" and "heavy" voices, of light and heavy mechanisms – referring to "head" and "chest" registers, and of course the head is higher than the chest. We speak of "holding" a tone, of "sustaining" a pitch, as if they were solid objects like books or chairs. We speak of voices that "carry" better than others.

We think about "attacking" and "releasing" tones, implying muscle effort and control, aggressiveness or passivity. We speak of "strong" and "weak" voices, "big" and "small" voices, voices of operatic "caliber," voices of "thin" or "thick" texture. But these associations with weight and gravity, motion and matter, do not translate accurately into the acoustical experiences of the singer, nor the sound-producing capacities of the vocal apparatus, nor the enhancing of dampening acoustical properties of the studio, auditorium, or theater.

Singers want to push their voices to "project." They want to take some deliberate action to "place" the sound. They tense abdominal muscles for "support." They clutch and try to stretch sublingual muscles and mandibles in order to "open"their throats. But with the exercises properly indicated by the Reculeur they can discover that the "chew and hummmmm" results in "placement," that the "yawn-sigh" naturally opens the throat, that the simulated cough, grunt, sneeze, or the "Huh! Huh! Huh! Huh!" results in natural support.

This is why the experience of "freedom" must precede settling on any particular terminology for describing it. After discoveries give students an authentic feel of freedom they can understand the sense in which the terms are being applied. And after that almost any agreed upon terms serve very well. The first thing students need to understand about voice-teaching terminology is that almost all terms that sound like verbs are much better understood as adjectives.

Even the terms describing vocal categories have inhibiting references, causing many of the self-misclassifications: Soprano, from "supra" for highest, Contralto, which used to mean "highest" male voice, and Tenor, derived from a term for "hold," and, of course, Bass for "bottom."

And some teachers either prefer or uncritically accept the term "voice building" to describe their work. And "building" clearly implies a process like the setting of brick on brick until a wall reaches the desired height. Students may hope to be able to "reach" a high F this year, and perhaps a G next year, if they can only build up their vocal strength. But the Reculeur metaphor affords a happier prospect; their entire phonating range is available to them, now, if they can discover it and then learn to produce it in conformity with the laws of acoustics – and the design of their own particular vocal instruments.

The semantic misconceptions are popular and pervasive: The non-singer says, "I can't carry a tune!" An impatient parent says, "Don't raise your voice at me!" The minister says from the pulpit, "Let us lift our voices in praise!"

*   *   *

*You can't have a science
if things hop about.*

– B. F. Skinner

Not too long ago – and at times, still – any gathering of five or
more singing teachers in one room constituted a babel of resonant
contradictions and mellifluous fictions, some benign, some
logical, some neither. These we have inherited from our teachers
and their teachers' teachers who for generations have been
describing physical sensations and acoustical events as personally,
often eccentrically perceived. Singers have always done this, and
still do, with an extraordinary disregard for "scientific" accuracy,
but, it must be said, with exquisite existential accuracy.

But in recent years an increasing professional self-
consciousness with some of the astonishments of our teaching
language has urged us toward a greater precision. And progress
has been made through closer contact with colleagues, in
professional associations, and reportings in professional journals
which provide us with a growing glossary of objective
terminology.

But it isn't clear how much this has significantly improved our
teaching effectiveness, perhaps because we have needed a more
precise terminology not so much for giving our studio lessons a
greater substantive content, but in order to have a more respectable
level of discourse with our colleagues and the academic peerage.
Some of our self-consciousness has been an effect of a cultural
distrust of intuition in an era of increasing regard for technological
precision. There is, for instance, an implied apology for the
imprecise nature of our teaching language in university classes in
vocal pedagogy when more time is spent on "vocal science" than
on the art of teaching. The fact is that now we must be fluent in
two professional languages; a poetic one for teaching, and a
scientific Lingua Franca for professional discussion and
publication.

Almost all voice teachers know – though we do seem to forget
– that many of the things we say in the studio are not only
unscientific but are often only improvised, ad hoc approximations
that we would never put in print. Many would be much more
comfortable if they could know that everything they said was

certifiably "right." And their hope has been that vocal science would do more than furnish us with a standard terminology; it might allow us to trace all vocal phenomena to observable, analyzable cause. And this longing for certainty – shades of the Given Word – can lead us voice teachers beyond mere hope; we like to believe we have achieved it.

Our interest in scientific precision began with Manuel Garcia's invention of the Laryngoscope – later adapted and better known as the dental mirror – which permitted direct observation of the vocal folds in action. Until then, it seems, no one knew or much cared how, exactly, the vocal folds behaved, up and down or in and out. With his mirror Garcia hoped to "dispel false ideas about voice production." He was, however, cautious enough to separate his scientific observings from his teaching practice. Some have been less cautious since.

Early in the century voice teachers began reflecting the growing cultural conviction that the dramatic scientific advances of the time were ushering in a new golden age. In 1915, writing in *The Natural Method of Voice Production,* Floyd Muckey presented a method of teaching as the "first scientific natural" approach to the teaching of singing. The term "natural" was used to suggest that other methods were not. Cures for all vocal ills were "in the area of physics and physiology," and therefore, methods must be "orderly."

There was an early and influential skeptic; in 1915 David Clippinger, in *Head Voice and Other Problems,* expressed reservations about the ultimate efficacy of "scientific voice teaching," reminding his colleagues that "determining which sounds are right or wrong is an aesthetic, not a mechanistic judgment." He distrusted methods that "mystify," and teachers with an "exquisite sense of detail." The basis for singing was simply a "beautiful tone" – which he struggled to define as a "mental product of the sound produced with the instrument provided for the purpose."

But momentum was building in the quest for the Given Word of scientific vocal pedagogy. In 1929, Douglas Stanley, writing in *Your Voice,* insisted that scientific research was singing's only hope for the future because the voice was "subject to physics and physiology," and progress in physics had now made it possible to "formulate absolute fundamentals without any fear of contradiction." Now, any voice teacher who had no association with "pure scientists" would have "little standing" in the field. His indoctrinees pledged themselves as "determined to learn the laws of voice, and to pass on our knowledge as pioneers in a new educational movement founded on scientific principles and techniques of singing." Later, writing in *Science of Voice,* Stanley concluded that the only difference between speech and song were the prolonged vowels in singing, the absence of vibrato in speech, the fact that consonants were less strong in speech, and that pitch did not change on single vowels in speech.

But for perfected faith in the Word, and for missionary zeal in spreading it, no writing surpasses Marchessi's *The Singer's Catechism and Creed,* published in 1932. Her method was "based on infallible principles," and those who disagreed were, variously, "Ignorant... Humbug... Conceited... Incredible... Tragic... Insolent... Preposterous... Outrageous bluffers... Disdainers of logic... Murderers of voices." There was hope. Her text would become "obligatory" once its values had been appreciated, because "there are never two truths; there can be only one."

The mechanists movement had a powerful supporter in the eminent psychologist Carl Seashore, who had carried on long-term research and experimental efforts to provide a scientific basis for pedagogical and aesthetic objectivity. In 1936 he published his conclusions in an *Objective Analysis of Musical Performance.* All aspects of singing "can be stated in quantitative detail by isolating and measuring the elements." Singing could now be, and ultimately would be, judged by "infallible machines" which could graph intonation and variations of loudness and duration. He was "troubled" by the apparent divergence between "aesthetic acceptance and the the explanation of the physical facts," but this was only because "present technology" was not yet perfected. The "divergence" would require "readjusting attitudes to pass from traditional introspectional and emotional attitudes of the musician to the laboratory attitudes of exact measurement and pains-taking analysis." But now we were able and obliged to progress from "mystic faith toward Science." Like Stanley, he was certain that the only differences between speech and singing were those of pitch and duration.

In *The Singing Voice,* published in 1947, Victor Fields expressed his profound concern that "singing teachers are prey to unscientific writings." There was a great need for a "scientific language and analytical study to avoid trial and error." Anything said about singing ought to be justified by "documented experimental evidence."

Enrico Caruso's personal physician, Marifioti, in Caruso's *Method of Voice Production,* wrote of his enjoyment "at living in an era in which all branches of human knowledge had progressed from empiricism to scientific principles and definite rules" – except for singing which still struggled along "on empirical crutches." If one correct method could be established there "could be no need for any other." And that exclusive method was to be founded on "physiological law and taught in a practical form," because "Art is based on Science!"

In *Emergent Voice* – a truly wonderful title – Kenneth Westerman, in 1955, joined the enthusiasm for technological teaching: "At last voice teaching has begun its final development in this beginning era of examined data." Now we had progressed "from the infancy of imitation, the youth of empirical findings, to the maturity of scientific investigation." But these investigations were made possible only with a "trust in technology: tapes, amplifiers, oscillographs, high-speed photography, X-ray, harmonic analyzers, stroboscopes, and all other engineering aids." With these, at long last, "We can have complete knowledge."

David McCloskey, in *Your Voice at its Best,* in 1959, like Westerman, reasserted the convictions of Seashore. Now, he felt, "We are beginning to understand some of the fundamentals upon which speech and song can be established," because of the "promise of new apparatus in related fields of scientific experimentation." And now there would be "fewer voice teachers deficient in physical facts."

All these have been influential and successful teachers, though, in strict truth, we actually know very little about the failure rate of any singing teacher, or about the number of students who were turned away as lacking "talent" who were not helped by the new technology. It seems very safe to say that the successes of any teachers have depended less on "scientific teaching" than on an obvious empirical truth: No matter what teachers say in the way of scientific explanation, they simply are not going to let their students sing sounds that offend their experienced, sensitive ears. What generally happens is that teachers attribute their successes to their "Given Word."

Anyway, the total trust in the ultimate values of technological teaching has since since been tempered by teaching experience. Most voice teachers believed that the wire recorders of the 1940s, and the much improved fidelity of the later tape recorders, would surely simplify their studio work. A student would only need to be told, "Just listen to this on tape, and hear what I meant." But we all have learned discretion in the use of recording devices in the studio sessions, and in our recommendations for their use in the student's practice. Listening to recordings of one's practice, let alone performance, is often more excruciating than educational, and not just for student singers.

It should have been – and still should be – of particular interest to voice teachers, self-conscious about the lack of precision and scientific respectability in their teaching lingo, that such a person as Paul Moses, thoroughly trained in a scientific discipline, could write in *The Voice of Neurosis,* in 1954, "Today's poetic voice teachers are better judges of the products of the larynx than many of us who claim the scientific approach. Their intuition is keen, their responses sensitive, and they grasp the totality, the gestalt expressed by the human voice. The complexity of the elements that form the particular human voice, their multiplicity, makes analyses very difficult. We should strive for creative hearing."

Later influential teachers have remained intensely interested in the findings of vocal science, but without the mechanists' former dogmatic insistence on the purity of its studio applications, or on the exclusivity of their methods. William Venard separated science from the act in the title of his *Singing, The Mechanism and the Technique,* first published in 1967 and since revised, telling us that "scientific terminology is insufficient for teaching," and that our poetic terminology was not meant to be "literally defended." We cannot be scientists and teachers at the same time. Terminology must be "adjusted to the individual." And Ralph Appleman, in *Science of Vocal Pedagogy,* agreed; "Singing defies science," and one may sing very well "without knowing why or how." The "best use of scientific information" is as a diagnostic tool, but, at least, we ought to keep our teaching practices "consistent with the best of current theory."

What, then, are the values of vocal science to the teacher and student? They are many. It can correct our empirical conclusions, and, properly practiced, does so in a manner unaffected by personal motives. No longer are any of our assumptions sacred; all are open to question and subject to continuing revision. Its methods provide us with common criteria against which we can test our differing methods, helping us to guide students toward healthy and beautiful conformity with singing's physical and acoustical realities. With its increasingly sensitive technical means it greatly extends the range of our perception, and we are surely less likely to abuse voices the more we can know about the mechanism and its actions. Informed students are protected against charlatanism. And the findings of any science are subject to confirmation by whomever troubles to repeat the experiments.

Whenever there are defensive evasions of instruction, technical or artistic, clear "scientific" descriptions of the physical blocks and acoustical effects are persuasive and reassuring. The teacher's knowledge is the rational basis for the student's "working faith," and, at the same time, solidifies the transference relationship. At times, there is a wonder-working power in the respect for "pure" knowledge.

But above all it should be understood that the proper applications of vocal science to the teaching are not so much to prevent us from saying something "wrong" as to provide us with fresher images and analogies. All scientific experiments are analogues, and, properly, much of our fascination with vocal science is due to the fact that newer and more sophisticated observational apparatus constantly generates new terminology. We, like poets, are always at a loss for words, always searching for fresh descriptive language, because the power of all analogy and metaphor fades with a few repeatings.

Still, the teaching values of scientific terminology are limited; no specific term or set of terms can be altogether adequate for describing or explaining the process or any of its parts. And this is because the actual act of singing cannot be scientifically examined. There is no way we can experiment with the complete and complex act of phonation, let alone the ultimate artistic product.

The vocal scientist must tease out some particular to examine and analyze, and considering parts, never wholes, objective science always limits or alters the reality of what is examined or described, simply because experimenting must be limited to the manageable and determined by the apparatus used. And in the selection of elements the all-at-once act of singing must be ignored. And it is that "whole" process that the voice teacher must somehow describe. The kind of absolute precision some teachers seek is an impediment to understanding just because it lacks the poetic ambiguity which makes communication possible between differing contexts. The fact is that there is not a single studio term, scientific or illusory, that does not have to be translated into some relevant reference for the student.

And the difficulties of the translation are compounded by the primary nature of scientific investigation; scientists are "visual" in their orientation; they observe, chart, graph, and publish their findings to be seen and read. But we are ear-oriented and must try to render the visual into the auditory. And in this semantic skirmish, all's fair. The language of the studio ought to be experimental and exploratory; students should be skeptical of teachers who overvalue their "precise" terminology. As someone said, it is not our knowledge of the law of gravity that keeps us from falling off ladders.

An explicit terminology can impede the process by fixing attention on some part of an indivisible act, narrowing an application to individual students, structuring students' expectancies in a manner that prevents discovery. We simply cannot describe "scientifically" what to do, think, or feel. Like the "total feel" of riding a bike – which we can't explain precisely either – one has to be singing in order to learn to sing.

It is safer and more effective teaching somehow to arrange for the students to have the desired vocal experiences, helping them to identify with those physiological internal events which only they can sense, and *then* try to make the experiences memorable, and repeatable, by using terms having common meanings for teacher and student. And, doing this, we cannot say the same things to all students. So, the desire to be "right" is always at odds with the need for teaching flexibility.

A central issue of teaching terminology is not whether it is either scientific or illusory, but whether or not it implies volitional control, for that certainly inhibits free vocal functioning. What we seek and are trying to learn to teach is a "disciplined spontaneity" – a very precise teaching term. So, things do indeed hop about in the studio. We should feel perfectly justified – no matter how we flap the air in certain ways with our tongues – that the truth of our terminology is to be judged, as it always has, by its results.

In yet another sense, a perfectly construed, objective terminology has limitations. The too-careful student must attempt "carelessness;" the too-defensive student must learn artistic assertiveness. The academically gifted may have to learn spontaneity; the technically gifted must develop sensitivity. The "too-dark and dramatic" tenor must learn to sing what may seem to him a weak and unmanly sound; the baritone may need to learn more about what the lyric voices feel like at the top of his range. The hypertense singer must "relax"; feeling lazier. The athletic type may need to feel a much softer sponginess in those powerful abdominal muscles – the muscularly disciplined dancer learning to sing may particularly need this. The shy singer must practice boldness and declamation; the exhibitionist must learn to let the music and the audience do some of the work. A consistent terminology, however "accurate," cannot serve all these. And this is why we must rely on all manner of logical and benign fictions, and enjoy making them up to suit the occasional need. But there are limits. A teacher has said, "When you are about to sing a high note, imagine you have a walnut between the cheeks of your buttocks and try to crack the walnut by squeezing." Another has said, "Imagine you have strings tied to your nipples which are pulled up and out when you take a breath for singing." Well now.

It is perfectly accurate to say, "You are to develop a technique for influencing the positioning process of the vocal apparatus at the instant of tonal inception," but it may be more helpful to say, "When the sound is 'right' it touches nothing on the way out."

While talking about an undesirable reflexive adjustment of sublingual muscles as a tone is attacked, we can still appreciate the aptness of the old master's metaphor: "Your voice is like a caged bird! Open the cage. Let the bird fly free!"

Of breath support we might say, "You must learn to control the rate of the reduction of thoracic capacity, keeping it in proper relation to your abdominal tension." Or we can help a student discover that resistant reflex through primitive vocal examples and exercises. Anyway, that relationship is never a constant; increasing, decreasing, dynamic, defined by need.

Once there was a soprano, seven months pregnant and unable any longer to hold her belly muscles tightly in, who suddenly began singing much more beautiful sounds. "Ah," she said, "That's what you meant about support!"

We can explain that a resonator is an apparatus for intensifying the loudness of a tone at its natural frequency, and that the only resonators the singer can adjust are the larynx and pharynx. But whatever students can "do" about this must be done by ear and confirmed by sensation.

"Ah," says the teacher when a student has done well, "now that was the kind of 'forward placement' I have been trying to describe!" "Really?" says the student, "I felt that way in the back of my head."

And of course there is no such thing as "chest resonance," or "nasal resonance," but every singer "knows" better. The terms express the singer's uncritical perception of an internal, undeniable perception. Experiment has shown that there is truly no such thing as nasal resonance, but the singer needs little science to prove this. While sustaining the vowel AH on any comfortable pitch, just pinch the nostrils closed with thumb and forefinger. If the sound has been properly produced there will be no change in the vowel's quality. But if there had already been a "nasal quality" – perhaps better called a "nosy" quality – the "nasality" will be dramatically increased. This is an easy way to bring to a student's attention the problem of an arched tongue and a sagging velum.

Singers talk endlessly about "focus," when we know full well that sound is omnidirectional. But "focus" describes the internal event. Every singer knows that when the sound is properly "placed", the bridge of the nose feels like a buzzing tuning fork, and such an impression, after finding the proper sound, confirms the production and helps the singer call up the desired functioning, correcting the nasality caused by the arched tongue and lowered soft palate. So, most vocal problems are best approached indirectly; one ought never to direct students to "raise the soft palate," for the students will surely try to do it.

Singers feel their skulls and recognize the "head resonance"; they feel their upper ribs and know about "chest resonance." Even the floor beneath their feet vibrates. So, they "know" where their voices "are," when singing well and, so, they learn to know where their voices "will be" before they open their mouths to sing. And, however they describe it, if they can keep that knowing "feel," whether the external acoustical environment may be "live" or "dull," their voices will be sounding their efficient best. No singer can do without such reassuring impressions.

One singer has said, "I warm up on a hum until I sense a little light turn on just inside my nose, and I keep the light on through the entire act of the opera."

We can identify and describe in accurate detail the extrinsic muscles which depress and elevate the larynx, that raise and shorten the wall of the pharynx, that tilt the larynx forward in the act of swallowing; or, we can say, "Put your finger under your chin and swallow. Those are the muscles that are in your way."

We can identify and describe the intrinsic muscle actions that abduct and adduct the vocal folds, to and from, toward and away from the medial axis, which, in so doing, tighten, elongate, and alter the mass of the folds. Or we can say, "You can trust the vocal cords to do all the work," or, "You should feel no muscle tension in the neck or in the jaw."

In an effort to improve the quality of the sound we might say, "The configuration of your vocal tract must be altered in order to produce those resonant frequencies which determine quality – the formants. And this is to be done without interfering with the fundamental frequencies produced by the cords themselves, or their resultant overtones. Thus, it is possible to alter the quality without disturbing the pitch, for the formants 'overlap' the phonemes, keeping the general quality of your voice the same." Or, we can lead the student toward discovery of the desired alterations by identifying the optimum quality of the desired phonemes by gliding through the Reculeur quadriphthongs.

A fine singer has said, "I inhale on the vowel I am to sing next."

Another has said, "I feel hollow and full of sound, like an
organ pipe that just contains the sound without doing anything to
it."
   And yet another, "I feel like a coke bottle that someone else is
blowing on."
   And, "That sound was a full foot out in front of my face. I
could wash my hands in it."
   Humpty-Dumpty said, "My words mean just what I want them
to mean, no more and no less."
   So, the best students learn that their best teachers seldom mean
"exactly" what they say.

The Demonstration Lesson

   A voice teacher of national reputation offered a series of
demonstration lessons at a convention of voice teachers, each
lesson to be devoted to one particular vocal problem. The problem
at one of the sessions: How to approach and sing through the
passagio upward into "Head Voice," a difficulty often encountered
by unwieldy young voices. Six young basses, from six different
local studios, had been volunteered as demonstration students for
this session.
   The Master Teacher explained his method: The students would
be asked to vocalize an ascending and descending five-note scale,
and as the pitch rose toward the top notes they were gradually to
anticipate the "next-more closed" phoneme. Thus:

   Ah would close toward AW
   AW would close toward O (as in Go)
   O would close toward oo (as in foot)
   oo would close toward U (as in moon)
   A (as in day) would close toward i (as in it)
   i would close toward E (as in me)

   And, he explained, as the voices reached the upper ranges to an
E^b, E, and perhaps an F or F$^{\#}$, the beginning vowels would
seem, to the singers, almost indistinguishable from the lower
"opener" ones.

This was intended to demonstrate the efficacy of two terms long in common empirical use by teachers and singers: "covering," and "vowel modification." These have been meant to help young singers refrain from pushing the lower "heavy mechanism" too high for efficiency or comfort. The hoped-for goal being to encourage the singers to sense and accept the acoustical fact that their voices should feel and seem "smaller" as they approach the highest range – as must be the case for fluent phonation. This proper sense of a smaller sound being partly the result of the fact that as the fundamental pitch being sung rises, the partials are relatively higher and fainter as they approach the upper limits of our hearing range.

And this effect reinforces the young singers' perception that their voices are leaving their bodies, leaving the familiar conversational "location," and this makes the sound seem unacceptably thin and weak, tempting them to drive the "heavier" sound upward while "holding" it down in the body. (Of course the correctly produced sound would seem rich and full to a passing bat.)

So, although "vowel modification" and "covering" are examples of those benign fictions common to voice teaching, sometimes the sense of slightly altering the vowel can be a useful approach to the feel of "head voice." Actually, the "modification" is meant only to keep constant the shade of phoneme pronunciation the exercise begins with; the desired modification offsetting the typical undesired modification toward a shouting quality at the top. Keeping the phoneme pure is the real goal; keeping it from "spreading," from becoming blatant, keeping it the *same,* makes the hoped for passage into "head voice" a more natural acoustical event.

The vocalisings began at an E^b up to B^b, in the middle range, in order to provide sufficient contrast between the lower vowels and the higher "closed" ones. The young singers were asked to sing the scales, first in unison, while the Master noted particular problems of each, after which he began working with individuals. But time was limited and results were not dramatic.

Finally, when one of the singers seemed to be having a particularly stubborn difficulty, the Master stood up from the piano and said, "No! NO! You're not getting it! Listen! Listen to this!" And he sang several scales to illustrate – his was a very beautiful voice. The young students listened, imitated, and immediately sounded much better.

The Master ended the session with a brief explanation of why his method worked so well.

Chapter Eleven

The Bel in Bel Canto

> *Fair is the fall of songs*
> *When the singer sings them.*
>
> – R. L. Stevenson

When we say "beautiful voice," or "beautiful singing," we often are referring only to elements of the act or art. It may be a response to the sensual qualities of the "warm," or "sweet," or "rich" sound. We may have admired the singer's technical command, or the range and power of a particularly impressive voice. We may have been charmed by the singer's style, or appearance, associating our sense of beauty with the singer's personality and presentation.

And there are other variables: the mood in which we approach the recital, the songs themselves, comparisons with other interpretations and other singers, preferences for certain kinds of voices. And, of course, all these judgments are made within the general and specific contexts of cultural and traditional associations. Here, we should be reminded that our particular preference for Bel Canto is indeed a cultural one; a Navaho medicine man singing a curing song, or an Asian folk-singer would surely not agree. But we justify our preference by pointing out that all we have learned about physiology and acoustics seem to support it, reinforcing all our empirically earned convictions that vocal beauty is the result of an automated coordination of body and breath, producing sounds with the most efficient use of the vocal apparatus. But this efficiency began as a performance necessity as recital halls grew less intimate and formal audiences larger. Then too, singers had to compete with the increasing tonal capabilities of instruments evolving at a technological rate, while voices remained as voices were when someone first blew across a hollow reed.

We know what "vocal beauty" is when we hear it; it is assumed as the goal and confirmation of the teaching methods we use to achieve it. But it eludes precise definition. We resort to all manner of metaphor and tautology in trying: "lyric line," or "flawless flow," or "pure and euphonious," or "sheer loveliness." Someone has said, "Beauty is a harmony of elements giving pleasure to the aesthetic sense," but it is not helpful to say that the beautiful is the beautiful – and it must be said that the faintest possible, most damning praise for singers is to tell them that their voices are "pleasing." Might as well tell them to go out in the woods and slit their throats.

Some have said that beauty is that which gratifies our aesthetic sense, or that which results in an aesthetic experience, circularities that leave out whatever "that" might be. Another has said that the beautiful vocal quality is the result of a certain distribution of overtones – partials – and this is certainly true without helping at all. Besides, widely differing distributions of partials can be thought beautiful.

The difficulty in defining "beauty," in general, should not surprise the singer; aestheticians have debated this for generations. The problem mainly seems to have been an inability to decide just what it might be that all sounds, sights, objects, people, and events that we find "beautiful" have in common. The general conclusion? Our disinterested contemplation!

For the most part there has been an insistence that the aesthetic experience is the result, as well as the state of a disinterested, distanced attitude in which we contemplate the "beautiful" for its own sake. If one contemplates, say, the "beauty" of a wooded area in the countryside, he is having an aesthetic experience *only* if not thinking about such things as the price of timber, real estate development, or clearing the area for growing corn; he must be contemplating the "beautiful" for its own sake. It is this kind of thinking that led to the cultural conviction of the utter impracticality of the arts, summed up in what is, for the singer, an infamous 19th century slogan, "Art for Art's Sake."

For singers, the sense of beauty and the aesthetic experience are never passive, never disinterested contemplations; they – and their audiences – are actively attending, participating in, and contributing to the experience, involved at unconscious, preconscious, and conscious levels all at once. We may continue to tolerate careless applications of the term "beauty" to describe a variety of perceptions, but we ought to reserve the term for its profounder implications. Vocal beauty is more than any of, and more than the sum of all such partial definitions; it is a multilayered aesthetic experience.

The fundamental requirement for the sense of beauty, in any and every of its instances, is transcendence; the appreciator of beauty must have the experience of being lifted out of a limited individual context into that of a greater "whole."

And this is what occurs when we "contemplate" any of the objects, sights, sounds, people, or events we term "beautiful," whether it is the woods, polished pebbles near the ocean's edge and turned by tides, a snowy Sierra mountain, a sunset, singer, or song. We are anguished with Romeo, and weep for Hamlet, recognizing universal human nature in ourselves. The pebbles, Hamlet, the woods, the singer and song, all remind us that we belong not just to ourselves, but to the entire process of evolution, to a culture, a species, a cosmos. We are reminded that we are a part of the movement of the stars we call "beautiful." Nothing could be more superficial than a definition of beauty as "disinterested contemplation." And no art – certainly not the art of song – exists for its own sake.

To be beautiful, the singer and song must evoke this transcendence; the listener must be moved toward wider contexts, richer relationships. Transcendence is the ultimate practicality of the aesthetic experience; it is proof that we are moving in the direction of evolution's arrow, becoming more human.

So, the perception of beauty in the beautiful singing is the confirmation of a multilayered experience; a unity of physical, intuitive, and intentional acts; the artistic exploration of the silent, sound, signal, and symbol modes, integrated, fused into song.

This requires, first of all, that the singers' sounds are produced with a flawless efficiency, an animal ease and grace, the physical perfection that inspires our appreciation for human perfectability; not merely conceived as an ideal, but present, perceived, in the flesh, an actualized example, here and now. The act of beautiful singing is a display of grace we admire in any perfected use of the human body, as in elegant dance, or in the fluent "form" of the medalled athlete. In our rapt attitudes of appreciation comes a realization, a sense of "I can do that!" Well, perhaps we cannot run or vault or sing "like that," but our awareness of beauty depends upon sensing our membership in a species that can. We partake of the perfection empathically, feeling potentially capable of that perfection, confirmed in this by the experience of others in the audience.

This beauty in singing depends upon the kind of sound we so desire and describe as "free." Only such a sound can contact the listener and evoke the transcendence. Even the slightest mechanical interference will distort the experience; contact with the audience faltering, interrupted, intermittent, incomplete, lost. And after the song we may say, "Ah, a good voice... but..." For whenever there is a noticeable, or even an unconsciously sensed staining of the basic sounds, the listener's empathy shifts to the singer's tensions; we descend from the level of the species to that of the self.

Still more is required. On the physical perfection of the silent and sound functions there must be imposed the authentic signal, the appropriate pathos, reflective of the mood and deep meanings of the music and text. We respond to these presentational sounds without analysis, as humans have throughout our species' evolution; ritually now as really before. Proof of this is in the concert hall where there will be measurable motor responses to the singing, our bodies remembering the need for survival action with variable effects on pulse rates, breathing, blood pressure, and metabolism. The signal's color, quality, pathos are heard with ancient associations with the profoundest of archetypal emotions.

But again, any physical interference will alter the pathos, rendering it inappropriate, incongruous, unauthentic, "unbeautiful." Because we will sense reservation, insecurity, a holding-back, a "hiding something," as if the singers did not trust us or themselves. With these emotional inaccuracies they cannot evoke the desired response; interpretations will be inadvertently, unintentionally versioned. Ah, one cannot but love the performers; they are so vulnerable, so brave, so at risk in a totally naked revelation of self.

Sing through the rests.
                                                        – Plunket Greene

Vocal beauty must have "line." Is ultimate reality a state of a process, a "being," or a "becoming"? Philosophers have debated this since language was invented. But the singers have no doubts about which side of the argument they support; they know that it is an indivisible "line" they must master and present. The succession of tones in the melody they sing are not a juxtaposing of discretes; the melody is and symbolizes "reality" as a flow, a changing, a ceaseless becoming, a prolongation of a past into a present already blending into a future.

The singing "line" symbolizes "reality" because creation and evolution are continuous processes. There can be a conceptual "being," but there is no actual stasis, subatomic, human, or cosmic. The singer intuitively understands, or must learn if the singing is to be "beautiful," that the "line" must be kept flowing and alive. Stop the flow, interrupt the line, and the maimed song dies.

Our appreciation for this indivisible process of the song's becoming is one of the significant ways in which our existentiality can be grasped and shared. It is reality made audible, expressive of our own individual reality – the "uninterrupted melody of self."

"Line" is crucial in all the arts; it is in the flow of the dancer through time and space, whose body, when we find the dancing beautiful, begins fresh flowing movements in new directions while still completing flowing movements in others. The unbeautiful dancer, stiff, technical, stops and starts.

A painter's "line" must suggest a "becoming," which is why we find a "beautiful" painting of a rose more "moving" than an ordinary photograph which stops the rose's time at some specific point – except, of course, for the wonderful time-lapse technique which permits us to watch events occurring in a time too slow for our unassisted sight; with this we can experience the reality of "roseness" as a single, indivisible, flowing, "beautiful" event.

From the earliest lessons singers must learn to keep the line alive, never to put periods where there should be commas, never to isolate elements, not to overemphasize single effects to the detriment of the overall line. And this is why Plunket Greene told us to "sing mentally" through introductions, rests, interludes, and postludes.

Consider the typical, tedious, heavy-handed, unmoving, gallumphing treatment of the superlatives in the Messiah chorus "For Unto Us a Child Is Born" – "Wonderful"... "Counsellor"... "The Mighty God"... "The Everlasting Father"... "The Prince of Peace," which so often sound as if the conductor and the singers forget all expressive intent in order to count beats until the next entrance, with no imagery in mind, just separate exclamations, all the same loudness and emotional intensity. Ah, if instead of the usual "Bump bumpbump"... Bump bumpbump... Bump bumpbump... the singers convinced themselves and the audience that they were only using the time between entrances for thinking up the next proper expression: "Wonderful!" (Ah, now, what might be even more reverent?) "Counsellor!" (But there must be something even greater! Ah!) "The Mighty God!" (And now more, more, something more to express our humility and reverence) "The Everlasting Father!" (And finally, some ultimate and glorious attribution!) "The Prince of Peace!" If that text was sung as if each new superlative flowed from a powerful need to express the nature of divinity, and our reverent dependence, then that choral line would have life, line, and beauty.

The function of "line" is easily illustrated in any consideration of the discursive nature of language. The tempo, manner, quality, and inflection with which one speaks the first part of any sentence is influenced and affected, colored and conditioned by the idea which can only be verbally completed later as the sentence ends and the idea is at last "whole."

The notes in the singing line are becoming wholes, phrases, and ideas. We don't sing words; we sing ideas. We don't sing notes; we sing phrases. These can be conceived as separable for the sake of analysis, but this can only be done analytically, not musically. The singer holds them in mind like the integral parts of the still uncompleted sentence, part of the flow, present with the past and with what is becoming present, with what is to come. Song is a process, beautiful in the becoming. "Reality," said Bergson, is an "elongated, stretchy nowness."

And a beautiful voice presents this continuity and coherence, giving unity to phrases and wholes, symbolizing, representing, reflecting, illustrating in an art form the uninterrupted flow of human and cosmic reality. The "line" is as indivisible as the flight of a bird.

> *God guard me from the songs men sing*
> *in the mind alone."*
>
> – Yeats

Beauty has form. Along with the sense of beauty stimulated by the sound, signal, and symbol elements of song, there is the added challenge and delight in an appreciation for the formal structure of the song. Through the form we are in contact with the creative intellect of the composers, hearing with their ears, ordering with their minds. But if the singing and the song are to be beautiful the musical materials and the forms in which they are set must be sharable.

Song forms, all art forms, are always dynamically evolving – this being part of the upsurge of novelty we find "beautiful" – but we will not think the singing or the song is beautiful if the musical materials or their setting are so radical that there is a gap in the art's evolution, or if we lag too far behind in ignorance of its grammar and syntax. Some familiarity with, or at least accessibility to the form permits a focus of attention on the musical message and text, just as our unconscious perception and acceptance of the deep structure of language allows us to understand the discursive Word.

An important part of our perception of beauty is an appreciation for the logic, the eloquence, economy, and the elaborations which constitute the "how" of what is being presented, because it is form that fixes the contours and boundaries of the essential musical message. But the "how" must not become the "what." This means that to contribute to the beauty – or at least not to detract from it – the form must not be too obviously an intellectual product. Where it becomes the message, the message is incomplete, unsatisfactory, and unbeautiful except in an arid "ideal" sense. The song is beautiful when form and freedom of expression are complementary.

The singing will not be beautiful if the song's composition is not vocally idiomatic, which is why the singers suffer more at the hands of the avant composer than do the instrumentalists whose instruments, not being human, are less troubled by successions of awkward intervals, extremes of range and intensity, and melodic lines which are removed, abstracted, too far from the Signal pathos to evoke our emotional attention. The singularities of formal structure and texture must not overpower the musical message; they must serve it.

Some experimentalist composers have argued that individual sounds or effects can exist in their music, and do, without a necessary relationship to those before or after. But this seems nonsense to the singer; it disregards the fact that the human mind cannot ignore associations of before and after, the mind's fundamental nature requires a striving to relate anything unfamiliar with something already understandable.

Beauty requires a perception of order, the human antidote for entropy, form's function. Disorder, even though it might be order unperceived, is distressing to the ear, the heart, and the mind. Some have argued that meaning in music lies only in perceiving relationships among the musical elements. Others argue that these very relationships are emotional expressions. But both, in a higher synthesis, are required for beauty.

Some have insisted that melody may be derived from an intellectual system of ordering successive tones. But where there is no reference to authentic human signal the listener will not be compelled to attend to the structural configurations. Where form is the primary significance its elements do not have their roots in archetypal human meanings. Vocal beauty cannot be cut off from our instincts.

And where the successive notes of a melody are either discretes or derived there can be no representation of reality as the "long stretchy nowness" Bergson described. There can be no "being" without a past or future, only discontinuity. There may indeed be an "upsurge of novelty," but it will be a novelty of interjections, not representative of an evolutionary or even an intellectual continuity. It may be striking, interesting, sensational, fascinating, but not beautiful. Contemporary song composers should know that the random, the probable, or the aleatoric are no longer even the current scientific models of "reality." At its profoundest, quantum theory represents a fundamental stability.

Of course contemporary composers have outgrown many of the traditional uses of the past, and naturally they have no desire to repeat or restate, no desire or requirement for comparisons with past greats. And singers can understand the composer's impatience with the limits of the human voice, but those limits must be understood and considered. As it is, human voices are required to perform Beethoven's Ninth Symphony a "whole-step" higher than he conceived the work – and there is little doubt that for his own expressive purposes he conceived the vocal demands to be very near the physiological limits – because instruments and orchestras seem brighter, richer, more impressive as their "concert pitch" is raised, and raised.

But when the title "Avant" is a conscious part of the composer's motivation, there is a splitting-off from evolving tradition, and from "present" time. The song's form, then, must be more than a solution to a technical problem, more than a test or a proof of a conceptual hypothesis. It may be different; it may be difficult to grasp, but it must yield to our attention. The aesthetic senses are not anarchists.

All formal elements of the song should be imbued with the character and personality of the composer, but they must be intelligible to the singers if they are to lead us through the form to satisfying interpretive solutions, to where we arrive with feelings of completion. We might – and this is part of the beauty and delight – have predicted other solutions enroute and compared them with our own, but those we finally hear must be as persuasive and appropriate. Part of the beauty of the singing and the song is the calm, cadential blessing of a harmony come home. Song composers should always remember the first act of Creation: the imposing of order on chaos. And part of that order, for "beautiful singing" is the recognition of affect.

We all have had the experience of thinking a particular song beautiful, and later, having outgrown it, no longer finding it so. To remain beautiful songs must have an inexhaustible inference; as the performer or listener matures it has other, newer, evolving meanings. But when all its implications are exhausted in a few hearings the song is no longer "beautiful." Songs have differential, radiant "half-lives" which determine their temporary or lasting beauty.

And understanding this "half-life," teachers of singing will not wish to impose, too soon, their own tastes and criticisms on young students. The perception of beauty and the intensity of the aesthetic experience are matters of degree, not of kind. A student might come to the studio knowing two songs and three chords on his guitar, but if there is talent for the art the two songs and three chords will not long seem beautiful; he will need greater means for self-expression. When his two songs become cliches more challenging materials will be sought. If not, he will have clearly failed the test of talent. But this relative nature of the perception of "beauty" should keep us all from inordinate pride in our advanced tastes and judgements.

Finally, the structuring of the formal elements must be such that the song symbolizes the tension and release of our internal states. It is not that certain specific elements in the musical materials express specific emotional states, but the ebb and flow, the suspension and release, the dissonance and resolution, the ritards and returns to tempi, the crescendo and decrescendo, all the musical elements, must represent the peaks and troughs of human experience. One's peaks may be higher or lower than another's, the troughs shallower or deeper, but both will recognize and respond to the singing and song as "beautiful" when the music guides or parallels our emotions. Beautiful singing always sounds the way our emotions feel.

Now, on the mechanical ease and the appropriate signal pathos the "Word" is to be grafted. And the poems are set, like the music, in forms, in intellectual organizations enabling the listener to share the insights and intentions of the poets. How well this is done depends on the unique perceptions and musical understandings of the singers themselves – the interpreters who fuse all the elements into a personal expressiveness, offering new and other ways of thinking about the art, the sounds, the songs, ourselves, and others in the audience.

*   *   *

An internationally acclaimed singer presented a lieder recital at a "Summer Workshop" for singing teachers, and that critical audience responded with a standing ovation.

The next morning the artist offered the first of a series of lecture-discussions on the interpretation of lieder, beginning the difficult task with enthusiasm and humor. One could see in his face an expression of, "Well, let's see. Just what is it I do?" He began with simple problems and common solutions. In a strophic song, like Schubert's *Das Wandern*, in which the melody is simply repeated for five verses, one might sing the first verse softly, the second mezzo-piano, the third mezzo-forte, the fourth forte, and the final verse fortissimo. Of course we must find some legitimate artistic reason for varying the mood, the dynamics, and perhaps the tempi when the music is repetitious.

He spoke of his regard for the texts, the precise meanings and the poetic allusions, and this led into digressions on the subtleties of German diction and pronunciation. He spoke about the prosody and meter of the language from which the lieder had evolved, pointing out how often the melodic lines of several of the songs he had performed the previous evening had been derived from a proper inflection of the spoken verses.

He mentioned the composers' techniques and styles: Brahms' counterpointing rhythms, Hugo Wolf's rapidly shifting harmonies, Schubert's episodic melodic lines, and of Schumann's elegant piano accompaniments which often make the singer into an accompanist.

But much of what had been so "beautiful" in his own singing seemed beyond his verbal expression; the manner in which his voice seemed to bloom into entrances and accented beats, the surge and fade of emotional intensities, the liberties with meter and tempo without disturbing the fundamental rhythms, the exquisite shadings of sound reflecting mood and meaning in the songs.

Someone suggested that his tempo for Brahms' *Wie Melodien* had been too fast and indicated a slower, "proper" tempo. "No!" he said, "No! You see, it goes faster than that, because, because... well, because it is right! Let me sing it again for you and you will hear." And after singing, "Can't you hear that it is right?"

Many other questions were treated with an engaging humility, "Well, you know, who am I to say?" Or, "It is very likely that you are the best judge since you were the audience." Or, "I listen very carefully to Fischer-Diskeau, for he is my idol."

What he seemed to be saying, without being able to say, was that a mature musical intelligence and a perfected technique allowed him a spontaneous freedom of expression in singing, that he had grown up in the culture which had inspired the verses and their musical settings, and that he reflected an unusually sensitive appreciation for them in his performance.

He taught best by performance, like most great artists who often don't know, exactly, what they are "doing," and find words inadequate. His artistry was most evident in a child-like delight at being immersed in the music, innocently showing off, inviting his audience to share the genius of the poets and composers. Everything he "did" was an animated expression of "Listen to this! Oh, just listen to this!"

> *To construe in the light*
> *of personal experience.*
>
>   – Webster

The "beautiful singer's" interpretive skills make the singing intelligible. But singers cannot express a context they do not occupy; they must make the song their own. They interpret according to their understanding of a composer's and a poet's ideas while reflecting visions of their own uniqueness. Their involvement with the songs must be personal, passionate, and authentic. But this is not license; they must give the composer and poet the benefits of interpretive doubts. They are free, however, to question all editing, arrangements, translations, and keys in which the songs are published. Discrete transpositions, though not approved by some composers, can make the songs fall into the singer's most expressive range. Commonly, publications do not. Keys are not merely to be the publishers' conveniences.

Beautiful singers interpret out of their own present beliefs, judgments, and interests, with fresh personal stamps which make interpretation not only what they "do," but also a revelation of "who" is "doing" it. All they are and know personalize the songs and the singing; their singular characters giving the songs a singular significance. They sing as if to say, "You see? This is how I felt going through this experience. This is what it meant to me to live through it and learn from it. Have you never felt like this?" Beautiful song is soliloquy.

But the singing will not be beautiful if the interpretation is strictly versioned, too explicit, too limited in its implications, either because of a lack of sensitivity or the result of some technical fault. Beautiful interpretations always have an element of exact ambiguity, in which the singer's performance leaves interpretive room for each member of the audience to accept and appreciate the song from an individual emotional and artistic context. Perception is always personal. A narrow explicitness will engage only those whose personal understanding and emotional sets are very near the singer's. The singing becomes beautiful when the audience is an accomplice in the interpretation. Then, everyone thinks, "How beautiful!" from as many contexts and for as many reasons as there are listeners. Their references differ but their humanity does not. Interpretation and reinterpretation meet the changing needs of the unchanging human heart.

This means that students must be taught, and permitted, to express themselves and not their teachers. And, apart from what seems innate in a particularly sensitive individual, interpretive abilities are best gained by singing song literature well within the student's present technical ability and artistic preference. The 18 year-old soprano's innocence is an indispensable part of the beauty of her singing – and of the song.

Student singers cannot offer "beautiful" – which is to say "authentic" – interpretations in languages truly foreign to them. And this presents a problem in our present educational practice. Colleges and universities offering vocal degree programs have unrealistic requirements for performance in Italian, German, and French, without providing student singers with time and opportunities for actual language study. We have tried to compensate with artificial means; there are "Lyric Diction" classes in which the basic phonetic characteristics of foreign languages are studied through a mastering of the International Phonetic Alphabet, which provides a most useful reference to pronunciations but not to meanings. We ought to insist that the singer's degree requirements be adapted to the real needs of the art.

The interpretive arts are best approached through the study and performance of songs in the native or a familiar language. But there is an exception; the common practice of beginning formal study with old Italian songs is justified. The purpose, here, is not primarily the development of interpretive abilities – though the student is doing so in acquiring an idiomatic vocal technique and an appreciation for a beautiful "line." This early exposure to Italian is usually for purifying phonemes stained by native conversational usage. Learning to produce these purest of phonemes – fundamentally responsible for a preeminent singing culture – has the direct and immediate effect of singing a more beautiful English.

This is not the case with German, and less with French and other languages phonetically distant from English. The Lied and Chanson ought not to be introduced to the student through phonetic imitation, an extravagant waste of studio time. And the struggle to approximate subtle shadings of unfamiliar sounds can interfere with technical progress. The songs of Schumann and Faure ought to wait for at least a concurrent and serious study of the languages. But there are exceptions here also; sometimes we are right to feel we ought not deprive a young and exceptionally talented student of these musical and expressive experiences. We can compromise; these songs may be studied and performed in the best available translations. But the trouble with this is that available translations are often unsatisfactory. Where they are literal they are often unidiomatic, as if meant to be understood rather than sung. And where they are "poetic" they often stray from meanings, and the "poetry" may consist of forced rhyming, awkward and even embarrassing to sing.

So, there is a critical need for translations into contemporary images, sufficiently disciplined to be properly faithful to literal meanings, but updated and free enough to evoke the originally intended emotional affect. To achieve this, however, the translator must be a poet-linguist-musician-singer; there cannot be many such and there are practical difficulties for the few. Publishers are reluctant to invest in new editions for limited markets. Teachers, students, and professional performers ought never to hesitate to improve on translations whenever possible.

Don't mistake movement for action.

– Hemingway

A vital sensitivity to body language and gesture preceded the Word, qualified it when it came, and has been inseparably associated with it ever since. Nothing the audience sees should detract from what it hears. "Body language" must not draw attention to the singer's internal concerns, expressive of something other than the mood and meaning of the song. Spoken or sung, the Word cannot be detached from the body.

It is a reciprocal relationship; poor habits of speech or singing, whatever the causes, distort body language into unintended interpretations, and neurologists have long been aware that articulation difficulties, from severe dysarthria to minor vocal tics, are associated with uncoordinated movements of facial muscles, eyes, jaws, tongue, neck, shoulders, arms, and hands, all compromising expressive intents.

The singing cannot be beautiful when there is a dissociation of action and affect, where the audience must make conscious efforts to disregard visual distractions in order to hear the song. Is the singer ill at ease? How to stand? What to look at? When to move? The physical indecisions have jarring effects, like the apparently inappropriate eye, mouth, and body movement of actors in foreign films when English has been dubbed on the soundtrack.

Some singers seem able to make personal mannerisms part of their interpretive styles, but there are many who sound ever so much better when we close our eyes to hear. But when the singer seems to be comfortable, confidently expressing himself rather than his teacher, or her coach, or his deference to tradition, or her concept of self-as-"singer," then the body language enhances, clarifies, and intensifies the song's affect, "beautifully."

There are always a few outstanding "pop" singers from whom art song singers might learn much about facial expressiveness and body movement, but a schizoid body language has become an obligatory part of much of "pop" performance, popularly accepted, it seems, as a demonstration of the performer's vital involvement with the music. Some of these movements, abstracted into rigid patterns, are imitations of the mannerisms of formerly successful performers for whom the movements were authentic personal expressions. Some are striking, pathological dissociations of the visual and vocal experience; the robotomorphic antics of featured singers, the surrealistic, "organized," wind-up-toy movements of "back-up" singers, the restricted pseudo-dance that began with the restrictions of microphone-cord length. Movement, for its own non-contextual sake separates style from substance. Along with social scientists we ought to speculate on the significance of the split between style and substance in the popular arts. Is this merely a temporary separation of what passes for entertainment from what strives toward art? Does its mechanical nature symbolize the triumphs of technology over taste and human expressiveness? Is it symptomatic of the deep division between thought and feeling in the social structure? Whatever the significance, there is a practical problem for young singers to consider; "organized movement" of some sort is presently an absolute requirement of agents and producers who "know what sells."

Popular styles in any of the arts formalize the effects of limited techniques into idiomatic fads. Singing teachers know that the inappropriate visual signals, just like the inappropriate vocal signals, are the results of a faulty technique. The art song singer strives to overcome the technical limitations; the song is more important than the singer. The personality of the "pop" singer is more important than the song; the technical limitations are exploited as "style."

The great physical effort required to sing badly results in all manner of visual inaccuracies: rage is read in the face of a singer singing about love, pain in a song about freedom, grins are seen in songs of lost love, cynicism in songs about friendship and loyalty, sexual arousal appears in songs of social reform. Enthusiasm and eroticism are perfectly justifiable, but neither of these is mechanical. Of course it is obvious that the perceived sexual persona of any performer is a potent part of the appeal in any singing. Who dares to say that physical attractiveness is not always a welcome and wonderful contribution to the beauty of any singing?

Vocally untrained listeners identify with the visual display of effort in popular singing – in any singing – feeling it themselves when they sing and expecting it in performers. The chronic hoarseness and more serious vocal fold pathologies which pop singers often force themselves to sing through, are accepted by the performers, and even admired by the fans, as proof that they are giving their all. And it is this popular empathy with effort that maintains the common impression that the trained singer possesses a special gift, and it is this identification with effort that causes young singers to imitate their idols, distrusting their own legitimate voices, and making them impatient with formal study. Conversely, it is the learned, earned ease of the trained singers that makes it difficult for them to "fake" the obligatory popular effort; even when musically comfortable with popular idioms they are rarely successful in the performance.

What we ought to remember is that physical expressiveness is more a matter of authenticity than of technique. Compare, for instance, the profound emotional affect in the untrained singing of the authentic folk or blues singer with that of their commercial imitators.

> *Awake my soul, I will sing*
> *and make melody.*
>
> — Psalm 58

And now, beyond the material cause of beauty in singing, the physical properties of the voice itself; beyond the formal causes of beauty, the patterns in which the musical and textual materials are set; beyond the efficient causes of beauty, the singers themselves in the act of interpreting Song, there is a final cause – that for the sake of which song is. To be beautiful the singing must satisfy the primary human need for ritual.

In *The Masks of God*, Joseph Campbell identifies two fundamental sources for all human values: the fear of death, and the fascination with life. From that fear derives our responses to the pain of loss, rejection, the retreats from ideals, the desire for security and for certainty. From the fascination derives the delights, fulfillments, growths, adventures, explorations, and ecstasies. The fears and fascinations are the sources of mysticism, science, and art. They are the substances celebrated in ritual and magnified in song.

There is no culture, subculture, or simple family unit without ritual. It relates us to others, reminds us of our delights, reconciles us to the mysteries and tragedies of life, to our mortality. It inspires us to accomplishment, instilling respect for social and spiritual order. And the performance of song is an artistic ritual, indistinguishable in emotional affect from the religious.

The singer – the artistic personification of the ancient shaman – leads the celebrants through a re-experiencing and contemplation of our significant survival values. Each song is a transformation of an ancient rite in which each of us is again initiated into the tribe, our membership validated. And in the mystique of this participation there is an increase in the amplitude of emotional waves in the concert hall. Individual fears and fascinations are transcended in a community of appreciators. "Beautiful singing" is a ritual that "takes us to the center of our spirit, and there," said Jung, "we meet with others of our species."

No wonder the ancients believed that song was the actual animated breath of the shaman-priest, carrying the soul-spirit-feelings of the singer to the celebrants, curing ills, banishing demons, pleasing the gods. And when the singing is "beautiful" it still does all these things.

Rituals are social events, which may explain why we find ourselves listening less often to recordings of our favorite performers when alone at home. For one thing, the upsurge of novelty ceases; it is always the same performance, often less satisfying than the live artistic happening. In the company of others we are co-interpreters of the song, our appreciation confirmed and intensified by that of others – the very reason why sunsets, seascapes, meteor showers, polished pebbles on the beach, and all things beautiful, are more so when shared.

The presentation is ritualistic; the shaman-singer's formal attire, appropriate for the most important member of the tribe; the walk-on, the bow that begins the ceremony, the celebrants applauding acknowledgement in anticipation of the magic to come, the rapt attentiveness – who would disturb the rite? Who leaves while the shaman sings? Who would applaud at inappropriate times?

The singer bows to our applause at the end of each group of songs; the songs have an almost liturgical ordering. We must not end the applause before the singer is out of sight backstage, and, out of respect, we recall the presence again to signify our appreciation. We bring offerings of flowers to the priestess, themselves symbols of gratitude for life and beauty, properest tribute to the Singer for performing the artistic rite.

A multilayered experience indeed; a fusion of physical grace, emotional empathy, sensual pleasure, intellectual delight. It is spiritual renewal with earthy roots. The singer's beautiful sound recapitulates our expressive evolution; the beautiful song reverberates with all human history. And while the singing lasts, the artificial dualisms of flesh-spirit, blood-brain, thought-feeling are closed up, all hyphens removed. The singer, the singing, and the song are whole. The listeners partake of that wholeness, their inarticulateness given a voice that expresses the ineffable; bringing the smile, the tears, the relief of recognition that only the beauty of another human voice can bring.

We sing because we cannot find a better use for breath.

Related Reading

Adler, Gerald, *Confrontation in Psychotherapy,* Science House, New York, 1973

Allen, Warren D., *Philosophies of Music History,* Dover Publications, New York, 1962

Appelman, Ralph, *Science of Vocal Pedagogy,* Indiana University Press, Bloomington, Indiana, 1967

Bacon, Richard M., *Elements of Vocal Science,* edited by Edward Foreman, Pro Musica Press, Champaign, Illinois, 1966

Beardsley, Monroe C., *Aesthetics from Classical Greece to the Present,* University of Alabama Press, University, Alabama, 1966

Bergson, Henri, *Creative Mind,* translated by Mabelle Andison, Philosophical Library, New York, 1946

Boone, Daniel, *The Voice and Voice Therapy,* Prentice Hall, Englewood Cliffs, New Jersey, 1983

Brain, Sir Walter Russel, *Speech Disorders,* Butterworths, London, 1961

Brodnitz, Friedrich S., *Keeping Your Voice Healthy,* Harper, New York, 1953

Bronowski, Jacob, *Origins of Science and Imagination,* Yale University Press, New Haven, Connecticut, 1978

Bronowski, Jacob, *A Sense of the Future, Essays in Natural Philosophy,* M.I.T. Press, Cambridge, Massachusetts, 1977

Bronowski, Jacob, *The Visionary Eye, Essays in the Arts, Literature, and Science,* M.I.T. Press, Cambridge, Massachusetts, 1978

Browne, Lennox, and Behnke, Emil, *Voice, Song, and Speech,* G.P. Putman's Sons, New York, n.d.

Campbell, Joseph, *The Masks of God, Creative Mythology,* Penguin Books, New York, 1977

Caruso, Enrico, and Tetrazzini, Louisa, *The Art of Singing,* Dover Publications Inc., New York, 1909

Chomsky, Noam, *Aspects of the Theory of Syntax,* M.I.T. Press, Cambridge, Massachusetts, 1965

Chomsky, Noam, *Knowledge of Language, its Nature, Origins, and Use,* Praeger Publications, New York, 1985

Chomsky, Noam, *The Logical Structure of Linguistic Theory*,
Plenum Press, New York, 1977

Clippinger, David Alva, *Head Voice and Other Problems*, Ditson,
Boston, 1917

Cooper, Morton, *Modern Techniques of Vocal Rehabilitation*,
C.C. Thomas, Springfield, Illinois, 1973

Critchley, MacDonald, *Aphasiology and Other Aspects of
Language*, Edward Arnold Ltd., London, 1970

Denes, Peter B., and Pinson, Elliot N., *The Speech Chain*,
revised edition, Anchor Press, Garden City, N.Y., 1973

Dewey, John, *Art as Experience*, Minton, Balch and Co., New
York, 1934

DeYoung, Richard, *The Singer's Art*, Northshore Press,
Waukegan, Illinois, 1958

Duey, Philip, *Bel Canto in its Golden Age*, Kings Crown Press,
New York, 1951

Eisenson, J., Auer, J.J., Irwin, J.V., *The Psychology of
Communication*, Apelton-Century-Crofts, New York, 1963

Fields, Victor Alexander, *Foundations of the Singer's Art*, second
edition, N.A.T.S., New York, 1984

Fields, Victor Alexander, *Training the Singing Voice*, King's
Crown Press, New York, 1947

Foulkes, S. H., *Group Analytic Psychotherapy*, Gordon and
Breach, London, 1975

Garcia, Manuel, *Hints on Singing*, Translated from the French by
Beata Garcia, E. Schuberth and Co., New York, 1894

Gililand, Dale V., *Guidance in Voice Education*, Typographic
Print Co., Columbus, Ohio, 1970

Gray, Giles W., and Wise, Claude M., *Bases of Speech*, third
edition, Harper and Brothers, New York, 1959

Grothjahn, Martin, *Art and Technique of Analytic Group Therapy*,
Jason Aronson Inc., New York, 1977

Hammar, Russell A., *Singing: An Extension of Speech*,
Scarecrow Press, Metuchen, New Jersey, 1978

Hebert-Caesari, Edgar F., *The Science and Sensations of Vocal
Tone*, Crescendo Publishers, Boston, Massachusetts, 1936

Henderson, William James, *The Art of Singing*, Dial Press, New
York, 1938

Henderson, William James, *Early History of Singing*, AMS Press, New York, 1921

Kelly, George, *The Psychology of Personal Constructs*, in two volumes, Norton, New York, 1955

Koestler, Arthur, *The Act of Creation*, Macmillan Co., New York, 1964

Kubie, Lawrence, *Neurotic Distortion of the Creative Process*, University of Kansas Press, Lawrence, Kansas, 1958

Kubie, Lawrence, *Practical and Theoretical Aspects of Psychoanalysis*, F.A.Praeger, New York, 1960

Lamperti, Giovanni B., *Vocal Wisdom, Maxims of Lamperti*, recorded and explained by his pupil and assistant, Wm. Earl Brown, Crescendo Publishing Co., Boston, Massachusetts, 1957

Langer, Suzanne, *Philosophy in a New Key*, Harvard University Press, Cambridge, Massachusetts, 1951

Large, John, editor, *Contributions of Voice Research to Singing*, College-Hill Press Houston, Texas, 1980

Lehmann, Lilli, *How to Sing*, translated by Richard Aldrich, Macmillan Co., New York, 1924

Levin, Nathaniel, *Voice and Speech Disorders*, Charles C. Thomas, Springfield, Illinois, 1962

Locke, Norman, *Group Psychoanalysis, Theory and Technique*, New York University Press, New York, 1961

Lucksinger, Richard, and Arnold, Godfrey, *Voice, Speech, and Language*, translated by Godfrey Arnold and Evelyn Finkbiner, Wadsworth Publishers, Belmont, California, 1965

Marchessi, Blanche, *Singer's Catechism and Creed*, J.M. Dent and Sons, London, 1932

Marifioti, P. Mario, *Caruso's Method of Voice Production, The Scientific Culture of the Voice*, Dover Publications, New York, 1949

May, Rollo, *The Discovery of Being, Writings in Existential Psychology*, Norton, New York, 1983

McCloskey, David B., *Your Voice at its Best*, Little Brown and Co., Boston, Massachusetts, 1959

Menninger, Karl, and Holzman, Philip, *Theory of Psychoanalytic Technique*, Basic Books Inc., New York, 1973

Menninger, Karl, with Mayman, Martin, and Pruyser, Paul, *The Vital Balance,* Viking Press, New York, 1963

Moses, Paul, *The Voice of Neurosis,* Grune and Stratton, New York, 1954

Muckey, Floyd, *The Natural Method of Voice Production,* Charles Scribner's Sons, New York, 1915

Muller, Friedrich Max, *Lectures on the Science of Language,* Longman, London, 1891

Nixon, Robert E., *The Art of Growing: A Guide to Psychological Maturity,* Random House, Toronto, Canada, 1962

Patterson, Cecil Holden, *Theories of Counselling and Psychotherapy,* Harper and Row, New York, 1980

Penfield, Wilder, and Roberts, Lamar, *Speech and Brain Mechanisms,* Princeton University Press, Princeton, New Jersey, 1959

Pines, Malcom, *The Evolution of Group Analysis,* Routledge and Keagan Paul, London, 1983

Reid, Cornelius, *Bel Canto, Principles and Practice,* Coleman-Ross Co. Inc., New York, 1950

Reid, Cornelius, *The Free Voice,* Coleman-Ross Co. Inc., New York, 1950

Rogers, Carl, *On Becoming a Person,* Houghton Mifflin, Boston, Massachusetts, 1961

Rogers, Carl, *On Encounter Groups,* Harper and Row, New York, 1973

Rose, Arnold, *The Singer and the Voice,* St. Martin's Press, New York, 1971

Rosenbaum, Max, and Berger, Milton M., *Group Therapy and Group Function,* Basic Books, Inc., New York, 1963

Rushmore, Robert, *The Singing Voice,* W.W. Norton, New York, 1984

Salter, Andrew, *Conditioned Reflex Therapy,* Creative Age Press, New York, 1949

Schiller, Johann Christoph Friedrich von, *On the Aesthetic Education of Man,* Letters, edited by Reginald Snell, Yale University Press, New Haven, Connecticut, 1958

Seashore, Carl, *In Search of Beauty in Music,* Ronald Press Co., New York, 1947

Seashore, Carl, *Objective Analysis of Musical Performance,* Iowa
    University Press, Iowa City, Iowa, 1936
Stanley, Douglas, *Science of Voice,* Carl Fischer, New York,
    1958
Stanley, Douglas, *A Singer's Manual,* Chadbourne Conservatory
    of Vocal Art, Harrison, New York, 1957
Tetrazini, Louisa, *How to Sing,* Da Capo Press, New York, 1975
Travis, Edward, *Handbook of Speech Pathology and Audiology,*
    Appelton-Century-Crofts, New York, 1971
Turner, J. Clifford, *Voice and Speech in the Theater,* second
    edition, Pitman, London, 1956
Van Dusen, Clarence, *Training the Voice for Speech,* second
    edition, McGraw-Hill, New York, 1953
VanKaam, Adrian, *Change Through Interaction,* Dimension
    Books, Wilkes-Barre, Pennsylvania, 1966
Venard, William, *Singing, The Mechanism and the Technique,*
    revised, Carl Fischer, New York, 1967
Waldman, Roy, *Humanistic Psychiatry,* Rutgers University Press,
    New Brunswick, New Jersey, 1971
Weaver, Andrew T., and Judson, Lyman S., *Vocal Science,*
    Appelton-Century-Crofts, New York, 1965
Westerman, Kenneth, *Emergent Voice,* second edition, C.F.
    Westerman, Ann Arbor, Michigan, 1955
Whitlock, Weldon, *Bel Canto for the 20th Century,* Pro Musica
    Press, Champaign, Illinois, 1968
Wilcox, John C., *The Living Voice,* Carl Fischer, New York,
    1945
Wilson, Colin, *New Pathways in Psychology, Maslow and the
    Post Freud Revolution,* Taplinger Publishing Co., New York,
    1972
Wolstein, Benjamin, *Theory of Psychoanalytic Therapy,* Grune
    and Stratton, New York, 1967

Index

"Adam's apple" 84, 157
Adler, Gerald 77
Aesthetic experience 196-197
Apollonian rites 125
Appleman, Ralph 186
Applied music 127
Aristotle 14
Art, bias in education 123
    "for art's sake" 136, 196
Articulation 56
Avant Garde 115

Bad singing, causes of 75-76
Beautiful singing, as multilayered experience of mechanical
    efficiency 197-198
    of "signal" pathos 198
    of Line as reality 199-201
    of perception of form 201-204
    of authentic interpretation 206
    of ritual 211-212
Behaviorism 55, 75, 124
Belly breathing 61, 165
Bergson, Henri 32, 111, 124, 200, 202
Body language 66, 209
Boethius 123
Brain, reptilian, limbic, neocortex 22
    Hemispheric dominance 129-130
Breath, control 165
    support 164-167, 190
Brodnitz, Friedrich S. 74

Campbell, Joseph 211
Canto ergo sum 71, 142
Caruso, Enrico 185
Case histories 33-45
Castrati 66
Chekov, Anton 122

Chest voice 63, 65
Chomsky, Noam 16
Class voice, justification for 79-80
    process of 87-93
    first lecture in 82-87
    peer teaching in 91
Clement, Pope 126
Clippinger, David 183
Concept vs. percept 112-113
Conceptual "deafness" 76
Counter-transferences 45-47, 49, 51

Dann, Hollis 136
Dewey, John 133, 134
Dichterliebe 149
Diction 174, 176

Einstein, Albert 130, 149
Ethos, doctrine of 123
Evolutionary order, as silence, sound, signal, symbol, song
    12-15
Evolution's "arrow" 122-123

Fauré, Gabriel 208
Fields, Victor A. 185
Fine Arts 133
Fischer-Dieskau, Dietrich 149
Formants 175
Frauenliebe und Leben 150
Freud, Sigmund 74, 75
Fromm, Eric 75
Frost, Robert 20
Fusion vs. fission, as symbol for human values 122

Garcia, Manuel 74, 183
Genesis 5, 7-8
Gestalt 172
Given Word error 10, 53, 76, 83, 85, 124
Group therapy 72-78

Handel 65
Head register 57, 161
Hegel 124

Inhibition 144
Inspiration 154
International phonetic alphabet 207
Interpretation 206-208
Intonation 178
Intuition 30, 128, 138

Jaspers, Karl 125
Jung, Carl G. 14, 29, 127, 212

Kant, Immanuel 125
Koestler, Arthur 124, 153

Langer, Suzanne 8
Language, acquisition 16-20
    Behavior 55, 73
Laryngologist 59, 74
Latin, as a mental discipline 131
Lerher, Tom 121
Levin, Nathaniel 74

Marchessi, Blanche 184
Marifioti, P. Mario 185
Mazzocchi, Vergillio 107
McCloskey, David 185
Menninger, Karl 77
Millay, Edna St. Vincent 122
Milton, John 6, 53
Moses, Paul 55, 186
Muckey, Floyd 183
Muller, Max 19
Muses 125
Myth 9

Navaho medicine man 195
Neuroses, causes of 75
Nixon, Robert 127, 144

Old Testament 126
Orphean oath 33
Orpheus 126

Paralinguistic signs 66-67
Passagio 161, 192
Phonemes 173-175
Phonic discrimination 176
Placement 159, 160, 164
Plato 110, 123
Play 130
Pliny 14
Plotinus 123
Plunket Greene 111, 199
Practice 10, 12, 146
Prometheus 7-8
Pythagoras 123

Rapport 32, 69, 71
Reculeur pour mieux sauter 153-157
Reduced cue 98, 104, 108
Renoir, Pierre Auguste 122
Ritual 211-212
    performance as 212

Schiller, Friedrich von 124
Schubert, Franz Peter 74, 205
Schumann, Robert 205, 208
Seashore, Carl 57, 184
Shapiro, Karl 6
Shaw, G.B. 174
Significant survival 122
Sing as you speak 57-58, 173
Skinnerian studies 129
Sound, as self 86

Stanley, Douglas 183-184
Stravinsky, Igor 66
Stress 149-150

Talent for singing 25, 28, 32, 69, 73, 100, 103, 142, 171, 185,
    204
Terminology 179-181
Third ear 73
Transcendence 197
Transference 28-32, 50, 52, 67-68, 107, 111-112, 114, 187

Venard, William 186
Vienna Boys Choir 135
Vocal abuses as personality requirements 76
Vocalises, as reculeur exercises 157-177
    efficacy of 30, 101
    values and limitations of 187-188
Voice, development vs. discovery 87, 145-146
    Building 146
    Coping with 178-179
Voice teachers, choice of 24
    roles of 25, 29
    Insecure, authoritarian 50-51
Voice teaching, stages in the process of 144-146

Westerman, Kenneth 185
Western culture 121
Whitehead, Alfred North 125
Wunderlich, Fritz 149